The Algonquins

Edited by: Daniel Clément

Mercury Series
Canadian Ethnology Service
Paper 130

Published by
Canadian Museum of Civilization
with financial support from
Research and Assessment Directorate, DIAND

© Canadian Museum of Civilization 1996

CANADIAN CATALOGUING IN PUBLICATION DATA

Main entry under title :
The Algonquins

(Mercury series, ISSN 0316-1854)
(Paper/Canadian Ethnology Service, ISSN 0316-1862 ; no. 130)
Translation of "Les Algonquins" issued in
Recherches amérindiennes au Québec, 1993.
Co-published by Recherches amérindiennes au Québec.
Collection of nine articles.
Includes bibliographical references.
ISBN 0-660-15961-9

1. Algonquin Indians — Ontario — History.
2. Algonquin Indians — Quebec (Province) — History.
3. Algonquin Indians — Ontario — Social life and customs.
4. Algonquin Indians — Quebec (Province) — Social life and customs.
I. Clément, Daniel, 1951- .
II. Canadian Ethnology Service.
III. Canadian Museum of Civilization.
IV. Recherches amérindiennes au Québec (Association).
V. Series.
VI. Series: Paper (Canadian Ethnology Service) ; no. 130.

E99.A349A3 1996   971.3'004973   C96-980050-9

PRINTED IN CANADA

Published by
Canadian Museum of Civilization
100 Laurier Street
P.O. Box 3100, Station B
Hull, Quebec
J8X 4H2

Senior production officer: Deborah Brownrigg
Cover design: Roger Langlois Design

Front cover: Algonquin man and woman, mid-18th century (Philéa Gagnon C51 Collection; photograph courtesy Public Library of Montreal, Salle Gagnon)

Canada

OBJECT OF THE MERCURY SERIES

The Mercury Series is designed to permit the rapid dissemination of information pertaining to the disciplines in which the Canadian Museum of Civilization is active. Considered an important reference by the scientific community, the Mercury Series comprises over three hundred specialized publications on Canada's history and prehistory.

Because of its specialized audience, the series consists largely of monographs published in the language of the author.

In the interest of making information available quickly, normal production procedures have been abbreviated. As a result, grammatical and typographical errors may occur. Your indulgence is requested.

Titles in the Mercury Series can be obtained by writing to:

Mail Order Services
Canadian Museum of Civilization
100 Laurier Street
P.O. Box 3100, Station B
Hull, Quebec
J8X 4H2

BUT DE LA COLLECTION

La collection Mercure vise à diffuser rapidement le résultat de travaux dans les disciplines qui relèvent des sphères d'activités du Musée canadien des civilisations. Considérée comme un apport important dans la communauté scientifique, la collection Mercure présente plus de trois cents publications spécialisées portant sur l'héritage canadien préhistorique et historique.

Comme la collection s'adresse à un public spécialisé, celle-ci est constituée essentiellement de monographies publiées dans la langue des auteurs.

Pour assurer la prompte distribution des exemplaires imprimés, les étapes de l'édition ont été abrégées. En conséquence, certaines coquilles ou fautes de grammaire peuvent subsister : c'est pourquoi nous réclamons votre indulgence.

Vous pouvez vous procurer la liste des titres parus dans la collection Mercure en écrivant au :

Service des commandes postales
Musée canadien des civilisations
100, rue Laurier
C.P. 3100, succursale B
Hull (Québec)
J8X 4H2

ABSTRACT

The purpose of this collection of essays featuring the Algonquin people, first published in French in *Recherches amérindiennes au Québec* (1993), is to provide a better understanding of this people and thus fill a gap in ethnological literature. The Algonquin proper, to be distinguished from the Algonquian linguistic family to which they belong with other First Nations such as the Abenaki, Micmac, Cree, and Innu, today occupy the Ottawa valley and the Abitibi-Témiscamingue region in Quebec. Their total population numbers 7,000 and they are attached to ten communities, residing within or outside them. The topics dealt with in this volume by nine different authors represent the Algonquin both diachronically and synchronically. They range from prehistory, history, social organization and land use to mythology, beliefs, material culture and the conditions of contemporary life. A selected bibliography intended to help and promote further research completes the volume.

RÉSUMÉ

La publication de cet ensemble d'articles sur les Algonquins, d'abord paru comme numéro spécial de la revue *Recherches amérindiennes au Québec* en 1993, vise à promouvoir une meilleure compréhension du peuple algonquin et, ce faisant, à combler un vide dans la documentation ethnologique. Les Algonquins proprement dits, qu'on doit distinguer de la famille linguistique algonquienne à laquelle ils appartiennent tout comme d'autres Premières Nations telles les Abénaquis, les Micmacs, les Cris, les Innus et plusieurs autres, occupent présentement la vallée de la rivière des Outaouais ainsi que l'Abitibi-Témiscamingue, une région du Québec. Les Algonquins forment une population de 7000 personnes réparties en dix communautés où vivent la plupart d'entre elles. Cette collection d'articles écrits par neuf auteurs différents prétend à représenter les Algonquins autant diachroniquement que synchroniquement. Les thèmes abordés sont variés et comprennent la préhistoire, l'histoire, l'organisation sociale, l'utilisation du territoire, les mythes, les croyances, la culture matérielle et les conditions de vie. Une bibliographie thématique visant à aider et à encourager de futures recherches vient compléter l'ouvrage.

CONTENTS

*I*NTRODUCTION

The term "Algonquin" probably comes from the word "Algoumequin" first used by Samuel de Champlain who met some Indians from the Ottawa River valley in 1603. These Indians had come to Tadoussac with the "Estechemins" (some of whom were called later Maliseet) and the "Montagnais" in order to celebrate a victory against their common enemy the Iroquois. Day (1972) suggests that this designation might be of Maliseet origin and that it could mean "they are our (inclusive) relatives or allies". However, this hypothesis is questionable for several reasons. Day did not consider all the etymologies proposed by others, namely that of Lemoine who says that : "As to Algonquin, it comes from *wanigan* or *waligan aking*, meaning *in the land full of pits* [...]" (Lemoine 1910 : 184). Furthermore, Day quickly dismisses certain etymologies because he apparently failed to recognize all the facts. He thus notes Father Charles Arnaud's proposition to the effect that "Algoumekuins - Montagnais say : Algoumekuots, those who redden themselves, who paint themselves red" (Arnaud in Day 1972 : 227). But he rejects this same proposition since he doubts the Algonquin used body paints, in spite of the fact that Champlain himself witnessed this custom during his 1613 trip in the Ottawa valley : "The soil is sandy, and there is a root which dyes a crimson color, wherewith the Indians paint their faces and their little trinkets, according to the custom in use among them" (Biggar 1922-1936 II : 269-270).

As early as the 17th century, the currently used expression "Algonquin", came to designate not only the inhabitants of the Ottawa valley, as Champlain called them, but also several neighboring Nations featuring similar languages and customs. Nowadays, in order to clear up the confusion still existing within older texts, the word "Algonquin" is only used to designate the Nation who occupies the Ottawa valley and the Abitibi-Témiscamingue region - the Nation featured in this book - whereby the word "Algonquian" refers to the large Algonquian cultural and linguistic family which in Quebec includes several other related Nations (Abenaki, Atikamekw, Cree, Micmac, Innu [Montagnais] and Naskapi) other than the Algonquin proper. This family is also vastly distributed accross North America ranging as far south as California (Wiyot and Yurok). Nevertheless, because of several factors such as the environment, migrations, external influences, etc, these

Nations, although related, remain different from one another whether from an economic, political, cultural, religious or any other point of view.

The Algonquin proper whose total population numbers 7,000 are attached to ten communities, either residing within them or outside them. These communities are Golden Lake, in Ontario, and in Quebec, Grand-Lac-Victoria, Hunter's Point (Wolf Lake Band), Kebaowek, Lac-Rapide (Barriere Lake Band), Lac-Simon, Maniwaki (River Desert Band), Pikogan (Abitibiwinni Band), Timiskaming and Winneway (Long Point Band). In addition, several political organisations represent the Algonquin, such as the Algonquin Nation Programs and Services Secretariat in existence since 1991 (first named Algonquin Council of Western Quebec) and the Algonquin Anishinabeg Nation Tribal Council, founded in 1992.

The Algonquin people designate themselves by the name "Anichinabe", (certain authors say "Anishinabe", "Nishnabe", etc.) which means "Indian; human; person; in plural form, the people" (McGregor n.d.). The Algonquin use the term "Anishinabe" in the same manner as the Ojibwa with whom they share many traits; however, their culture and language are distinct even though linguists consider the Algonquin language to be a northern dialect of Ojibwa (see Spielmann in the present book).

In fact, if one were to simply draw an outline of Algonquin culture historical development, this would probably require several volumes. First, from a political point of view, one would need to offer details about Algonquin chiefs known since the 17th century for their eloquence, their pride and their leadership : in the 17th century, Tessouat, Iroquet, Pieskaret and Ki8et; in the 18th century, Paginawatik, the founder of Maniwaki; and in the present, for example, Kermot Moore, now deceased, who founded an important organization called the Laurentian Alliance of Métis and Non-Status Indians of Quebec. Then, to properly understand the evolution of Algonquin bands one would need to describe all their activities throughout the centuries. This portrait of a group of hunters, fishermen, trappers, gatherers but also farmers, lumberjacks, steel workers, and seasonal workers on fur and poultry farms in the United States, would be from the start like a mosaic design, obviously rich and complex, but not always easy to define.

With this collection of articles featuring the Algonquin people, first published in French in *Recherches amérindiennes au Québec* (1993), we truly aim at a better understanding of this fascinating mosaic and thus fill a huge gap in ethnological literature. As we know, in comparison with other Native populations in Quebec, little research has been accomplished on Algonquin subjects. This book therefore plans to represent the Algonquin diachronically as well as synchronically. Thus it

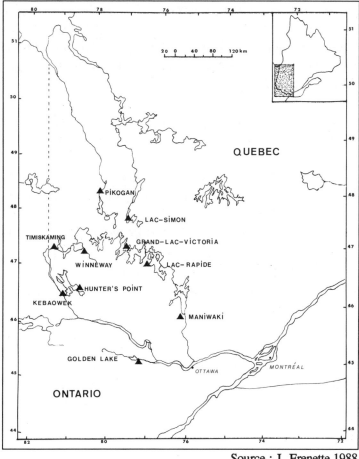

Source : J. Frenette 1988

begins with an article by Marc Côté on Abitibi-Témiscamingue prehistory and on the presumed ancestry of the Algonquin in that region. Maurice Ratelle then discusses the location of the Algonquins from 1534 to 1650, while Jacques Frenette concentrates specifically on the River Desert Band (Maniwaki) and on their land use and occupation from 1850 to 1950. This same band is discussed in the following article in which Pauline Joly de Lotbinière carefully examines a speech by its former chief, William Commanda, concerning Algonquin wampums.

The XXth century provides the context for all the other articles. Daniel Clément and Noeline Martin give voice to the Algonquin themselves by presenting legends and custom descriptions collected by Juliette Gaultier de la Vérendrye at the beginning of the 1940s, in the Upper Gatineau region. Sue Roark-Calnek describes and analyses an Algonquin wedding ceremony which took place at Lac-Rapide in 1988. For his part, Roger Spielmann examines an Algonquin bear dream account recorded in Pikogan in 1985, which he compares with similar data collected in an Manitoulin Island Odawa community in 1992. Christiane Montpetit presents a picture of the Algonquin and Métis of Algonquin origin who were residing in 1988, permanently or temporarily, in Val-d'Or, Abitibi-Témiscamingue.

Finally, a thematic bibliography should enable other researchers to further explore several aspects not dealt with in the present group of essays. This book devoted to the Algonquin does not pretend to be exhaustive and in spite of our efforts the communities are not all represented. Nevertheless, a variety of themes ranging from prehistory to history, social organization, mythology, beliefs, material culture and the conditions of contemporary life offers a fairly complete picture of the Algonquin. Hopefully, this publication will foster greater concern for this Nation and inspire other researchers, no matter how few; when this happens we will have reached our objective. The Algonquin should never again be considered as one of the most unknown Native groups in the literature.

Daniel Clément
Translated by Louise Beaudry

ACKNOWLEDGEMENTS

I particularly wish to thank my wife, Christiane Pelletier, who drew the map accompanying this introduction.

WORKS CITED

BIGGAR, H.P., 1922-1936 : *The Works of Samuel de Champlain in six volumes*. Toronto, The Champlain Society.

DAY, Gordon M., 1972 : "The Name 'Algonquin'". *International Journal of American Linguistics* 38 (4) : 226-228.

LEMOINE, George, 1910 : "Les Algonquins du Canada". *Bulletin de la Société de géographie de Québec* 4 (3) : 184-196.

McGREGOR, Ernest, n.d. : *Algonquin Lexicon*. Maniwaki, River Desert Education Authority.

PREHISTORY OF ABITIBI-TÉMISCAMINGUE

Marc Côté, Archaeologist
Corporation Archéo-08

Translated by Nicole Beaudry
with the collaboration of Moira McCaffrey

For reasons that remain unknown, little anthropological research has been done on the Algonquin people of Abitibi-Témiscamingue, who call themselves the Anicinabe[1]. Moreover, our knowledge of their ancestors' history before the arrival of white people remains in as nascent a state as their ethnohistory or ethnography.

More than two hundred archaeological sites have been recorded by Quebec's ministère de la Culture in the Abitibi-Témiscamingue region. Excluding brief evaluations resulting from recent surveys (about one hundred sites), eight loci have been partially excavated since 1964 (Lee 1965; Marois and Gauthier 1989; Côté 1989 and 1992). The excavated sites are spread across an area of approximately 1200 square kilometers surrounding Rouyn-Noranda (fig.1), which represents less than two percent of the total Abitibi-Témiscamingue territory. Much work remains to be done therefore, in order to complete a geographical coverage of the region. The archaeological sites are extremely rich. Thus, two of the four sites excavated by Archéo-08[2] produced more than 100,000 artifacts over an average excavated surface of 55 square metres.

The results of our research establish a link between the contemporary Anicinabe and Abitibi-Témiscamingue's ancient occupants going back as far as the Late Woodland period (Côté 1993). This association represents only ten

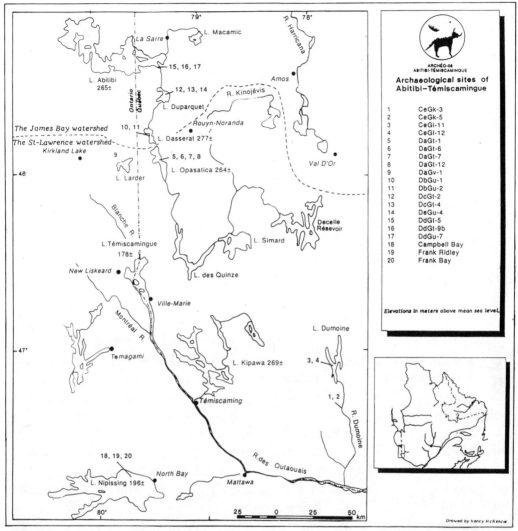

Fig. 1
Abitibi-Témiscamingue physiographic characteristics and identification of the main locations and archaeological sites mentioned in the text.

percent of the temporal range for which a human presence is confirmed in the study area. Beyond the 14th century a direct link with contemporary Native peoples fades. Although it is reasonable to hypothesize that this direct link is very ancient, this remains to be proven. Due to the limited amount of research as yet carried out, we can only point to a clear-cut kinship with the wider Algonquian cultural family, much discussed by other authors.

At this stage in our research it would be an exercise in futility to attempt an explanation of the processes that ensured the development of human groups in the Abitibi-Témiscamingue region. Increasing archaeological research and evidence will soon make it possible to tackle this theoretical problem with more detailed evidence. Huge spans of history remain to be deciphered and many hazy areas still veil the temporal plot. In this article we present the main lines of a picture that still needs to be completed.

We have purposely excluded the Historic period in this overview. This time period is amply illustrated in various ethnohistorical sources and to include a discussion here would have taken up too much space. We suggest that readers interested in this subject consult the monograph by Ethnoscop (1983) where they can find a good overview of the Protohistoric and Historic periods.

Our main objective is to document human presence. The use of analogy and typology were the methods chosen to facilitate an understanding of the cultural relationships surmised after the study of the too few sites that were correctly excavated and of numerous surface collections gathered by local people. These methods, although limited and far from perfect, enable us to draw a general picture of the situation. This exercise also reveals that cultural development in the region was neither static nor linear. The archaeological reality of Abitibi-Témiscamingue is very complex. In fact, due to its geographic location, the region is situated at the confluence of large and varied hydrographic, climactic and ecological systems that foster all forms of life. Abitibi-Témiscamingue was situated at a crossroads where populations and ideas from diverse origins met and influenced one another. Figure 2 summarizes in schematic form the cultural history of the region.

THE ANTIQUITY OF OCCUPATION

Traces of occupations dated to before 6000 B.P. have been found in Quebec. The Plano site in Rimouski, dated to 8150 B.P., is the oldest human occupation known in Quebec (Chapdelaine and Bourget 1992). Several Early Archaic occupations on the Lower North Shore have also been dated to before 7000 B.P. (Beaudin et al. 1987).

Years before present	Period	Culture	Stage	Sites and dates
0(1950 AD)	Recent		Post-confederation	DcGt-37, DcGu-4
200	Historic	Anicinabe	English Regime	DcGu-4, DcGt-9
			French Regime	DaGt-1, DcGu-4, DdGt-5, (270±60)
400			Wendat	DcGu-4, DcGt-12, DcGt-14 ,DdGt-5 (310± 60)
			Black Creek-Lalonde	DaGt-1 (480±70), DdGt-5
600	Late Woodland	"Proto-Algonquin" ?	Middleport	DaGt-1 (660±70, 680±70, 640±70), DcGt-2 (620±45)
800			Uren	DaGt-1 ?
1000		Blackduck	Pickering	DdGt-5 CeGl-11
				DcGt-4 (900±50 et 940±90), DdGt-5, DdGt-9b, DcGt-10
1200		Laurel	Eastern Laurel	DcGt-2, DcGu-4 ? (1300±70AA), DcGt-4 (1170±70), DaGt-1,DdGt-9b (1635±150AA), DdGt-5 (1600±90AA)
1400				
1600	Middle Woodland			
1800				
2000		?	?	
2200				
			Middlesex ?	Ville-Marie ?
2400				
2600	Early Woodland		Meadowood	Pearl Beach (DaGu-1), DaGt-1, DdGt-5, Meath (BiGj-1) Deep River (CaGi-1), Rosebury Lake (BkGr-1)
2800				
3000			"Small Point" ?	DdGt-9b (2760±50AA)
3200 3400 3600		"Post- Laurentian"	Lamoka ?	Hynes (BlGf-2) (2870±50AA)
3800 4000	Late Archaic			DaGt-1 (4230±70AA), DdGt-5, Pearl Beach (DaGv-1) Traverse Lake (BlGm-1), Lake Dumoine (LA-101, LA-103, LA-104A)
4200 4400 4600 4800		Laurentian		
5000 5200 5400 5600 5800	Middle Archaic ?			DdGt-5 (6225±160) ? DaGt-7, DaGt-12 ?
6000 6200 6400 6600 6800 7000 7200	Early Archaic ?			
7400 7600 7800 8000 8200	Late Paleoindian?			

Fig. 2

Preliminary archaeological sequence of the Abitibi-Témiscamingue region.

Nevertheless, there is currently no concrete evidence to support the hypothesis that the Abitibi-Témiscamingue region was occupied at such an early date. However, we should point out that at the time when groups of Plano hunters ranged across the Laurentian axis, the region situated south of Ville-Marie bordered the south shore of glacial Lake Barlow. This territory had drained several centuries prior to that time (Jean Veillette[3], pers. comm.) and had a complex flora. About 8000 B.P. a coniferous forest was present, similar to the forest covering the present territory (Richard 1980). A diversified fauna was probably also present. Theoretically, nothing prevented hunters from exploring and exploiting the territory. To this day, no research geared specifically towards discovering these early traces has been undertaken.

Excavations directed by Roger Marois were carried out between 1970 and 1975 in the estuary of Duparquet River, one of Lake Abitibi's "principal" headstream. Numerous samples suitable for radiocarbon (C14) dating were collected. In 1979, while pursuing his analyses, Marois sent several samples of charcoal and of food remains collected at the Joseph Bérubé site (DgGt-5) to a specialized laboratory. Along with other results, he obtained the date of 6280 ± 160 B.P. (S-1932). The corrected date corresponds to events which might have taken place between 7358 and 7642 B.P. (Taillon and Barré 1989).

This date was obtained from fragments of calcine bone discarded from meals eaten by the site's occupants. Unfortunately, the bones were scattered in a haphazard fashion throughout an excavation unit. They were not associated with a hearth structure or with a feature, which would have confirmed the hypothesis of a very early occupation on this site. In addition, the other dates obtained for site DdGt-5 from calcine bone are not reliable. The standard deviations are too extreme and indicate that several of the samples constitute an average date between different events.

Nevertheless, an important segment of the material from the Bérubé site is obviously of Archaic origin (Marois and Gauthier 1989); thus, discarding the early date is hardly justified. Basic prudence requires that we wait for future discoveries that will enable us to compare and properly situate the assemblage that was recovered.

The discovery of sites DaGt-7 and DaGt-12 in 1987 and 1988 on the shores of Lake Opasatica (Côté 1988 and 1989) might offer part of the solution. Both sites are located on a ten metre high terrace situated 35 metres inland from the three metre high terrace that borders the lake. In both cases, another site was located on the three metre terrace. DaGt-7 and DaGt-12 are situated at the edge of an old beach line resulting from a rather long stabilization period of the paleolake Opasatica, a remnant from the drainage of Lake Barlow (Gaétan Lessard[4], pers. comm.). This event, which illustrates one stage in the formation of the lake's present shoreline, has not been carefully studied by geomorphologists. Those consulted decline to suggest even an approximate date without undertaking further research.

Site DaGt-12 is located on the ancient terrace behind site DaGt-1. Logically, the formation of this terrace predates the earliest occupation encountered on DaGt-1. As we will later see in more detail, feature 3 of site DaGt-1 produced a date older than 4000 B.P. The location of DaGt-7 and DaGt-12 on this paleo-terrace and their distance from the lake's present shores do not guarantee their antiquity. However, these appear to be small sites without pottery, perfectly suited to small hunting groups who would have roamed the region before 5000 B.P.

THE EARLIEST UNCONTESTED OCCUPATION : LATE ARCHAIC

As was already indicated, feature 3 on site DaGt-1 (Lake Opasatica), excavated in 1988, produced a date of 4230 ± 70 B.P.[5] (Beta 33899) [Côté 1989]. Associated with this feature were several objects typically found on sites of the Laurentian Archaic tradition (pl. 1 : 12 to 16). The attribu-tion of Archaic material from site DaGt-1 to the Laurentian tradition is now supported by an ever growing list of Laurentian artifacts identified in numerous private collections from the region.

During the summer of 1992, a ground schist projectile point was discovered in the course of exploratory excavations by Parks Canada at the historic site of Fort Témiscamingue. This point can now be added to the half-dozen ground schist projectile points typical of the Laurentian Archaic (pl. 1 : 3) already inventoried. Laliberté made two similar discoveries on the upper part of Dumoine River (sites CeGk-3 and CeGk-5) in the Témiscamingue region :

> These are ground stone objects attesting to this region's occupation for at least 4000 years and to the inhabitants' participation in the Laurentian Archaic cultural sphere. (Laliberté 1993 : 6)

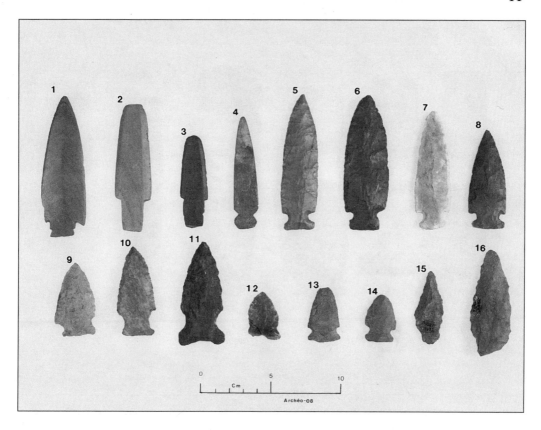

Pl. 1
Laurentian Archaic points from Abitibi-Témiscamingue. 1 to 11 : various origins; 12 to 16 : Lake Opasatica site DaGt-1.
(Photograph by Maurice Boudreau)

In addition, Noble (1982 : 43) mentions that while he was digging at the Pearl Beach site (DaGv-1), "a bevelled ground slate stemmed projectile was found along with two greywacke ulus and a cache of three large rough pecked and ground maroon slate tools".

Noble (1982) also mentions numerous finds of ground schist points, gouges and ulus at Lake Temagami (Boyle 1905), at Lake Timiskaming (Knight 1977), on the shores of an unnamed waterway near the village of Swastika, south-west of Kirkland Lake in Ontario (Pollock 1976), as well as at Lake Abitibi (Jordan

Pl. 2
Artifacts from Abitibi-Témiscamingue, associated with the Laurentian Archaic period. 1-3, 11 : gouges, 1, 2 also axes (proximal part); 4, 5 : large polished axes; 6: pecked-groove pestle; 7, 9-10 : semi-circular knives; 8 : pear-shaped object.
(Photograph by Maurice Boudreau)

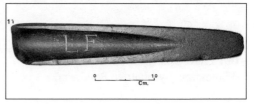

and Jordan 1978). Knight (1977) obtained a date of 5030 B.P. for his Lake Timiskaming finds. All these objects were found less than 30 kilometres from the interprovincial border. Several objects in private collections from the Quebec side of the border should be noted, of which some of the most significant are illustrated here (pl. 1 : 1, 2, 4 to 11; pl. 2 : 1 to 11).

Therefore, during the fourth millennium before the present, the region was occupied by groups who had close contacts with Laurentian people, who at the time occupied the St. Lawrence Valley, southern Ontario and northern New England. Langevin (1990 : 59) has reached a similar conclusion after typological analyses on the collection from site DdEw-12, in the Lake Saint-Jean region. He believes that between 5000 and 3000 B.P., the Lake Saint-Jean region was occupied by Laurentian Archaic groups.

What about the Shield Archaic tradition? This concept was defined primarily by Wright in 1972 to organize the growing number of archaeological discoveries made in the boreal or semi-boreal environment of Quebec, Ontario and eastern Manitoba. At that time, the creation of this new tradition was based on a number of hypotheses.

According to Wright, the Shield Archaic tradition would originate from the development of Plano populations from the southeastern part of the Northwest Territories. The new culture spread from west to east, across the Canadian Shield as floral and faunal colonization made occupation possible. The relative stability of lifeways and of available resources would have resulted in a minimal amount of change, even cultural stasis among most of the groups living north of the 45th latitude.

The Archaic period in the western part of the Canadian Shield gradually transformed into the Woodland culture of Laurel, Blackduck and Selkirk, from 1500 B.P. onward. In the case of the easternmost groups, the Shield Archaic may have persisted until the protohistoric period.

Wright's definition of the Shield Archaic concept is based on the analysis of eleven archaeological sites, of which three are located in Abitibi-Témiscamingue[6]. A thorough evaluation of these loci was made during the summer of 1991. In each case, the sites studied had been reoccupied many times during the Middle and Late Woodland periods. In the three cases, the undeniable presence of pottery, in relatively large amounts, was noted (Côté and Cadieux 1992).

Wright did not personally gather the Quebec collections used to define the Shield Archaic concept. These artifacts were found on the surface by well-meaning amateurs, but whose aesthetic imperatives led them to retain only lithic objects such as points and bifaces. Wright was conscious of the problem and made a point of mentioning it at the beginning of his description of Quebec sites:

> It is fully realized that the major weakness of the following descriptive chapter rests with the fact that eight of the eleven sites consist of surface collections. [...] Future

data will undoubtedly alter the present reconstruction, including errors of interpretation arising from the use of surface collections lacking desirable temporal controls. (Wright 1972 : 7)

It would appear therefore, that the Quebec sample used by Wright to define the Shield Archaic is not even representative of an ancient time period, since a new study of the Bancroft, Beach and Pinder's Paradise sites shows that they are primarily associated with the Middle and Late Woodland period. In view of the non-representativeness of Wright's sample it follows that in Abitibi-Témiscamingue, the notion of Shield Archaic needs to be redefined completely.

In any case, between 6000 and 4000 B.P. Archaic populations in Abitibi-Témiscamingue lived at the northern margins of Laurentian influence. At present, evidence backing this assumption is stronger and more tangible than an association with the Shield Archaic, whose definition is based on collections assembled out of curiosity rather than to fulfill scientific goals.

END OF THE ARCHAIC IN ABITIBI-TÉMISCAMINGUE

Further south, post-Laurentian history remains poorly defined until about 2800 B.P., with the exception of certain Lamoka and Susquehanna episodes. In particular, note the vast transitional period covering half a millennium that precedes the establishment of Early Woodland culture. This interval is characterized by the amorphous nature of its archaeological assemblages. Indeed, few distinguishing characteristics are obvious, apart from some vaguely fish-shaped point forms and the occasional practice of making bowls out of steatite. The artifactual production of the post-Laurentian period was neither remarkable nor highly standardized.

Between 4000 and 2500 B.P., our tenuous information about Abitibi-Témiscamingue prehistory is muddled even further. Half-formed images are perceived which are poorly supported archaeologically. However, even if the signal is weak and discontinuous, communication with the groups who came after the Laurentian people is not interrupted. Next, we will discuss some evidence which allows us to draw a tenuous line back to the Woodland period.

A certain number of projectile points found in private collections and on a few sites allow us to postulate a continuous occupation and at least sporadic contacts between local populations and the occupants of more southern regions.

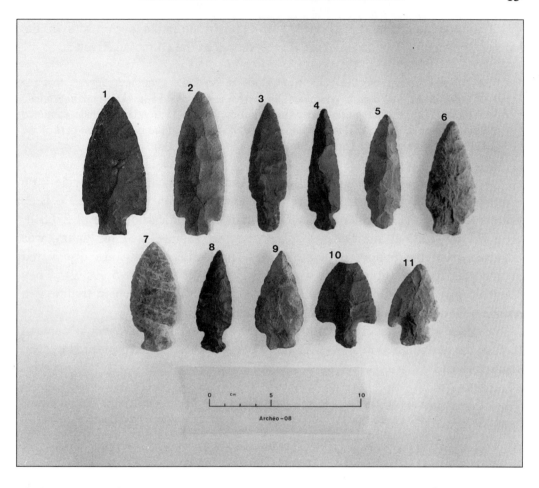

Pl. 3
Points associated with the post-Laurentian Archaic period in Abitibi-Témiscamingue.
Source : Joseph Bérubé collection.
(Photograph by Maurice Boudreau)

As can be noted from plate 3, several points discovered in Abitibi-Témiscamingue could easily be mistaken for artifacts from a post-Laurentian assemblage. For example, a Genesee point (pl. 3 : 1) was manufactured from siltstone that is macroscopically similar to the siltstone used by Susquehanna people at Pointe-du-Buisson (Clermont and Chapdelaine 1982).

Laliberté mentions the discovery of a post-Laurentian period site in the southern portion of Témiscamingue, on the shores of the Dumoine River :

> A chipped stone projectile point from CeGl-12 on Lake Dumoine suggests that the occupation in the region continued after the dispersal of the Laurentian Archaic tradition. The artifact presents certain affinities to post-Laurentian Archaic stemmed points dating to the second millennium before the present in the northeastern part of the United States and the St.Lawrence Valley. (Laliberté 1993 : 6)

At present, excavations carried out in Abitibi-Témiscamingue provide little information on occupations dating to the interval between 4000 and 2500 B.P. Marois (Marois and Gauthier 1989 : 54) obtained a radiocarbon date of 2760 ± 70 B.P.[7] (S-1150) at site DdGt-9b. The charcoal sample used for dating was collected from the bottom of a pit. A few projectile points were discovered around this feature (Marois and Gauthier 1989, pl. XV : 3, 5, 7, 9). They resemble projectile points that define the Small Point Late Archaic tradition in southern Ontario (Ellis et al. 1990 : 108; Woodley 1990 : 69).

Certain authors, such as Pollock (1975) and Noble (1982), would contend that for the period 3500 to 3000 B.P. there exists a phase called Abitibi Narrows, characterized by

> ...large percussion flaked predominantly greywacke implements, large bifaces, ovate blades, leaf-shaped bifaces, predominantly large cresentic end scrapers (over 10 grams), some small end scrapers, bifacial core chopping tools, corederived lanceolate and stemmed projectile points (Pollock 1975 : 10).

This description could also apply to Marois' assemblage from site DdGt-9b. Pollock thinks this phase is a regional variant of the Shield Archaic. Nevertheless he has not commented on the connection he sees between this expression and the Narrow Stemmed Point Tradition.

At present, although the evidence is slim, we can present the hypothesis that the occupants of the Abitibi-Témiscamingue region from 4000 to 2500 B.P. would have to some extent contributed to the development of a diagnostic trend popular throughout the Northeast, the Narrow Stemmed Point Tradition (Clermont and Chapdelaine 1982 : 33).

REGIONAL PARTICIPATION IN THE "MEADOWOOD PHASE" DURING THE EARLY WOODLAND?

William A. Ritchie created the Meadowood phase concept in 1944, and redefined it in the 1960s (Ritchie 1980). It distinguishes the earliest archaeological evidence associated with the Woodland period. At first considered to be primarily a New York phase, discoveries of similar sites multiplied rapidly in Ontario and Quebec. South of the St. Lawrence River, Meadowood components are found within the time span of 2900 to 2400 B.P.

The identification of Meadowood culture is based on a certain number of diagnostic elements. In the first place, Vinette 1 pottery, the earliest found in the Northeast, then appears. In addition, a unique lithic assemblage appears dominated by three types of objects exclusive to this period : Meadowood points, fan-based or box-based; cache blades; bifacial scrapers manufactured from distal fragments of blades or points and secondarily retouched along their broken edges (Ritchie 1980). The abundant and nearly exclusive use of Onondaga chert also constitutes tangible evidence of Meadowood culture. This type of stone is found only in a geological formation located between southern Lake Champlain and the north shore of Lake Erie, on either side of the Canadian-American border.

In the last thirty years the interaction sphere associated with this culture has considerably expanded. Excavations at the Batiscan site in 1962 and the ensuing analysis in 1963 (Levesque et al. 1964) made it possible to double its area of distribution. In addition, for the first time it was possible to examine a habitation site. Prior to this discovery, this cultural phase was known only through cemeteries and complex mortuary rituals. Station 5 on the Pointe-du-Buisson site, contained numerous mortuary pits notable for their spectacular furnishings. A date of 2380 $\pm$ 130 was obtained on this site (Clermont 1990). The Oka (Chapdelaine 1990 : 23) and Cadieux (Pinel and Côté 1985 : 40) sites represent temporary stopovers of this group. About twenty Meadowood artifacts were identified during the analysis of the Hamel site (CdEx-2) in Lotbinière (Côté 1986). A recent discovery by Chrétien (1992) at Saint-Nicolas, near Québec City, resulted in excavations at the Lambert site (CeEq-12), a site of comparable wealth to that of Batiscan. Clermont (1990) even indicates the existence of a Meadowood assemblage near Baie-Comeau, 400 kilometres east of Québec City.

North of the St. Lawrence Valley, identification work is clearly less advanced. However, near Maniwaki we note the existence of a birdstone typical of this culture (Townsend 1959), as well as several Meadowood objects such as

Vinette 1 pottery found on sites at Deep River on the Quebec side of the Ottawa River (Mitchell 1966), and at Montgomery Lake (BlGj-1) on the shores of the Petawawa River in Ontario (Mitchell et al. 1967).

Numerous artifacts discovered in Abitibi point to an interesting fact. Indeed, in private collections as well as in excavations, a significant number of points were identified that are similar in shape and size to box-based Meadowood points (Marois and Gauthier 1989, pl. vii : 11; pl. ix : 5; pl. xiv : 8 and pl. xvii : 8; and Côté 1989). Noble (1982 : 42) made the same observation at the Pearl Beach site in northeast Ontario. We have identified a similar point in a collection gathered by Wintemberg (1931) in the Ontario county of Temiskaming.

Nevertheless, none of these points is made from Onondaga chert, with a single exception found at the mouth of Duparquet River. Most of the points are made from diverse local materials such as Cadillac quartzite, a local rhyolite and a whitish, chalky chert that is heavily patinated. A specimen discovered at Lake Larder was flaked out of pelite, a material with poor flaking properties (Noble 1982 : 42). This represents a significant variation since further south, the vast majority of this kind of artifacts are made from Onondaga chert. Langevin noted a similar practice in Lake Saint-Jean, at site DdEw-12.

> At DdEw-12, Onondaga chert is very rare. In fact, more of this chert is found in Chicoutimi in a Middle and Late Woodland context than at DdEw-12 in a Meadowood context. On the other hand, among the points that resemble the Meadowood type, few were flaked from materials which probably have a southern origin. (Langevin 1990 : 67)

In the collections examined we did not see any Meadowood points with a fan-shaped base except at the Deep River site, as illustrated by Mitchell (1966, pl. 2 : 1). No small scrapers made out of the distal end of a point or a cache blade were noted. In Joseph Bérubé's collection (pl. 4 : 1 and 2) there are two finely flaked box-based point preforms. Typologically and technologically they could pass as cache blades.

What do these cultural expressions mean? Do they represent the adoption by Native people in Abitibi-Témiscamingue of a trend they might have observed elsewhere in the course of sporadic exchanges? Do these points represent a technological throw-back that survived at the periphery of the network at the start of the Middle Woodland period? This last hypothesis might explain the presence

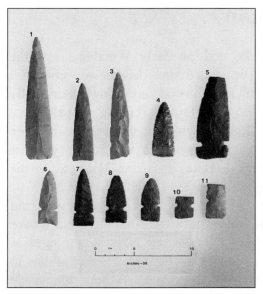

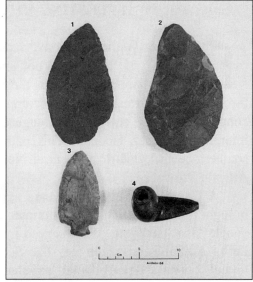

Pl. 4
Meadowood points and cache blades (1 to 3) from Abitibi-Témiscamingue. 1 to 7, 9 and 11 : Joseph Bérubé collection; 8 : Laliberté collection; 10 : DaGt-1.
(Photograph by Maurice Boudreau)

Pl. 5
1 and 2 : large leaf-shaped bifaces from the Joseph Bérubé collection; 3 : Ville-Marie Middlesex bifacial leaf-shaped point from the Société d'histoire du Témiscamingue collection; 4: platform pipe from the Joseph Bérubé collection.
(Photograph by Maurice Boudreau)

of a specimen in the Middle Woodland assemblage at DaGt-1, level 2 (pl. 4 : 10). Whatever the case, the distance involved and the sporadic nature of contacts with the region providing Onondaga chert forced local craftsmen to use locally available materials rather than this chert during the Early Woodland.

As soon as some of these artifacts are discovered in dateable contexts, they will shed light on a situation that appears to be similar in several regions of the Canadian Shield's southern fringe. Nevertheless, even an indirect participation in a cultural network that was much more active in the south tells us about the diffusion of ideas and techniques. This fact also emphasizes the well-known dynamic nature and wide-spread influence of Meadowood culture prevalent in a large portion of the Northeast during the first half of the third millennium before the present.

A FLEETING MIDDLESEX PRESENCE

The cultural period that overlaps the end of Early Woodland and the beginning of Middle Woodland is called the Middlesex complex. Middlesex populations, like those of Meadowood, are known principally through their mortuary sites. Accompanied by offerings (tubular pipes, native copper ornaments, shells and a range of lithic objects), the deceased were often interred in earthen mounds. This pattern is found over a vast territory, from southern-central Ontario to central New York State, and from Michigan to the Atlantic Provinces.

A discovery made some years ago near Ville-Marie, Témiscamingue, and brought to our attention in the summer of 1992, raises the possibility that Native people associated with or influenced by Middlesex culture might have ranged as far as Abitibi-Témiscamingue. The Société d'histoire du Témiscamingue has in its collections a large bifacial leaf-shaped point (pl. 5 : 3). A bone tool made from black bear cubitus was found with this point.

The point was manufactured from brown chert with beige spirals which we think is exotic to the region. Both in shape and size, this artifact is similar to points discovered in several Middlesex mortuary sites such as Sillery (Clermont 1990), See Mound and Pike Farm (Spence et al. 1990).

It is not possible to elaborate much on the presence of this object. However, it joins a long list of preliminary clues that will help guide future research.

MIDDLE WOODLAND IN ABITIBI-TÉMISCAMINGUE

EASTERN LAUREL

During the Middle Woodland period, the occupants of Abitibi-Témiscamingue join the circle of pottery users. Two phases can be identified within the time span that corresponds roughly to the years 1800 to 900 B.P. The first phase is culturally linked to the Laurel tradition. The other, at the end of Middle Woodland, clearly denotes a Blackduck influence.

As early as the mid-1950s, Wilford (1941 and 1955) had established the existence of the Laurel tradition on the basis of excavations he directed on the sites of Pike Bay, Smith and McKenistry in northern Michigan near the Canadian border. The discovery of similar sites north of the Great Lakes rapidly led

Wright (1967) to redefine and describe in detail the traits characteristic of the Laurel tradition. Among other things, he identified diagnostic styles of ceramic decoration.

Several Ontario archaeologists (Knight 1970; Pollock 1972, 1973, 1976; Stothers 1973) identified a regional variant of the Laurel tradition, "Eastern Laurel", on the basis of pottery styles. Eastern Laurel applies to the region between Manitoulin Island in the southwest and Lake Abitibi in the northeast. Although this concept was created more than fifteen years ago, no reexamination of this cultural construct has been undertaken.

Reid and Rajnovich (1991) were interested in diffusion and the chronology of the Laurel tradition. Their statement can be summarized in a few words. Laurel culture emerged around 2200 B.P. on both sides of the Canadian-American border that separates southwestern Ontario from the states of Wisconsin and Michigan. This expression soon spread northward, extending into Manitoba and reaching the western shore of Lake Superior. Between 1750 and 1200 B.P., Laurel culture attained its broadest extent, reaching Abitibi-Témiscamingue. After 1200 B.P., one notes the collapse of this phenomenon with the result that Laurel pottery is found only in western Ontario and in the center of eastern Manitoba. These cultural expressions last until about 750 B.P., in unison with Blackduck components that gradually replace them completely.

Laurel influences have also been noted in the Middle Woodland ceramic collections from Lake Saint-Jean. Therefore this network had strong ramifications on the Canadian Shield :

> Among the Pss decorated sherds attributed to the Middle Woodland period, some attributes suggest Laurel influences. The latter would include the presence of small punctations driven from the interior to form small bosses on the exterior surface. (Moreau et al. 1991 : 52)

The work of Reid and Rajnovich is important because it defines the temporal and spatial limits during which Eastern Laurel developed and prospered. Consequently, a Laurel presence in Abitibi cannot date to earlier than 1750 B.P. or later than 1050 B.P. As we will see later, the existence of Blackduck sites immediately following the Laurel-influenced sites bridges the gap between Laurel occupations and those clearly identified as Late Woodland.

Therefore, what took place in the time interval between 2400 B.P. and 1750 B.P.? At present, this remains a mystery. The date of 2130 $\pm$ 260 B.P., obtained by Knight (1970) and associated with Middle Woodland material on the Montréal River site, suggests an affiliation with a group using Point Peninsula pottery.

Compared to Western Laurel, the behavior of Eastern Laurel pottery users (pl. 6) is characterized by a strong preference for three decorative elements : pseudo scallop shell, dentate stamp and dragged stamp. Compared to Western Laurel groups we also note a marked decline in the use of punctate stamp impressions (less than 20%). Meanwhile, among Laurel groups in northwestern Ontario, the presence of this decorative technique is greater than 70% (Clermont and Chapdelaine 1982 : 81). The Eastern group also shows a stronger tendency to decorate the rim and the interior of the pot, whereas Western groups rarely do this. For example, note that less than 8% of Laurel pots from the Wanasaga Rapids site feature interior decoration. Less than 4% of the rims are decorated (Hamilton 1981 : 57). More than 60% of Middle Woodland pots from sites DaGt-1 and DcGt-4 have rim and interior decoration. In addition, rocked stamp impressions nearly absent from Western Laurel collections are regularly noted in the Abitibi-Témiscamingue collections.

Pl. 6
Laurel pottery from the following sites :
DaGt-1 (2-3-6-7-8-10-11-12 and 13); DaGt-6 (1); DcGt-4 (5 and 9) and Joseph Bérubé collection (4).
(Photograph by Maurice Boudreau)

These events perhaps illustrate the attraction for the Point Peninsula tradition felt by the Middle Woodland groups who inhabited Abitibi-Témiscamingue. We must not forget that the Ottawa River is an effective access route into the territory, not only for people and goods, but also for ideas and modes of behavior.

DaGt-1 is a site where we have examined a component associated with Middle Woodland. Level 2 of this site produced ten pots, a large lithic assemblage and several hearths. Two sites on Lake Duparquet (DcGt-4 and DcGu-4) were also occupied during Middle Woodland times. They were excavated in 1989 and 1990 respectively. On DcGu-4, a radiocarbon date of 1300 ± 70 B.P.[8] (Beta-33896) was obtained, and is associated with part of the as-

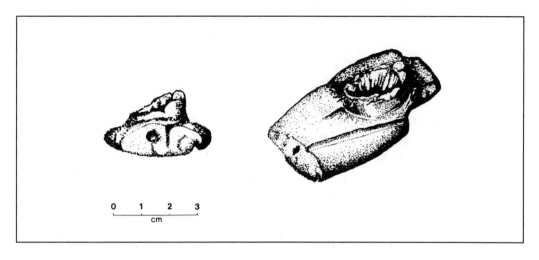

Fig. 3
Platform pipe in the René Levesque collection housed at the Centre muséographique de l'Université Laval.
(Drawing by Nancy McKenzie)

assemblage that was collected (Côté 1992).

The Joseph Bérubé collection (pl. 5 : 4) and the collection gathered by René Levesque in the early 1960s (fig. 3) each contain a steatite platform pipe. These objects are associated with the Middle Woodland period and can be situated chronologically within a broad time span. Thus in Ohio, the Hopewell culture from which this type of artifact originates is dated to between 2150 B.P. and 1650 B.P. In northwestern New York State and in southern Ontario, such pipes are rarely dated earlier than 1450 B.P. At the site of Pointe-du-Buisson, eight platform pipes are associated with occupations dating to between 1450 B.P. and 1000 B.P. (Chapdelaine 1982). The pipe in the Bérubé collection has an unusual shape, with a bulbous bowl and the absence of a front platform. The liberty taken with a form generally standardized in the older sites might lead one to believe, like Chapdelaine (1982 : 213), in a late manufacture date. The pipe from the Levesque collection and the one from the Bérubé collection were found in the estuary of Duparquet River which flows into Lake Abitibi. The sites on which these objects were found constitute the northern limit of platform pipe distribution.

BLACKDUCK

Towards the end of the Middle Woodland period, ceramic assemblages undergo a profound change. Laurel pottery is replaced by a different ceramic tradition, decorated with corded stamps and linear punctate motifs which form bosses on the interior collar of the vessels. The pots' exterior is decorated with a corded-wrapped stick motif which is sometimes smoothed. This kind of pottery is associated with Blackduck culture of the Canadian Shield.

Blackduck culture was first identified in the southern portion of the boreal forest bordering Lake Superior's north shore. In this region, the time frame attributed to Blackduck culture ranges from the end of Middle Woodland to the end of Late Woodland (1350 to 350 B.P.). In its terminal phase, Blackduck coexists with Selkirk culture (Hamilton 1981). In the Abitibi-Témiscamingue region, the presence of Blackduck culture was already noted by Wright (1979 : 83). The time frame for this manifestation is quite well-defined since it appears to be absent from approximately 750 B.P. onward, as we will later see.

Blackduck culture is essentially an Algonquian manifestation. The discovery of this kind of pottery in significant quantities implies that the occupants of Abitibi-Témiscamingue were receptive to influences from Western Algonquian groups. Much research remains to be done to fully understand the participation of the region's inhabitants in this cultural network. Given the current state of the research, the evidence paints a static picture. The reality was surely more dynamic. It is plausible to think that, for a time, the occupants of Abitibi-Témiscamingue were an integral part of this network, thus participating in its development and diffusion.

Pottery associated with Blackduck culture has been recovered on sites DcGt-2, DcGt-4, DcGt-10 (Côté 1988), DdGt-5, DdGt-9b (Marois and Gauthier 1989) and DdGu-7 (Lee 1965). On site DcGt-4, a few pots (pl. 7 : 3 and 5) were left by a family who occupied for a certain time the rocky outcrop rising five metres above Lac Duparquet. The presumed orientation of the habitation seems to indicate a desire for protection from dominant winds.

The lithic collection from this site is large and characterized by the following four features. Projectile points are on average smaller than those found on older sites; several points are unifacial, and were made on minimally retouched flakes. We have identified a large number of unifacial tools such as retouched flakes and utilized flakes. The vast majority of lithic artifacts are made from two local materials, rhyolite and Cadillac quartzite; there is less evidence

Pl. 7
Blackduck pottery from Abitibi-Témiscamingue; site DcGt-4 (5 and 10); Joseph Bérubé collection (1 to 4, 6 to 9 and 11 to 15).
(Photograph by Maurice Boudreau)

for extra-regional exchange of lithic raw materials than on other sites we have excavated. Finally, there is a surprisingly large number of ovoid bifaces; we have yet to determine if this is related to the proximity of lithic sources and therefore to a technological process, or if this reflects a particular stylistic preference. Site DcGt-4 is presently being analysed and dates are not yet available[9].

The Blackduck occupation sequence, although apparently quite short, must have been intensive since pottery associated with this culture is frequently found in collections.

LATE WOODLAND IN ABITIBI-TÉMISCAMINGUE :
A REALIGNMENT OF EXCHANGE NETWORKS

Our view on the start of the Late Woodland period in Abitibi-Témiscamingue is hampered by a lack of data for this time period. In fact, what we know about the period spanning from 1000 to 750 B.P. is based only on a few discoveries, which suggest that there were contacts between the Algonquians of Abitibi-Témiscamingue and the Iroquoians of southern Ontario.

Laliberté made the first discovery at site CeGl-11 on the shores of Lake Dumoine. It consisted of several fragments from the same pot whose collar is decorated with horizontal dentate tool impressions. The vessel's neck is decorated with a horizontal chevron pattern made by the same kind of tool (Laliberté 1993). Another pot found at site DdGt-5, excavated by Marois and Gauthier (1989 pl. III : 2) at Lake Abitibi, features a collar decorated with horizontal dentate stamps. The limit between the body and the collar is emphasized with a row of oblique incisions made with the edge of a stick. The neck, encircled by a double row of linear horizontal incisions, is not pronounced. The beginning of the shoulder is marked by a series of oblique stamps whose top points to the right. This decoration is made using a cord-wrapped object. The rim of this vessel is decorated with a spout which follows the rounded contour. The base of the collar features a band of punctations made from the inside that form bosses on the outside. The body of the vessel is covered with cord-wrapped stick impressions. These two pots are similar to those produced by Iroquoian groups from Ontario during early Late Woodland period (Williamson 1990).

In 1991, during the evaluation of site DbGu-7 on the shores of Lake Dasserat, a collarless rimsherd was discovered. It was decorated with horizontal linear incisions placed above exterior bosses, created by interior punctations (Côté and Cadieux 1992). This sherd is comparable to those collected in Ontario and associated with the Pickering phase. In addition, Brizinski notes the presence of several Pickering vessels on three Lake Nipissing sites (Campbell Bay, Frank Ridley and Frank Bay) :

> Regardless of which model is correct, three general trends are noticeable: (1) by A.D. 800 corded pottery became a popular design type; (2) Pickering vessels were the most popular type at A.D.1000; (3) from A.D. 1200 to Contact, Iroquoian vessel dominated the Nipissing collection. (Brizinski 1980 : 250)

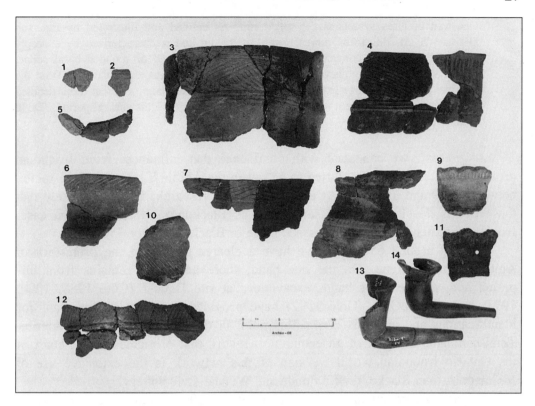

Pl. 8
Late Woodland pottery from Abitibi-Témiscamingue. 1 and 2 : rolled rim pots from the Uren phase; 5 to 7 : Middleport pots from DaGt-1; 3 and 4 : Black Creek-Lalonde pots from DaGt-1; 8 to 12 : Wendat pots (8 to 11 : Joseph Bérubé collection; 12 : DcGt-12); 13 and 14 : pipes from DcGu-4.
(Photograph by Maurice Boudreau)

Around 670 B.P., the Pickering phase is followed by the Uren phase, which continues until about 620 B.P. (Dodd et al. 1990 : 324). To our knowledge, no sites in our region have produced a date or an assemblage typical of this period.

Nevertheless, two pots have been recovered that bear characteristics associated specifically with the Uren phase. One was found on site DaGt-1 (Côté 1993) and the other comes from a surface collection gathered by René Ribes in 1977 (pl. 8 : 1 and 2). In both cases they are pots with rolled rim :

> One trait of Uren vessels is the rolled rim. As defined and illustrated by Emerson (1956a : 3, 5), this form curves inward at the lip and is characterized by a deeply channeled interior, a convex exterior, and a poorly-defined or rounded basal collar. [...] It would appear, however, that the rolled rim form was a popular trait from the terminal part of the Early Iroquoian stage to the Uren substage, and that more detailed analysis may demonstrate it to be a quantitative diagnostic of this general period. (Dodd et al. 1990 : 330)

At present, we can state with confidence that influences from Iroquoian groups in southern Ontario started to be felt in the Abitibi-Témiscamingue region between 1000 and 750 B.P. At this point in our research, it appears likely that these events developed at the same time as Blackduck. If this was the case, Iroquoian influences rapidly surpassed those of Blackduck after 750 B.P.

Starting around 650 B.P., we have a clearer picture of the prehistory of Abitibi-Témiscamingue. On the one hand, there are more remains from this period and, on the other hand, excavations at site DaGt-1 (Côté 1988, 1990, 1993) and site DcGu-4 (Côté 1992) have provided data that is important for identifications and analyses. From this point in time, the occupants of Abitibi-Témiscamingue are part of an economic network that originates in the heart of the Ontario Iroquoian world. A sign of this network is the extensive use of Middleport, then Black Creek-Lalonde and Wendat-style pottery.

Neutron activation analyses of clays (Côté 1993) point to a discrepancy between the material used to make the pots on site DaGt-1 and the type of clay available in the Abitibi-Témiscamingue. The vessels found on DaGt-1 were not made there: they were most likely imported.

The presence of proto-Wendat pottery in Quebec Algonquian assemblages is poorly documented. This phenomenon is better known in Ontario where it is often the subject of debate. On the other hand, the presence of such sherds in the James Bay region, the Mauricie, the Laurentians, Lake Saint-Jean, and along the Ottawa River has not raised any controversy. Only recently have Quebec archaeologists been questioned and more extensive research been undertaken (Moreau et al. 1991; Laliberté 1993; Chapdelaine 1993; Côté 1993).

The presence of proto-Wendat pottery sometimes far from its presumed place of origin, emphasizes the strong political, economic and cultural influence these Amerindians had on their allies, the northern Algonquian populations. Observations made by Europeans in the 17th century support this assertion :

> Various Algonquin groups were allies of the Huron. Some of these Algonquins wintered with the Huron [...] and they seem to have come in numbers. In April of 1637, the Bissiriniers returned to their country after the ice had broken and the lake was opened, carrying with them in seven canoes the 70 bodies of those who had died while wintering among the Huron [...]. In the winter of 1623-24, the Epicerinys [...] camped in Huronia. (Tooker 1964 : 19)

Other researchers such as Wright (1966:150) have suggested that a well-organized and very efficient system of exchanges and exogamous marriages explain the presence of this pottery. Still others, like Fox (1990) and Brizinski (1980), think that Algonquian groups manufactured and distributed this pottery - groups located in different parts near Huronia such as the Odawas, the Nipissing and the southern Algonquins. This hypothesis rests on the assumption that close interactions existed between Iroquoians and the Algonquians. Some researchers have suggested the idea that Algonquians shared and influenced the nature of the Ontario Iroquoian ceramic tradition from its onset. The greater mobility of the Algonquians would account for the diffusion of this tradition.

> It appears then that the presence of such Iroquois ceramics across the north is not solely the result of intermarriage, trade or Iroquoian hunting parties but rather that Algonkians have shared in the Iroquois ceramic tradition from the beginning, although not consistently or uniformly. (Dawson 1979 : 27)

During the historic period certain Algonquians had the reputation of being great travellers. Their contacts with at times very distant populations constituted a major asset for the efficiency of the French trade system during the first half of the 17th century.

> They [the Epicerinys] told the Recollets that they traded once a year with a nation a month's or 6 weeks' journey by land, lake, and river. (Tooker 1964 : 19)

This type of interaction is not unique. Four hundred years before the arrival of white people on the continent there existed a well-organized exchange and cultural interaction network. This network facilitated the diffusion of Iroquoian-like pottery made in the St. Lawrence Valley among Algonquian populations living in far-reaching areas such as the Lower North Shore (Chapdelaine 1986).

Further clay analyses will no doubt nourish this debate by adding samples collected in regions occupied by the Wendat and their ancestors. Samples must also be taken in the territories of those Algonquian Nations who acted as intermediaries in the spread of this pottery.

At site DaGt-1, the chronological and typological affiliation of the domestic vessels is clear. The decoration, the shape, the height of the collar, the shape of castellations, and the preferred surface treatment confirm that this pottery is of typical Iroquoian manufacture. These Iroquoians were the ancestors of the Wendats, the Neutrals and the Petuns who occupied the region located between Georgian Bay and Lake Simcoe in Ontario.

The relationship between the radiocarbon dates and the style of the vessels supports this assertion. The Amerindians who occupied site DaGt-1 participated in two consecutive and distinct cultural episodes. Some of the vessels are associated with three radiocarbon dates[10] obtained from charcoal in three different hearths. Ontario archaeologists call this cultural episode the Middleport phase of the Ontario Iroquoian tradition (pl. 8 : 5, 6 and 7). For this episode, Dodd et al. (1990) propose a time span that covers a seventy year period between 620 and 550 B.P.

Other vessels on site DaGt-1 are typical of a ceramic style known as Lalonde high-collar (pl. 8 : 3 and 4). This pottery is the primary evidence for proto-Wendat occupations between 550 and 500 B.P. We now designate this time span as the Black Creek/Lalonde Period (Ramsden 1990).

A date of 480 ± 70 B.P.[11] (Beta-33897) was obtained from feature 4 on site DaGt-1. This hearth partially covered feature 8 that was associated with a contemporaneous Middleport phase occupation. Part of one of the Lalonde vessels was found in the ash layer at the center of feature 4.

A few ceramic pipes and several lithic objects characteristic of Late Woodland occupations have been found in addition to the vessels from DaGt-1. Let us mention the small triangular, bifacial projectile points, a Middleport point of Onondaga chert and a few grinding-stones usually associated with the Late Woodland (Côté 1993).

From this time onward, a direct link between the present Anicinabe and "proto-Algonquians" can be postulated. In fact, although artifacts are typologically associated with Iroquoian cultural groups, this is not the case for habitation remains which strictly respect the construction methods prevalent among northern Algonquian cultures. For example, hearths consisting of a structure of stones supporting the fireplace characterize Algonquian Nations from Manitoba to the shores of the Atlantic Ocean, since at least the end of the Middle Woodland. Two styles of habitation can be deduced from the position and the number of hearths at site DaGt-1 - a conical tent and a multi-family dwelling containing several hearths. These constructions, whose origins go back to prehistory, have changed very little since the time of the Late Woodland occupations on DaGt-1 and Champlain's visit in the Ottawa valley at the start of the 17th century, the first missionaries' accounts of Témiscaminque in the 19th century, and McPherson's arrival (1930), the first ethnographer to have visited the Abitibiwinnis. Thus an ethnohistorical link in the style of housing can be drawn (Côté 1993).

Some of the occupations identified on sites DcGu-4, DdGt-5 and DdGt-9b are related to Algonquian occupations from the early part of the Late Woodland period. Certain types of pottery we have encountered are usually discovered in protohistoric contexts or on late prehistoric sites (pl. 8 : 8, 9 and 12). In addition, the discovery on site DcGu-4 of two pipes (pl. 8 : 13 and 14) with bowls of a capacity largely exceeding prehistoric norms could, according to Norman Clermont (pers. comm.)[12], be an indication of how recent this occupation is and a reflection of a greater abundance of certain trade items such as tobacco. Although no radiocarbon date is presently available, we believe that a date close to 350 B.P. is plausible for the Late Woodland occupation on site DcGu-4. Site DdGt-5 has been dated to 380 B.P. (310 $\pm$ 60 B.P., S-1152).

CONCLUSION

We have shown how the prehistory of the Algonquian groups who occupied the southern fringe of the Canadian Shield is slowly coming to light. This vast region, situated far from large urban centers and from the main lines of development, was neglected by archaeologists. Consequently, few sites had been excavated and analysed.

Sites that were studied were often multi-component occupations spread over a long time period. In those instances, it is often difficult, without sites to use for comparison to distinguish the observed occupations.

In some cases, the available collections were gathered by amateurs. The context and dates that would have made it possible to better identify and interpret the artifacts have, for the most part, been destroyed or are non existant. We have emphasized a good example of this situation, that of the Abitibi-Témiscamingue sites that were used to illustrate the nebulous Shield Archaic concept.

Nevertheless, the future appears promising and stimulating. Inevitably, future discoveries may cause us to question what we have discussed here. We have presented, in this article, some of the questions, conclusions and intuitions that we are currently considering. Although preliminary, our propositions indicate that the territory occupied by the Anicinabe for centuries had a much longer and more complex history than was generally thought.

It is now possible to trace human occupation in the Abitibi-Témiscamingue region back forty centuries. The thread that extends from one era to another is often tenuous, nevertheless we can already suggest the possibility of continuous occupation over this vast territory.

Available evidence indicates that the Amerindians who occupied the Abitibi-Témiscamingue region during prehistory took part in interaction networks based to the west or southwest. However, on the basis of the data at our disposal, very few links can be established with the St. Lawrence Iroquoians and their ancestors.

Influences originating to the east and north may, at times, have been quite strong and relatively important. This assertion is supported by the constant presence, albeit in small amounts, of certain lithic materials such as James Bay Lowland chert, Mistassini quartzite and Ramah quartzite. Unfortunately, the typology of assemblages in these regions is still too poorly understood to allow us to discern influences or an adaptive sharing of traits, as is the case, for example, of settlement patterns.

Use of typological analogy is very useful as it makes it possible to establish basic parameters from which Abitibi-Témiscamingue prehistory may be developped. That was our intention here. Unfortunately, this method leaves little room for regional variation. It overemphasizes elements from archaeological assemblages which correspond to "types" identified elsewhere, to the detriment of less standardized elements that are both new and unknown. From now on, we must pay special attention to these less striking elements. In this way the particularities that escape us today will be brought to light. As such, the intriguing Laurel pottery and the "Meadowood-style" points may constitute the beginning of traditions that will gradually become clearer.

The problem of ethnicity is more delicate. Our research indicates that the ancestors of present-day Anicinabe already occupied Abitibi-Témiscamingue during the Late Woodland period. However, beyond this time, the relationship is unclear. Nevertheless, to say that the populations who occupied Abitibi-Témiscamingue before the Late Woodland belong to the Algonquian family constitutes a workable hypothesis, supported by analogies derived from the discoveries of many researchers. The history of a people is often comprised of changes, migrations, disasters and demographic leaps. The subtle mechanisms of the events are sometimes difficult to recognize from an archaeological perspective.

NOTES

[1] Concerning the term that "Algonquins" use when naming themselves, the reader may turn to note 2 in Jacques Leroux's text ("Le tambour d'Edmond") published in *Recherches amérindiennes au Québec* XXII (2-3) : 42.

[2] Archéo-08 is a non-profit organization created in 1985 by the citizens of Abitibi-Témiscamingue to develop their archaeological heritage. Archéo-08 is supervised by a seven member executive board. In 1986, they hired a resident archaeologist. Since then, the Corporation has had the mandate to set in motion and work on a long-term, archaeological research plan.

[3] A geomorphologist affiliated with the Geological Survey of Canada.

[4] A geographer, geomorphologist, geologist, and a teacher at the Abitibi-Témiscamingue CEGEP.

[5] Calibrated date according to the Maska table, 4890 B.P.

[6] Bancroft site (DcGt-1), Beach site (DbGu-1) and Pinder's Paradise site (DbGu-2).

[7] Calibrated date according to the Maska table, 2935 B.P.

[8] Calibrated date according to the Maska table, 1265 B.P.

[9] We have just received radiocarbon dates from three charcoal samples found at DcGt-4 in 1990. These results support the existence of two distinct occupation periods. The first charcoal sample is related to Laurel vessels and was taken from feature 3; the occupation took place around 1155 B.P. (1170 $\pm$ 60 B.P. Beta-61780). The second sample is associated with feature 2 and with several Blackduck vessels; the occupation took place approximately two centuries later, around 900 B.P. (900 $\pm$ 50 B.P. Beta-61782; 940 $\pm$ 90 B.P. Beta-61780). These results also support the hypothesis that Blackduck influence in Abitibi-Témiscamingue overlaps with the end of Middle Woodland and the first quarter of Late Woodland.

[10] Feature 2: corrected date, 610 B.P. (660 $\pm$ 70 B.P., Beta-33898); Feature 8: corrected date, 600 B.P. (650 $\pm$ 80, Beta-33900); Feature 12: corrected date, 625 B.P. (680 $\pm$ 70, Beta 33901).

[11] Calibrated date according to the Maska table, 520 B.P.

[12] Archaeologist and professor in the Department of anthropology, University of Montréal.

ACKNOWLEDGMENTS

I wish to express my sincere thanks to Claude Chapdelaine, Daniel Chevrier and Jean-François Moreau for their invaluable comments on the different versions of this text. Nancy McKenzie has drawn the figures while Maurice Boudreau made the photographs. Diane Bernard has processed part of the text. I wish here to acknowledge their professional competence. Finally, I wish to express my appreciation of the Direction régionale de l'Abitibi-Témiscamingue employees, a section of Quebec's ministère de la Culture, and of the employees and deputies of the Rouyn-Noranda MRC, who, since 1986, have supported our work and helped us immensely.

WORKS CITED

BEAUDIN, Luc, Pierre DUMAIS, and Gilles ROUSSEAU, 1987 : "Un site archaïque de la baie des Belles Amours, Basse-Côte-Nord". *Recherches amérindiennes au Québec* XXII (1) : 17-32.

BOYLE, David, 1905 : "Notes on Some Specimen". *Annual Archaeological Report 1904 being part of Appendix to the Report of the Minister of Education Ontario*, Toronto, pp. 17-39.

BRIZINSKI, Morris J., 1980 : *Where Eagles Fly : An Archaeological Survey of Lake Nipissing.* Master's thesis, Department of Anthropology, McMaster University, Hamilton, Ontario.

CHAPDELAINE, Claude, 1993 : "Algonquins et Iroquoiens dans l'Outaouais : Acculturation ou confrontation", in Marc Côté and Gaëtan L. Lessard (eds.), *Traces du passé, Images du présent : Anthropologie amérindienne du Nord-Ouest québécois.* Rouyn-Noranda, Quebec, pp. 177-187.

– , 1982 : "Les pipes à plate-forme de la Pointe-du-Buisson : Un système d'échanges à définir". *Recherches amérindiennes au Québec* XII (3) : 207-217.

– , 1986 : "La poterie amérindienne du site EbEx-1, île du Havre de Mingan : Identification culturelle et position chronologique". *Recherches amérindiennes au Québec* XVII (2-3) : 95-102.

– , 1990 : "Un site sylvicole moyen ancien sur la plage d'Oka (BiFm-1)". *Recherches amérindiennes au Québec* XX (1) : 19-37.

CHAPDELAINE, Claude, and Steve BOURGET, 1992 : "Premier regard sur un site paléoindien récent à Rimouski (DcEd-1)". *Recherches amérindiennes au Québec* XXII (1) : 17-32.

CHRÉTIEN, Yves, 1992 : *Le site Lambert (CeEg-12) à Saint-Nicolas, intervention 1991*. Paper presented at the XIth Annual Conference of the Association des archéologues du Québec held in Montréal, April 24-26, 1992.

CLERMONT, Norman, 1990 : "Le Sylvicole inférieur au Québec." *Recherches amérindiennes au Québec* XX (1) : 5-19.

CLERMONT, Norman, and Claude CHAPDELAINE, 1982 : *Pointe-du-Buisson 4 : Quarante siècles d'archives oubliées*. Recherches amérindiennes au Québec, Montréal.

CÔTÉ, Marc, 1986 : *Le site Hamel (CdEx-2) : Un site à occupations multiples de la moyenne vallée du Saint-Laurent*. Master's thesis, Department of Anthropology, University of Montréal.

– , 1988 : *Reconnaissance archéologique 1987*. Corporation Archéo-08, report submitted to Quebec's ministère des Affaires culturelles, Québec.

– , 1989 : *Intervention archéologique 1988 : La fouille du site DaGt-1*. Corporation Archéo 08, report submitted to Quebec's ministère des Affaires culturelles, Québec.

– , 1990 : *Intervention archéologique 1989 : Fouille au site DaGt-1 (lac Opasatica)* Corporation Archéo 08, report submitted to Quebec's ministère des Affaires culturelles, Québec.

– , 1992 : *Le site Baril (DcGu-4)*. Paper presented at the XIth Annual Conference of the Association des archéologues du Québec held in Montréal, April 24-26, 1992.

– , 1993 : "Le Site DaGt-1 : un établissement algonquin du sylvicole supérieur en Abitibi-Témiscamingue", in Marc Côté and Gaëtan L. Lessard (eds.), *Traces du passé, Images du présent : Anthropologie amérindienne du Nord-Ouest québécois*. Rouyn-Noranda, Quebec, pp. 5-59.

CÔTÉ, Marc, and Denis CADIEUX, 1992 : *Inventaire archéologique 1991 : Lac Dasserat "Obadowagacing Sagahigan"*. Corporation Archéo-08, report submitted to Quebec's ministère des Affaires culturelles, Québec.

DAWSON, Kenneth, C. A., 1979 : "Algonkian Huron-Petun Ceramics in Northern Ontario". *Man in the Northeast* (18) : 14-31.

DODD, Christine F., et al., 1990 : "The Middle Ontario Iroquoian Stage", in Chris J. Ellis and Neal Ferris (eds.), *The Archaeology of Southern Ontario to A.D. 1650*. Occasional Publication of the London Chapter, OAS (5) pp. 321-360.

ELLIS, Chris J., Ian T. KENYON, and Michael W. SPENCE, 1990 : "The Archaic", in Chris J. Ellis and Neal Ferris (eds.), *The Archaeology of Southern Ontario to A.D. 1650*. Occasional Publication of the London Chapter, OAS (5) pp. 65-125.

ETHNOSCOP, 1983 : *Étude synthèse sur l'occupation amérindienne en Abitibi*. Report submitted to Quebec's ministère des Affaires culturelles, Québec.

FOX, William A., 1990 : "The Odawa", in Chris J. Ellis and Neal Ferris (eds.), *The Archaeology of Southern Ontario to A.D. 1650*. Occasional Publication of the London Chapter, OAS (5) pp. 457-474.

HAMILTON, Scott, 1981 : *The Archaeology of the Wenasaga Rapids*. Archaeological Research report 17, Ontario Ministry of Culture and Recreation, Toronto.

JANZEN, Donald E., 1968 : *The Naomikong Point Site and the Dimensions of Laurel in the Lake Superior Region*. Publications of the Museum, Michigan State University, Anthropological Series 36.

JORDAN, J. C., and M. M. JORDAN, 1978 : *1977 Report to the Archaeological Committee of the Ontario Heritage Foundation*. Manuscript on file at Ontario Ministry of National Resources, Toronto.

KNIGHT, Dean H., 1970 : *The Montréal River Site CgGu-1*. Canadian Museum of Civilization, Library, Archaeology document Ms. No. 53, Ottawa.

– , 1977 : *The Montreal River and the Shield Archaic*. PhD dissertation, Department of anthropology, University of Toronto, Toronto.

LALIBERTÉ, Marcel, 1993 : "La rivière Dumoine, une route commerciale aux confins du Témiscamingue au cours de la préhistoire", in Marc Côté and Gaëtan L. Lessard (eds.), *Traces du passé, Images du présent : Anthropologie amérindienne du Nord-Ouest québécois*. Rouyn-Noranda, Quebec, pp. 151-162.

LANGEVIN, Erik, 1990 : *DdEw-12 : 4000 ans d'occupation sur la grande décharge du lac Saint-Jean*. Master's thesis, Department of Anthropology, University of Montréal.

LEE, Thomas, 1965 : *Archaeological investigations at Lake Abitibi, 1964*. Centre d'études nordiques, Université Laval, Travaux divers 10, Québec.

LEVESQUE, René A., Francis F. OSBORNE, and James V. WRIGHT, 1964 : *Le gisement de Batiscan*. Musée national du Canada, Études anthropologiques 6, Ottawa.

MacPHERSON, John T., 1930 : *An Ethnological Study of the Abitibi Indians*. Canadian Museum of Civilization, Library, Ethnology document III-G-38M.

MAROIS, Roger, and Pierre GAUTHIER, 1989 : *Les Abitibis*. Archaeological Survey of Canada, Mercury Series 140, Canadian Museum of Civilization, Ottawa.

MITCHELL, Barry M., 1966 : *Preliminary Report on a Woodland Site Near Deep River, Ontario*. National Museum of Canada, Anthropology Papers 11, Ottawa.

MITCHELL, Barry M., et al., 1967 : "The Multi-Component Montgomery Lake Site". *Ontario Archaeology* (9) : 4-24.

MOREAU, Jean-François, Erik LANGEVIN, and Louise VERREAULT, 1991 : "Assessment of the Ceramic Evidence for Woodland-Period Cultures in the Lac Saint-Jean Area, Eastern Quebec". *Man in the Northeast* (41) : 33-64.

NOBLE, William C., 1982 : "Algonkian Archaeology in Northeastern Ontario", in M. G. Hanna and B. Kooyman (eds.), *Approaches to Algonquian Archaeology*. Proceedings of the Thirteenth Annual Conference, Archaeological Association of the University of Calgary, Alberta, pp. 35-55.

PINEL, Lyn, and Marc CÔTÉ, 1985 : *Fouille archéologique du site Cadieux (1985)*. Report submitted to Quebec's ministère des Affaires culturelles, Québec.

POLLOCK, John W., 1972 : *Report on Archaeological Sites of Swastika District 1972*. Manuscript on file at Ontario Ministry of National Resources, Swastika, Ontario.

– , 1973 : *Salvage Archaeological Excavations in Kirkland Lake District*. Manuscript on file at Ontario Ministry of National Resources, Cochrane, Ontario.

– , 1975 : "Algonquian Culture Development and Archaeological Sequences in Northeastern Ontario". *Canadian Archaeological Association Bulletin* (7) : 1-53.

– , 1976 : *The Culture History of Kirkland Lake District, Northeastern Ontario*. Archaeological Survey of Canada, Mercury Series 54, National Museum of Man, Ottawa.

RAMSDEN, Peter G., 1990 : "The Hurons : Archaeology and Culture History", in Chris J. Ellis and Neal Ferris (eds.), *The Archaeology of Southern Ontario to A.D. 1650*. Occasional Publication of the London Chapter, OAS (5) pp. 361-384.

REID, C. S., "Paddy", and Grace RAJNOVICH, 1991 : "Laurel : a Re-evaluation of the Spatial, Social and Temporal Paradigms". *Canadian Journal of Archaeology* (15) : 193-234.

RICHARD, Pierre J.H., 1980 : "Histoire postglaciaire de la végétation au sud du lac Abitibi, Ontario et Québec". *Géographie physique et Quaternaire* XXXIV (1) : 77-94.

RITCHIE, William A., 1980 : *The Archaeology of New York State*. Natural History Press, New York (Revised Edition).

SPENCE, Michael W., Robert H. PIHL, and Carl R. MURPHY, 1990 : "Cultural Complexes of the Early and Middle Woodland Periods", in Chris J. Ellis and Neal Ferris (eds.), *The Archaeology of Southern Ontario to A.D. 1650*. Occasional Publication of the London Chapter, OAS (5) pp. 125-170.

STOTHERS, David, and Marci STOTHERS, 1973 : "The Buck Lake Sites : Two Prehistoric Settlement Sites in Muskoka District, Northern Ontario". *Toledo Area Aboriginal Research Club Bulletin* 2 (2) : 13-22.

TAILLON, Hélène, and Georges BARRÉ, 1987 : *Datation au ^{14}C des sites archéologiques du Québec*. Dossiers 59, Quebec's ministère des Affaires culturelles, Québec.

TOOKER, Elisabeth, 1964 : *An Ethnography of the Huron Indians, 1615-1649*. Bulletin 190, Bureau of American Ethnology, Washington, D.C.

TOWNSEND, Ernest C., 1959 : *Birdstones of the North American Indian*. Privat Printed, Indianapolis.

WILFORD, Lloyd A., 1941 : "A Tentative Classification of the Prehistoric Cultures of Minnesota". *American Antiquity* 6 (3) : 231-249.

– , 1955 : "A Revised Classification of the Prehistoric Cultures of Minnesota". *American Antiquity* 21 (2) : 130-142.

WILLIAMSON, Ronald F., 1990 : "The Early Iroquoian Period of Southern Ontario", in Chris J. Elis and Neal Ferris (eds.), *The Archaeology of Southern Ontario to A.D. 1650*. Occasional Publication of the London Chapter, OAS (5) pp. 291-320.

WINTEMBERG, William J., 1931 : "Distinguishing Characteristics of Algonkian and Iroquoian Cultures". *Ottawa, National Museum of Man, Annual Report for 1929* (67) : 65-125.

WOODLEY, Philip J., 1990 : *The Thistle Hill Site and Late Archaic Adaptations*. Occasional Papers in Northeastern Archaeology No 4, Copetown Press, Dundas, Ontario.

WRIGHT, James V., 1966 : *The Ontario Iroquois Tradition*. National Museum of Canada, Bulletin 210, Ottawa.

– , 1967 : *The Laurel Tradition and the Middle Woodland Period*. National Museum of Canada, Bulletin 217, Ottawa.

– , 1972 : *The Shield Archaic*. Publications in Archaeology No. 3, National Museum of Man, Ottawa.

– , 1979 : *Quebec Prehistory*. National Museum of Canada, Van Nostrand Reinhold Ltd., Toronto.

LOCATION OF THE ALGONQUINS FROM 1534 TO 1650

Maurice Ratelle
Direction des Affaires autochtones
Ministère de l'Énergie et des Ressources

Translated by Michael J. Ustick

A clear grasp of the history of the aboriginal peoples of North America is not possible without taking into account the fact that the ethnic and demographic profile of many major regions has been transformed, sometimes radically, by population migrations. This is a fundamental reality in the history of the indigenous peoples of Quebec. Entire populations emigrated or sometimes even disappeared within very short periods of time. Evidence of this may be found in this country's earliest historical sources. In 1534, 1535 and 1541 Jacques Cartier encountered Iroquoian populations frequenting Gaspé and Tadoussac and occupying the Québec and Montréal regions. Some 60 years later, Samuel de Champlain met with Algonquian nomads (Montagnais, Etchemins and Algonquins) travelling on the St. Lawrence River in summer. If sedentary groups could vanish from so large an area in a short span of time, leaving few traces, what of the nomadic groups who were more flexible in their visits to the territory?

The Algonquins present themselves to us as a subject of study which is wholly appropriate to the issue of the ethnic upheavals subsequent to contact with the Europeans. Situated on each side of the Ottawa River, they faced threats which together serve to explain the disappearance of other Amerindian groups :

epidemics, the Iroquois wars, and assimilation following upon the scattered flights which those wars provoked. After the disintegration of their former tribes, the Algonquins managed to preserve sufficient strength to organize and define themselves as a new homogeneous "nation".[1]

THE 16TH CENTURY EVIDENCE

The disappearance of the Iroquoian groups which had settled in the St. Lawrence valley in the 16th century can chiefly be explained as a result of climate, epidemics and war. However, our data on climate and its impact are at present insufficient to draw any significant conclusions. For example, a cooling in the 16th century (the little Ice Age) might have adversely affected these populations, for whom corn growing was important, more particularly in the Québec region than in the Montréal region. Hunting and fishing, which were substantial sources of food, apparently remained available, as did the marine resources harvested by Iroquoians from the Québec area visiting the regions of Tadoussac and Gaspé in the summer.

Epidemics, on the other hand, seem to have constituted a real threat. On Jacques Cartier's second voyage, it was noted that in December 1535 over 50 Stadaconans had already died of a severe disease (Cartier 1981 : 225), yet we cannot conclude that epidemics were the sole cause of the Iroquoians' disappearance. We must investigate how much responsibility can be attributed to warfare, a fact confirmed by the fragments of Amerindian oral tradition collected at the time by the first European observers.

The voyages of Jacques Cartier inform us that the Stadaconans (from Québec) had the Toudaman as enemies, and the Hochelagans (Montréal) feared the Agojuda. In 1533, 200 Stadaconans on their way to the Gaspé were killed by Toudamans who surprised them on an island in the St. Lawrence by the mouth of the Saguenay (Cartier 1981 : 210). As to the identity of the Toudaman, the only options are Micmacs or Maliseet (Etchemins) : specialists tend to favour the Micmacs, while taking care not to conclude that they may have been responsible for the disappearance of the Stadaconans. As we shall see, it is in fact probable that the greatest aggressive threat to the Stadaconans came from upriver and not downriver. As for the Agojuda, not long ago historians tended to identify them with the Algonquins. Yet everything seems to indicate that the Algonquins were interested in being commercial partners with the Hochelagans and profiting from complementary trade goods[2], as they did with the Hurons of Lake Simcoe (Trigger 1985 : 147). On the other hand, the Iroquois located in the northern part of present-day New York State seem to have been potential enemies of the St. Lawrence Iroquoians, and the recent tendency has been to consider them as the aggressors (Trigger 1985 : 144-146). The Mohawks, for example, located not far from the headwaters of the Richelieu, south of Lake George, could travel via Lake Champlain and the Richelieu and attack both Hochelaga and Stadacona. However, archaeological research suggests that groups of Hurons in the Trent River valley had already been responsible for the disappearance of the West Laurentian Iroquoians between Lake Ontario and Lake St-François (Trigger 1985: 144-146). The extension of these wars to the Montréal region could be confirmed by information gathered by Father Vimont, who stated in 1642 regarding the island of Montréal :

> Jacques Cartier, the first of our French who discovered it, writes that he found on it a village called Ochelaga. This fully agrees with the accounts of the Savages, who call it "Minitik outen entagougiban", "the Island on which stood a town or a village". The wars have banished its inhabitants. (J.R., Vol. 22 : 205-207)

Further on, Father Vimont reports the words of two Algonquin chiefs (probably Onontchataronons) who, standing on the summit of Mont Royal, said :

> . . . that they belonged to the nation of those who had formerly dwelt on this Island. Then, stretching out their hands towards the hills that lie to the East and South of the mountain, "There," said they, "are the places where stood Villages filled with great numbers of Savages. The Hurons, who then were our enemies, drove our Forefathers from this country. Some went towards the country of the Abnaquiois, others towards the country of the Hiroquois, some to the Hurons themselves, and joined them. And that is how this Island became deserted." "My grandfather," said an aged man, "tilled the soil on this spot." (J.R., Vol. 22 : 215)

While these were Onontchataronon Algonquin chiefs speaking to Father Vimont, there is no doubt that the ancestors to whom they refer, who lived in "Villages filled with great numbers of Savages", were St. Lawrence Iroquoians, that is, Hochelagans. Since these chiefs claimed that at the time the Huron were their enemies, one must conclude that they were the descendants of certain Iroquoians who took refuge with the Onontchataronon, and that through oral tradition they kept alive the memory of an occupation of the island of Montréal.

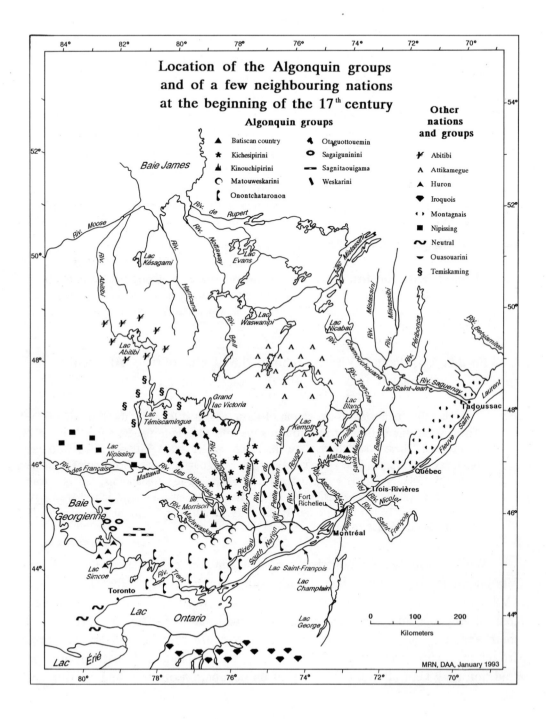

Location of the Algonquin groups
and of a few neighbouring nations
at the beginning of the 17th century

Algonquin groups

▲ Batiscan country
★ Kichesipirini
▲ Kinouchipirini
○ Matouweskarini
(Onontchataronon
◢ Otaguottouemin
◖ Sagaiguninini
— Sagnitaouigama
\ Weskarini

Other nations and groups

⚥ Abitibi
Λ Attikamegue
▲ Huron
▼ Iroquois
◖◗ Montagnais
■ Nipissing
~ Neutral
▼ Ouasouarini
§ Temiskaming

Baie James

Riv. Moose
Riv. Abitibi
Lac Késagami
Riv. Harricana
Riv. Nottaway
Riv. de Rupert
Lac Evans
Riv. Bell
Lac Waswanipi
Lac Nicabau
Riv. Mistassini
Lac Mistassini
Riv. Mistassini
Riv. Mistassibi
Riv. Péribonca
Riv. Betsiamites
Riv. Chamouchouane
Lac Saint-Jean
Riv. Saguenay
Saint Laurent
Tadoussac
Lac Abitibi
Lac Témiscamingue
Grand lac Victoria
Lac Kempt
Lac Blanc
Riv. Trenche
Riv. des Français
Lac Nipissing
Mattawa
Riv. des Outaouais
Riv. Coulonge
Riv. Gatineau
Riv. du Lièvre
Riv. Rouge
Riv. Petite Nation
Fort Richelieu
Riv. Assomption
Matawin
Riv. Saint-Maurice
Vermillon
Riv. Batiscan
Fleuve Saint Laurent
Québec
Trois-Rivières
Riv. Nicolet
Riv. Saint-François
Montréal
Baie Georgienne
Riv. Morrison
Île
Riv. Matawaska
Riv. Richelieu
Rideau
South Nation
Lac Saint-François
Lac Champlain
Lac George
Lac Simcoe
Riv. Trent
Toronto
Lac Ontario
Lac Érié

0   100   200
Kilometers

MRN, DAA, January 1993

To make this text consistent with that of Cartier, the Agojuda must therefore be identified as Hurons. This would suggest the hypothesis that the Huron wars against the West Laurentian Iroquoians (located between Lake Ontario and Lake St- François) continued until the dispersal of the Hochelagans. These Agojudas apparently came down via the Ottawa River, which was the classic connection between the Montréal region and Lake Huron and the best route for travelling to Montréal, whether for purposes of war or trade. The Algonquin were the natural allies of the Huron, and thus would not only let them pass but possibly even accompany them on their war campaigns. While all this is no more than conjecture, it is certain that the Hochelagans were defeated by one of these groups and that the survivors found refuge among both of them. These three aboriginal groups – Huron, Iroquois and Algonquin – had different versions of this past, and felt that they had been present in the Montréal region at a given point in their history. Every descendant of these "refugees" probably had his own view of events, influenced by his adopted nation – whence the variety of traditional interpretations.

It is strange that, even in the early 17th century, the Algonquins, like the Montagnais, seem to have had no clear recollection that Iroquoians once inhabited the St. Lawrence valley, and that they formed distinct groups of Hurons and Iroquois situated further to the south. It should be noted, however, that early in the French regime the Algonquins spoke of periods of friction and quarrels with both the Iroquois and Huron regarding occupation of the territory. We must therefore locate the conflicts with the St. Lawrence Iroquoians within a triangle whose delimiting lines extended from Huronia to Iroquoia, down the Richelieu and then the St. Lawrence rivers, well short of Québec, and then back toward Huronia. In Jacques Cartier's time, this area was probably a battlefield. It was a territory of changing borders (if it is possible to speak of borders for the 16th-century Amerindians), an area of combat but also of trade, and consequently of temporary or permanent alliances. In Champlain's time, this area was empty, and remained a no man's land until the French established themselves there and offered tactical support to the Algonquins and Montagnais.

Having established the existence of population movements prior to the 17th century, we can now move to the heart of our study. Entering the Gulf and ascending the river in the manner of the first French explorers, we shall attempt to detect the presence of the Algonquins between the years 1603 and 1632.

PRESENCE OF ALGONQUINS BETWEEN
TADOUSSAC AND QUÉBEC : 1603-1632

In 1603, the Tadoussac region was a nerve centre for the Montagnais that was testimony to their predominance. With a population of 1,000 (R.J., Vol. 1, 1611 : 15), they received their various trading partners there, both European and Amerindian. It was only by virtue of their commercial and war alliances that the Algonquins, Etchemins and later Hurons had a presence in Tadoussac. The Algonquins who were there at the very beginning of the French regime came from the Ottawa valley or the region west of the St-Maurice, depending on one's sources. The Algonquins of the Island (the Kichesipirini, whose main encampment was on present-day Morrison's Island[3]) and the Iroquet Band (the Onontchataronon, south of the Ottawa River in Eastern Ontario) are most frequently mentioned. They had the same enemy as the Montagnais : the "Iroquois", southeast of Lake Ontario, who were trying to seize control of the river whose shores had recently been abandoned by the Laurentian Iroquoian peoples.

PRESENCE OF ALGONQUINS BETWEEN
QUÉBEC AND TROIS-RIVIÈRES

It is estimated that in 1603 the Montagnais had imposed their presence in the Québec region for probably less than 30 years, shortly after the disappearance of the Stadaconans (Trigger 1985 : 146-148). The Algonquins sometimes encountered in this region came from the Ottawa valley, further upriver. They came there to trade, knit alliances and undertake minor war campaigns (Giguère 1973, Vol. 1, 1603 : 108; 1609 : 348). The Algonquin headmen Iroquet and Tessouat, who came from the Ottawa valley, and chief Batiscan (who, as we shall see, was not from the Québec region either) met with Montagnais there (Sagard 1866, Vol. 1 : 103-104). When the Montagnais saw the Jesuits preparing their installations in Sillery, they were the first to ask to settle on that mission's lands (R.J., Vol. 2, 1638 : 18-19). According to the *Jesuit Relations*, in 1640 the Québec region north of the St. Lawrence River still seemed to be essentially defined by the Montagnais who "are those who reside nearer Kebec, and are thus called on account of our high mountains. The Algonquins are further back." (J.R., Vol. 23 : 303).[4] But it must be made clear that the Algonquins were divided into two groups : in addition to those of the Ottawa valley, near the Hurons east of Georgian Bay, there were those who "are neighbors of the Montagnets, and as if mingled with them" (J.R., Vol. 23 : 305). Such a statement might lead us to infer that there were Algonquins in the Québec region who were culturally close to the Montagnais. This would be an incorrect inference, however, since the Attikamegues (Poissons Blancs) themselves, although remote from Québec, demonstrated on the occasion of their temporary settlement at the Sillery mission that they felt culturally closer to the Montagnais than to the Algonquins. In our opinion, the expression "mingled with them" conveys more a co-existence on certain hunting grounds or meeting places than it does ethnic similarity.

Furthermore, it is difficult to establish that specific groups of Algonquins might have frequented the lands north of the St. Lawrence between Québec and Trois-Rivières. If such groups existed in the early 17th century, they had no specific designations. Only the name of chief "Batiscan" has been assigned to a band and the river that this chief used for trading. It is difficult to decide whether chief Batiscan was a Montagnais or an Algonquin (Trudel 1966 : 170; Jury 1966: 80). If we rely on Champlain's map of 1612, the "Bastisquan country" was west of the St-Maurice River. This map suggests that chief Batiscan and his band frequented the sources of two rivers, one of which can only be the present-day Mattawin, which flows into the St-Maurice, while the other may be the Maskinongé, Yamachiche or Assomption (Giguère 1973, Vol. 1, 1612 map appended). However, the 1632 map suggests that this second river might be Rivière du Loup (Giguère 1973, Vol. 3, 1632 map appended). Champlain said that the Algonquins sometimes used the Batiscan River as a travel route (Giguère 1973, Vol. 1, 1603 : 91). Hence this would not yet have been customary for chief Batiscan himself, of course, if he was an Algonquin. We should point out that, at the end of its course, the Batiscan afforded an excellent route for travelling by canoe. It was also used by other bands, including those of Iroquet (Onontchataronon Algonquin) and Ochateguin (Arendaronon Huron), who came in 1609, for example, to assist their allies in their wars against the Iroquois (Mohawks) (Giguère 1973, Vol. 1, 1609 : 323-324; Vol. 2, 1609 : 803). Their stopping-place was on an island named Saint-Éloi, opposite the Batiscan church and a league and a half from the mouth of Ste-Anne River (Giguère 1973, Vol. 1, 1603 : 93, note 2; Vol. 1, 1609 : 323, note 1; Vol. 2, 1609 : 803, notes 1 and 2). This place was on the route from Huronia which led down the Ottawa River, the Gatineau (or other tributaries such as the Dumoine), the St-Maurice, the

Batiscan, and then the St. Lawrence as far as Québec and even Tadoussac. In this way attacks by the Iroquois, which were frequent along the Ottawa valley, could be avoided. In 1637 the Trois-Rivières region was still at the junction of the territories frequented by the Algonquins and Montagnais. The hunting grounds extending to the north, including those in the direction of Québec, were exploited by a Montagnais group during the winter (J.R., Vol. 12 : 189-191).

Consequently it is definitely not true to say that the Algonquins controlled the comings and goings of the Montagnais in this region. In fact, both the Montagnais and the Algonquins accompanied Champlain on his explorations of the St. Lawrence; both Montagnais and Algonquins seem to have used the river route, and they could do so only by helping each other.

THE TROIS-RIVIÈRES REGION

Although Algonquins have been found to be present between Québec and Trois-Rivières in 1603, they were newcomers in this region. When Champlain ascended the river that year, it was clear to him that even though they were assisted by the Montagnais and Etchemins, the Algonquins did not really control the river route :

> . . . a settlement at Three Rivers would be a boon for the freedom of some tribes who dare not come that way for fear of their enemies, the said Iroquois, who infest the banks all along the said river of Canada; but if this river were inhabited we might make friends with the Iroquois and with the other savages, or at the very least under protection of the said settlement the said savages might come freely without fear or danger, inasmuch as the said Three Rivers is a place of passage. (Biggar 1922, Vol. 1, 1603 : 137)

At that time, Algonquins from the Ottawa valley area were gradually taking over the old hunting grounds of the Iroquoians who had formerly frequented the region north of Lake St-Pierre. These Iroquoians must have been a presence on the north shore of the St. Lawrence, and for their winter hunting would have had access to a territory which could extend, where the St-Maurice was concerned, up to present-day Coucoucache on Lake Blanc. This would explain the subsequent location of the boundary between the hunting grounds of the Attikamegues and the Algonquins of Trois-Rivières at this place (Parent 1985 : 237). Despite their sedentary way of life, the St. Lawrence Iroquoians needed hunting territories, which lay north of the St. Lawrence River between Stadacona and Hochelaga. On the other hand, the French built their dwellings in Trois-Rivières on the very site of an old Iroquoian village (J.R., Vol. 8 : 27-29).

From the beginning of the Christian missions, Trois-Rivières was a place where Algonquins, Montagnais and Attikamegues met (Gouger 1987 : 81). It was because of the Iroquois threat that Trois-Rivières, founded in 1634, seemed destined to shelter several nations. This threat was also perceived as an effective way of forcing the Algonquins and Montagnais to settle in Trois-Rivières (J.R., Vol. 12 : 171; Beaulieu 1987 : 146). The Jesuits established the Conception mission there in 1634 (Trudel 1979, III, Vol. 1 : 138), but in the beginning few Algonquins chose this site for settlement. In 1637 there were only two families on what is commonly called the Pachiriny estate, situated "on the third lot of Jesuit lands" (Trudel 1983, III, Vol. 2 : 377, note 29), but a major defeat suffered in the same year by the Algonquin and Montagnais warriors (then on a campaign against the Mohawks) drove them to fortify themselves near French settlements (J.R., Vol. 12 : 157-171, 191; Parent 1985 : 325). The *Jesuit Relations* mention that in 1639 over 800 Algonquins from the Ottawa valley arrived in Trois-Rivières (J.R., Vol. 16 : 37, 43). As a rule, however, these Amerindians would remain there only temporarily. In 1640-1641 the missionaries of Trois-Rivières tended to a number of nations, including, among the Algonquin, the Kichesipirini, Weskarini, Onontchataronon and Oukotoemi (Otaguottouemins), as well as Attikamegues, Montagnais and several others (J.R., Vol. 20 : 259). Many baptisms administered at Trois-Rivières show that those who can be identified as Algonquins came from the Ottawa valley (Parent 1985 : 176, 227-229); they are also referred to as "the upper Algonquins" (J.R., Vol. 24 : 191). In fact, the Trois-Rivières mission was structurally similar to the Québec mission, which embraced a number of nations, as if these two regions were situated on a borderline and not within the specific territory of one nation.

In the 1640s, the Algonquin refugees in Trois-Rivières were affected by a major population shift. In 1641 two large groups fled the Iroquois menace : one took refuge in Sillery and the other returned to the Ottawa valley, where it was massacred by the Iroquois all the same; a third group, however, replaced these first two in Trois-Rivières (Trudel 1983, III, Vol. 2 : 377). In 1645 the Ottawa valley Algonquins assembled in Trois-Rivières and were still capable of a war effort to bring the Mohawk Iroquois to conclude a peace, which however was only temporary (Parent 1985 : 344-345; R.J., Vol. 3, 1645 : 23-35). All of them believing that peace had been won, these Algonquins frequented the hunting grounds in the Nicolet and Yamachiche river regions (Perrot 1973 : 107).

Those who hunted on the south side, around Nicolet River, were Onontchataronon Algonquins led by chief Taoutskaron (R.J., Vol. 4, 1647 : 4). The Yamachiche River group, led by Simon Piskaret, a chief of the Island Algonquins (Kichesipirini), suffered heavy losses at the hands of the Iroquois, who returned to the warpath. The Assomption River Band, if there was one, had no specific name, but we note that the Algonquin name of this river is *Outaragauesipi* (R.J., Vol. 3, 1642 : 36). This band could be that of chief Batiscan, if his band can be linked to certain Algonquins who frequented the area west of the St-Maurice in the early 17th century.

THE UPPER ST-MAURICE

Probably well before visiting the hunting grounds of the Trois-Rivières region, the Algonquins, like the Montagnais, used the Trenche and Bostonnais rivers to reach Lake St-Jean, and the Vermillon-Lièvre route to reach the Ottawa River (Parent 1985 : 226-227). However, up the St-Maurice River, beyond Coucoucache, began the territory of the Attikamegues, or Poissons Blancs (Parent 1985 : 237; Hodge 1913 : 52-53). Here it should be clarified that the Attikamegues were not the ancestors of the present-day Attikameks of the Upper St-Maurice, who in the 1970s were still identified as "Têtes-de-Boule" (Clermont 1982). However, the oral tradition of the present Attikameks (Têtes-de-Boule) suggests that a group called the "Omami" might have occupied lands situated to the north, east and south of Lakes Kempt and Manouan (Burger 1953 : 33). The Omami, reduced by epidemics and war, are said to have been driven further east by the arrival of the Têtes-de-Boule. The *Jesuit Relations* do not mention that such a group might have frequented a territory situated between that of the Algonquins of Trois-Rivières and that of the Attikamegues of the Upper St-Maurice. It is true that oral tradition, as recounted by the Têtes-de-Boule, can only refer to the period between 1720 and 1750, since that is approximately when an initial band of Têtes-de-Boule settled in the watershed of the St-Maurice (Ratelle 1987 : 92). In our opinion, the term "Omami" identified any group generally situated downstream, like the Oumamiweks of the North Shore, whose name means "down-stream people" (Hodge 1913 : 380). Similarly the Nipissing called the Algonquin

Oma'mi'wininiwak, that is, people from downriver (Day and Trigger 1978 : 797). Consequently the Omami, as reported in Tête-de-Boule oral tradition, would simply be Amerindians who, starting from approximately 1720 – hence in the 18th century, but not before – were situated downriver, that is, Algonquins of the Lower St-Maurice.

One of the main meeting-places of the Attikamegues was a lake named Kisakami (R.J., Vol. 4, 1651 : 26). This lake, christened St-Thomas by Father Buteux, has been identified as Lake Mandonac, but according to Albert Tessier (1934 : 19), without real proof. The true centre of Attikamegue territory was the heights where the Huron came to trade (Tessier 1934 : 30-32). In 1609 Champlain learned that those "great hunters" the Attikamegues could reach the North sea in under six days (Giguère 1973, Vol. 1, 1609 : 327). In 1648 three bands of Attikamegues, one of which had 40 canoes of its own, came down to Trois-Rivières (J.R., Vol. 32 : 283). Ethnically, these Attikamegues were closer to the Montagnais than the Algonquins.

We learn that the Attikamegues had as neighbours "three or four other small nations which are North of their country", including the Kapiminakouetiiks (J.R., Vol. 18 : 227; Vol. 29 : 119-121). There were also Ouramanicheks, many of whom came to trade with the Attikamegues in the early 1640s (J.R., Vol. 26 : 91). The Outakwamioueks, who were probably a branch of either the Mistassini or the Montagnais (or even the Naskapi, according to Bailey 1969 : 41), also came to trade with them. One of the principal meeting-places of these nations was Nicabau (Maouatchihitonnam), on the heights between the three major basins of Lake St-Jean, James Bay and the St-Maurice River (J.R., Vol. 46 : 275; R.J., Vol. 3, 1643 : 38). Further west, the Attikamegues probably adjoined the hunting grounds of a group of Algonquins known as Otaguottouemins (or Kotakoutouemi, possibly the same as the Oukotoemi). To the south, the Attikamegue hunting grounds lay beside those of the Kichesipirini and the Petite Nation (Weskarini).

CAP DE LA VICTOIRE (ANTHRANDÉEN) OR FORT RICHELIEU

The Algonquins did not venture onto the south shore of the St. Lawrence without good reason. They occasionally visited the mouth of the Richelieu to trade with Europeans or conduct guerilla warfare against the Iroquois. In 1603, the Algonquins, Montagnais and Etchemins erected a demi-fortress there of posts and oak bark which began on the shores of the St. Lawrence and ended on the banks of the Richelieu. This tactic allowed them to flee quickly by canoe if the Iroquois were to surprise them (Giguère 1973, Vol. 1, 1603 : 97-98). In 1609 a campaign was launched against the Mohawk Iroquois south of Lake Champlain. On their return, the allies halted at Chambly, divided up the prisoners and separated. The Algonquins did not return to Trois-Rivières or Québec, and neither did they remain in the Richelieu region, of course : they headed in an almost straight line to Sault St-Louis with some Hurons on their way back to Huronia (Giguère 1973, Vol. 2, 1609 : 825), and then returned to the Ottawa valley. Only the Montagnais accompanied Champlain back to Québec.

Champlain believed that the edges of Lake Champlain, like those of the Richelieu River, had been vacated of the populations who had once farmed there (Giguère 1973, Vol. 1, 1609 : 337). Champlain's writings may suggest that these shores were abandoned because of war between Algonquins and Montagnais on one side (joined on occasion by Etchemins) and Mohawks on the other. It is more probable, however, that the St. Lawrence Iroquoians, who no doubt visited these shores solely in order to hunt and fish, were driven out by the Mohawks themselves, who on their subsequent march to Québec found other enemies – the Algonquins and Montagnais (Trigger 1985 : 144-148).

A victory in 1610 not far from the mouth of the Richelieu, where Algonquins, Montagnais, Hurons and a few Frenchmen defeated some 100 Mohawks, afforded the Algonquins greater security on the river between Montréal and Québec, even though sporadic Iroquois raids were always to be feared (Giguère 1973, Vol. 1, 1610 : 359-360; Vol. 2, 1610 : 826-827). In fact, only the lands north of the river continued to be safe for seasonal hunting. However, even before the founding of Trois-Rivières, Cap de la Victoire was occasionally selected in periods of calm as a trading destination. In 1623, for example, Sagard comments that Hurons coming from Huronia had sojourned there for this purpose (Sagard 1976 : 41-42). With the approach of the peace of 1624, Cap de la Victoire tended to become a mandatory stop for the Hurons, from whom the Island Algonquins (Kichesipirini) and Montagnais attempted to obtain "presents" before allowing them to move on toward Québec (Sagard 1976: 260-261; 1866, Vol. III : 752-754).

The French presence at Fort Richelieu assured the Algonquins and others frequenting the region of safety during the winter hunt, which was particularly profitable there because the land was unoccupied (J.R., Vol. 24 : 115, 195). In the 1640s, it was Algonquins who had taken refuge both in Québec and Trois-

Rivières, as well as Algonquins of the Island (Kichesipirinis), who went to hunt around Fort Richelieu (J.R., Vol. 24 : 59, 113-115, 195, 209). When spring came, they would set out again for Trois-Rivières or Montréal. Algonquins must have frequented the watersheds of the Nicolet and Bécancour rivers only seldom in the early 17th century. Therefore, resituating Nicolas Perrot's remarks in their correct context (1973 : 107-108), we must conclude that there were Algonquins in this region just before they were defeated in 1647.

The Richelieu was thus an open door between the Algonquins and the Mohawks. While the Iroquois posed a direct threat to the Montréal region and even the Ottawa valley, the first clashes chiefly took place in the Richelieu corridor. This was so because the Mohawks were the main belligerents in the war for control of the communication channel of the St. Lawrence, one of the gates to which was Cap de la Victoire, situated at the very origin of the Richelieu.

The entire region south of Lake St-Pierre was therefore not Algonquin territory, but a no man's land, a battlefield, and the Richelieu was the warpath. The Lake St-Pierre region was in fact part of a war zone which extended to Lake Champlain. It is clear that the Algonquins, no more than the Iroquois or any other group, had no regular hunting ground south of Lake St-Pierre in 1603 and 1650. Their presence depended on the support of their Montagnais, Etchemin, Huron and French allies.

THE MONTRÉAL REGION

In the early 17th century, the Montréal region had also just been emptied of its former occupants. When Champlain arrived in 1603, it had probably been abandoned for less than 25 years. It is possible, however, and even quite probable, that groups of Hochelagans had taken refuge with a number of surrounding peoples, including Iroquois, Hurons and Algonquins.

Champlain learned that Algonquin country lay along the Ottawa River, then called the river of the Algoumequins. For the Algonquins, this was the Grand River, or *Kichesipi* (Hodge 1913 : 241). Rivière des Prairies was occasionally regarded as an extension of the Ottawa River, but apart from the fact that the territory of the Weskarini Algonquins bordered Rivière des Prairies and the group frequenting the Assomption River must have been in the vicinity, we are led to believe that Rivière des Prairies must have been just as deserted as the island of Montréal itself.

The Montréal region as well, therefore, was no more than a somewhat irregular passageway for the Algonquins : this is the drift of the information collected by Champlain. The entire area east and south of the Montréal region, i.e. the navigable routes of the Richelieu, the St. Lawrence, and the lower course of the Ottawa River, were directly threatened by the Iroquois raids, a fact which ruled out any stable Algonquin presence. Hence the assembly of 2,000 Amerindians at Sault St-Louis in 1612, including 1,200 warriors, can be explained only in terms of a conjunction of trade and warfare (Giguère 1973, Vol. 1, 1613 : 459). This site also saw a gathering of Amerindians in 1623, but it was of a temporary nature, on the trade route (Sagard 1976 : 42).

Champlain tried to induce the Algonquins to farm near Sault St-Louis by promising to build a French settlement there (Giguère 1973, Vol. 1, 1613 : 456-457). In 1613 Tessouat, chief of the Island Algonquins (the Kichesipirini of Morrison's Island) considered the possibility of moving to Sault St-Louis, but only if Frenchmen were there (Giguère 1973, Vol. 2, 1613 : 869-870). For the time, however, it was unthinkable for the Algonquins to come and settle in the Montréal region, since war was being waged virtually in that very spot, as well as at the mouth of the Richelieu. And it was probably not in the merchants' interest to provide for the needs of a settlement in this region which, for the time, was fairly far inland.

The Algonquins did not have a meeting-place in Montréal that afforded a minimum of safety until the foundation of Ville-Marie in 1642. The project had constantly been postponed since 1611 for lack of resources (Trudel 1983, III, Vol. 2 : 147). The missionaries hoped to attract there "the Mataouachkariniens, Onontchateronons, Kinonchepirinik, Weweskariniens, those of the Island, and others, – who speak the dialect of that region" (J.R., Vol. 24 : 269). As a result, starting in the winter of 1642-1643, Algonquins from the Ottawa valley, some of whom had hitherto ventured only to hunt near Fort Richelieu, were able to hunt around Montréal (J.R., Vol. 24 : 219, 267). However the Iroquois, armed by the Dutch, were quick to destroy this feeling of security.

THE OTTAWA VALLEY

An Algonquin legend alludes to former occupation of land situated near salt water at the time of first contact with the French (Speck 1929 : 107). This legend may be rooted in two historical realities. First, it seems that in the

16th century, some Iroquoians from the Québec region who frequented the salt waters of the St. Lawrence River at Tadoussac and of the Gulf at Gaspé, when dispersed, found refuge among one or more groups of Algonquins, thus contributing to the enrichment of oral tradition. The second explanation is simply that groups of Algonquins from the Ottawa valley going to trade at Tadoussac supposedly encountered Frenchmen there in the late 16th century.

Despite the lack of information concerning the Algonquins in 1535 and 1541, and in view of the historical certainty of an Iroquoian presence in the St. Lawrence valley, we must acknowledge that the Algonquin people must have occupied a territory adjoining that of the Iroquoians, i.e. at the very least, the Ottawa River valley. The documentation indicates that the Ottawa River extended "to the dwelling-place" of the Algonquins (Biggar 1922, Vol. 1, 1603 : 153). Champlain mentions this dwelling-place as being situated 60 leagues from the river, which would correspond to the location of the Algonquins of the Island, the Kichesipirini of Morrison's Island. Champlain himself in fact distinguished six principal groups of Algonquins following his expeditions of 1613 and 1615.

The first Algonquins identified north of the Ottawa River were the Weskarini (or Petite Nation). They most certainly frequented the Rouge, Petite Nation and Lièvre rivers, and their territory stretched north for at least four days' journey from the mouth of the Petite Nation River (Giguère 1973, Vol. 1, 1613 : 447). They might also appear in the Montréal region, and those who hunted north of Jésus Island, and possibly even on Assomption River, were doubtless from this band, or closely related to it.

To the south, the Onontchataronon (or Iroquet Band) frequented the South Nation River and possibly the Rideau River (Day and Trigger 1978 : 792; Giguère 1973, Vol. 1, 1613 : 448). Some observers have felt that they were part of the Weskarini (Petite Nation), probably because maps long identified a Petite Nation River in the area of the present-day South Nation, but historical documentation affirms that they were distinct from this band. The Onontchataronon are said to have once occupied the island of Montréal. This is possible, but as we saw earlier, it would be more plausible to conclude that Hochelagan survivors took refuge among the Onontchataronon. It is a fact that the way of life of the Onontchataronon demanded that they trade products that were complementary to those offered by the Hochelagans. In Champlain's time, this complementary trading persisted with other Iroquoian groups, such as the Neutral and Huron of the Great Lakes region.

However, the Onontchataronon did not visit the hunting grounds between the St. Lawrence and Ottawa rivers until after the disappearance of the West Laurentian Iroquoian groups who once occupied the river banks between Lakes Ontario and St-François. We cannot lend too much credit to the Nicolas Perrot text in which he states that the Algonquin territory in this region lay within the lines formed by the Ottawa River, Lake Nipissing and the French River, and beyond to Toronto (Perrot 1973 : 9). This territory can be superimposed upon Huronia; certain Algonquin groups wintered near the Huron, and the Onontchataronon sometimes even went into Neutral territory (Sagard 1866, Vol. III : 803). In reality, the Montréal region and Huronia were simply extreme points of the Onontchataronon territorial presence.

The Onontchataronon had on the one hand an alliance with the other Algonquins, the Montagnais and the Etchemins, and on the other an alliance with the Huron, especially the Arendaronon. They were the ones most threatened by the Iroquois in their trading with the French. The Iroquois could strike at the Onontchataronon via the Ottawa, the St. Lawrence and Lake Ontario. Once they arrived at the headwaters of the Rideau River, they could easily reach the Ottawa River and attack the nerve centres of this artery of Algonquin "territory" (Giguère 1973, Vol. 1, 1613 : 448).

Other Algonquins travelled further up the Ottawa River to hunt on the Gatineau. Champlain assigned them no particular name other than "Algoumequins" (Giguère 1973, Vol. 1, 1613 : 447-448). Note that the term "Algoumequins" most often corresponds to the Algonquins of the Island (Kichesipirini). Hence it would be Kichesipirinis whom Gabriel Sagard encountered when he came upon a small "hamlet of Algoumequins" between Morrison's Island and the Chaudière (Asticou) (Sagard 1976 : 254-255, 257). On the Ottawa River route, Morrison's Island was a summer meeting-place for the Kichesipirini. This band, one of whose chiefs bore the hereditary name of Tessouat, settled on Morrison's Island and the vicinity (including Allumette Island) as they came to require farmland, and gathered there in the summer to grow corn and squash, as well as peas, recently obtained from the French. Their hunting grounds covered the region north of Allumette Island, and certainly the downriver watersheds of the Gatineau and Coulonge as well; their northern limits are not clear. These were the richest and most powerful Algonquins in this early part of the 17th century. From Morrison's Island they attempted to control trade circulating on the Ottawa River. They also came to trade at the trading sites on the St. Lawrence, as far as Tadoussac.

On the south shore of the Ottawa, at the mouth of the Madawaska, lived the Matouweskarini (Giguère 1973, Vol. 1, 1613 : 450-451), whom Champlain had met at Chats Lake in 1613. This group, which in fact lived south of the Kichesipirini (R.J., Vol. 2, 1640 : 34; Vol. 3, 1643 : 61; Vol. 3, 1646 : 34; Vol. 5, 1658 : 22), fled to James Bay during the height of the Iroquois wars between 1647 and 1661, and was still there in 1672 (R.J., Vol. 6, 1672 : 54).

South of the Kichesipirini, in the Muskrat Lake region on the south side of the Ottawa River, were the Kinouchipirini (Keinouche, Quenongebin[5]) [Giguère 1973, Vol. 1, 1613 : 446], who were at once gardeners, hunters and fishermen. Champlain first met them above Long Sault (Quenechouan), when 15 canoes came down to trade at Sault St-Louis. Later at Muskrat Lake he met a chief called Nibachis, who in all probability was a Kinouchipirini (Giguère 1973, Vol. 1, 1613 : 452; Vol. 2, 1613 : 867; Day and Trigger 1978 : 792).

Northwest of the Kichesipirini, the Otaguottouemins lived off hunting and fishing. Champlain met them in 1615 at the mouth of the Mattawa River (Mataouan) (Giguère 1973, Vol. 2, 1615 : 508, 900). The Jesuits called them Kotakoutouemi and Otokotouemi (R.J., Vol. 2, 1640 : 34; Vol. 6, index : 20). As they were said to be neighbours of the Kichesipirini in lands to the north, Parent (1985 : 236) believes that they led a nomadic existence north of the Gatineau, in the region of the present-day Cabonga Reservoir, and in the Grand-Lac-Victoria region. It is probable that the Kotakoutouemi (Otaguottouemin) were the Outaoukotouemioueks with whom certain Trois-Rivières Algonquins went off to trade (J.R., Vol. 18 : 229 and 258, note 14; R.J., Vol. 4, 1650 : 34; Hodge 1913 : 375, 619; Giguère 1973, Vol. 2, 1615 : 508, note 6). If this was so, the Otaguottouemin, who did not farm and lived on hunting and fishing, could have frequented the territory north of the Ottawa River, possibly from the Lake Kipawa region to the Dumoine River, inclusive. They would then have been free to make regular contact with the Attikamegues.

WESTERN QUEBEC

Other groups of Amerindians whom the records do not associate with Algonquins were to be found northwest of the Algonquins : these were the Temiskaming, Abitibi and Temagami, and to the west, the Nipissing.[6] Still further west were groups related to the Ojibwa (or Chippewa) (Day 1978 : 787). The Nipissing, who in Huron were called *Askik8anehoronon*, were distinct from the Algonquins. In the present day, however, the Abitibi and Temiskaming are incorporated in the Algonquin nation within the territory of Quebec. These groups or "nations" were identified by the name of the principal lake where they would gather in the summer.

The Nipissing lived in the vicinity of the lake of the same name, and probably all around it. Culturally, the Nipissing are doubtless more similar to the Saulteux or Chippewa, but we shall see that they were later to be closely allied with the Algonquins. Champlain visited them in 1615 and estimated their population to be from 700 to 800 (Giguère 1973, Vol. 2, 1615 : 510). He noted that, like a number of other Algonquins from the Ottawa valley, certain Nipissings wintered in Huronia. Sagard reported that they spoke the Huron language in addition to their own tongue (Sagard 1976 : 74). In 1640, the Jesuits opened the mission of the Holy Ghost among them (R.J., Vol. 2, 1641 : 81), but a few years later, in 1650, violent attacks from the Iroquois forced the Nipissing to flee to Lake Nipigon (R.J., Vol. 4, 1650 : 26; Vol. 6, 1667 : 24).

SOUTHEASTERN ONTARIO

Champlain's voyages and the *Jesuit Relations* show that the Algonquins wintered regularly among the Huron. Three main groups of Algonquins frequented southeastern Ontario. The first of these, under chief Iroquet, was identified by the name of that chief as the Iroquet Band, but also by the word "Onontchataronon", which is of Huron origin. The second group was the Matouweskarini, located on the Madawaska River at the time. Finally there were the Kinouchipirini or Quenongebin, one of whose chiefs was undoubtedly Nibachis. However, three other minor groups must also be added : the Sagaiguninini (Sagahiganirinioueks, Sagahiganisini), the Sagnitaouigama, and the Ouasouarini. The Sagaiguninini and Sagnitaouigama reportedly lived southwest of the Ottawa River, near the Ottawa valley Algonquins, or even near the Huron (J.R., Vol. 18 : 227-229; Vol. 29 : 145; R.J., Vol. 2, 1640 : 34; Vol. 3, 1646 : 34; Vol. 4, 1648 : 62). The Ouasouarini, on the other hand, were more similar to the Chippewa, and belonged to the Algonquian groups of the Georgian Bay region (Hodge 1913 : 379). One must therefore avoid classifying all so-called "Algonquian-speaking peoples" living near the Huron as Algonquins. For example, the Ouachaskesoueks, Nigouaouichiriniks, Outaouasinagoueks, Kichkagoneiaks, Ontaanaks, Outaouakamigoueks, Ouasaniks, Atchougues,

Amikoueks, Achirigouans, Nikikoueks, Michisagueks and Paouitagoungs were not Algonquins, but Algonquian groups from the Great Lakes (Tooker 1964 : 19; J.R., Vol. 16 : 253; Vol. 33 : 149-151; Vol. 44 : 241-243).

The Christian missions were also responsible in part for the Algonquin presence in this region. The principal Jesuit missions were as follows : Holy Ghost, among the Nipissing (J.R., Vol. 30 : 109, 119); St. Charles, among the Ouasouarini (Waswarini) and Sagahanirini (R.J., Vol. 2, 1640 : 34; Vol. 4, 1648: 62; Vol. 4, 1650 : 21); and St. John the Baptist, among the Arendaronon Huron, who admitted certain Onontchataronons as neighbours in 1641 (Hodge 1913 : 467; R.J., Vol. 2, 1640 : 94; Vol. 2, 1641 : 83). The regularity with which the Onontchataronon took refuge in this place led the Jesuits to establish their own mission of St. Elizabeth for them (R.J., Vol. 3, 1644 : 100).

THE ALGONQUIN TERRITORY

D rawing up a 16th-century borderline between the Algonquins and the other ethnic groups is a very risky proposition.[7] By observing certain criteria characteristic of the cyclical way of life of the nomadic Amerindian populations, however, certain researchers have attempted to establish that the northern boundary of Algonquin territory ought to resemble the one that can be drawn for the early 17th century. Hence this boundary would respect the nomadic Algonquians' custom of dividing up hunting grounds on the basis of watersheds (Parent 1985 : 76-77). Yet one should be cautious in making this kind of extrapolation. In reality, at the turn of the 17th century the Algonquin people were advancing to the east, and appearing on hunting grounds and fishing sites frequented not long ago by the St. Lawrence Iroquoians.

Furthermore, one must beware of all generalization. One ethnic group did not necessarily occupy the entirety of a hydrographic system. The St-Maurice River seems to divide the Algonquins from the Montagnais, and Lake Blanc appears to be a border with the Attikamegues. It is probable that, around 1600, the Algonquin groups did not occupy all the northern tributaries of the Ottawa River, and this could apply to the southern ones as well. The Weskarini hunted at a distance of four days' canoeing and portaging to the north. The Kichesipirini, on the Coulonge and Gatineau rivers, probably went just as far inland.

The Attikamegue, Oumamiouek, Outakamiouek, Abitibi, Temiskaming and Nipissing bands were recognized as Algonquin by neither the Amerindians nor the French. The Barrière Lake and Grand-Lac-Victoria region was not frequented by the Kichesipirini, but rather by the Koutakoutouemi (Otaguottouemin) [Parent 1985 : 236]. Later, this region was not visited by Algonquins, but by Têtes-de-Boule from the west.

With regard to the area south of the Ottawa valley, the hunting territories might have extended as far as Toronto, as Perrot maintains. Further west, these territories should not have crossed the Canadian Shield or encroached upon Huron lands in Huronia.

POPULATION

In the face of an obvious lack of adequate data, any attempt to establish a population estimate for the Algonquin people for the mid-16th and early 17th centuries may seem pure speculation. We will therefore confine ourselves to reviewing certain previous estimation efforts and testing the method of projection based on population density, i.e. the individuals-to-area ratio.

Clearly, researchers are obliged to respect a certain order of size. Benjamin Sulte's estimate of 5,000 for the entire Algonquin people is doubtless exaggerated (Sulte 1898 : 124). A prudent estimate for the contact period would rather be 3,000, in view of the fact that certain groups could be assimilated to the "Algonquin" identity (Viau 1986 : 23). Unfortunately, we cannot establish a count for each Algonquin nation (or tribe). The count that has been attempted by the contributors to the *Historical Atlas of Canada* (1987 : pl. 18) is based on so-called ethnohistorical data. This is in fact nothing more than an honest guess, which sets the maximum Algonquin population for the early 17th century at 3,250 (*Atlas* 1987 : pl. 18). Certain researchers, basing themselves too narrowly on Nicolas Perrot's work, have accepted the figure of 400 warriors in 1650 for the Kichesipirini of Morrison's Island alone (Day and Trigger 1978 : 794; Sulte 1898 : 134). Yet if we assume as our basis of calculation that an average coefficient of 4.5 persons per family corresponds to each warrior, we obtain a total of 1,800 individuals for the Kichesipirini Band alone – a figure which, in our opinion, is far too high. Here one might make use of certain estimates based on the predatory economies model which researchers are attempting to apply to the nomadic Algonquian groups, a model which provides us with a rigid framework for the estimation process. Some specialists have proposed territorial occupation ratios, which could usefully be tested. Such calculations are mainly directed to a period prior to the European presence. This model prescribes that, based on various ecosystemic requirements, a predator Algonquian group frequenting a given territorial unit cannot exceed a certain demographic weight, for it would then endanger its viability in terms of the ecological equilibrium (a homeostasis) that it maintains on its territorial unit (Clermont 1977 : 182).

If we can establish that a pre-1600 nomadic Algonquian population can be calculated using an occupation ratio of 1.5 to 2 individuals per 100 km^2, as suggested by Hubert Charbonneau (1984 : 31), based on the territorial delimitation established earlier (which estimates the area occupied by the Algonquin groups for the mid-16th century to be approximately 40,000 km^2), we would arrive at a maximum population of around 800 individuals. For Algonquin occupation in the early 17th century (the area of which – shared with other groups – we estimate at approximately 94,000 km^2), there would be close to 2,000 individuals. These two estimates are certainly low, and would probably have to be doubled. A useful comparison can be made with eastern James Bay, where the territory might have contained a population of 0.001 to 0.004 individuals per square kilometre (Séguin 1985 : 68). Applied to the Algonquin territory, such a calculation would yield a population of only 160 to 380 persons. The wildlife resources of the territory with which we are concerned are obviously superior to those of the region east of James Bay. Consequently we prefer the estimate of Norman Clermont, who takes into consideration an occupation rate of one individual per 15 square miles for a nomadic Algonquian territory situated just north of an Iroquoian population – that is, after conversion, one individual per 39 km^2 (Clermont 1980 : 161). If we adopt a ratio of 1/39 km^2, we then have a population of 1,000 for the 40,000 km^2 that we estimate for 1535, and a population of 2,400 for 94,000 km^2 after 1600. However, the Algonquins were not strictly nomads : groups engaged in some amount of horticulture, and hence were able to support a larger population. They also engaged in trading complementary products with Iroquoian growers. These trading ties doubtless improved the living conditions of the peoples in question; therefore we must be prudent in all population estimates for the Algonquins. Lastly, we emphasize the imponderable of culture. In its cultural baggage, every human society carries empirical know-how with regard to its environmental constraints. Any population estimate for the early 17th-century Algonquins therefore remains highly relative.

The Amerindian populations, Algonquins included, suffered from the Iroquois wars of the 1630s to 1660s, but also from epidemics. As early as 1611,

Champlain noted a serious epidemic among them (Giguère 1973, Vol. 1, 1611 : 409). These misfortunes were to weigh heavily upon the Algonquins. They could have vanished completely, like other groups. They survived by fleeing great distances, as well as by getting closer to the French settlements, even though the latter tactic could aggravate the disastrous effects of the epidemics. It was these flights that were responsible for the fact that the name of the Algonquin River, as it was called in Champlain's time, was changed to the Ottawa River.

CONCLUSION

Setting out like the first French explorers in search of the Algonquins, we have covered an extensive geographical area stretching from Tadoussac to the Great Lakes. By Champlain's first voyage in 1603, the St. Lawrence Iroquoians whom Cartier had encountered had disappeared two or three decades ago. At that time the Algonquins, Montagnais and Mohawks were found to be trying to impose their presence in the Laurentian valley, which had become a no man's land.

The regions of Tadoussac and Québec were essentially controlled by the Montagnais. The Trois-Rivières region was no more than a passageway for the Algonquins coming from the Ottawa valley, who appeared there only after the disappearance of the Iroquoians. In winter, the Montagnais hunted north of the St. Lawrence River between Québec and Trois-Rivières. In the Upper St-Maurice, beyond present-day Coucoucache, were the Attikamegues (Poissons Blancs), who were to vanish without a trace as a result of the Iroquois wars and epidemics, and be replaced by the Têtes-de-Boule, a distinct cultural group from north of Lake Superior which adopted the name of Attikameks in the 1970s.

The six Algonquin groups or "nations" described by Champlain were located on each side of the Ottawa River, which was originally called the Algonquin River. But the history of the location of the Algonquins does not stop there : in fact, it has only just started. Furthermore, it is very difficult to attempt to define an "Algonquin territory", for the outline of such a territory can only be vague. Likewise, within that same territory, approximation is the best one can do.

The Algonquins were to be subjected to harsh attacks by their enemies the Iroquois, who forced them to abandon the Ottawa valley for many years. These attacks, accompanied on occasion by epidemics and famines, served to aggravate the general situation and threaten the survival of the Algonquin groups. Apart from the refuges of Québec, Trois-Rivières and Montréal, the Algonquins chiefly escaped to Huronia, the French forts, and well into lands north of a long line from Tadoussac to James Bay to the Great Lakes (J.R., Vol. 46 : 109; Vol. 50 : 297). During this period, efforts to settle the Algonquins failed, for two main reasons : epidemics and the persistence of nomadism. They temporarily registered at missions, but unlike the Huron and Iroquois did not really resolve upon settling there before the end of the 19th century.

The Algonquins managed to avoid breaking up completely, but no longer could they present the image they used to have. No longer were they the six distinct nations (or tribes) encountered by Champlain, living as neighbours along the Ottawa River. By the end of the French regime, they stood forth as two distinct groups : one from Trois-Rivières frequenting the hunting grounds of the Lower St-Maurice, and one from Lake of Two Mountains frequenting the hunting grounds of the Ottawa valley.

NOTES

[1] The sources offer us a plethora of names to designate the "nations", bands or clans. The basis of these names may be a meeting-place, a presumed quality, a totem, a chief's name, etc. At a stage prior to this study, we differentiated between references to the term "Algonquin". Given the limited framework of the present study, however, we confine ourselves here to the most adequate information for sketching a picture of the situation of the groups that can be included in a definition of "Algonquin" that is specific to the first half of the 17th century. Such an approach indicates that, as of the turn of the 17th century, this definition was constantly changing. While the Algonquins managed to avoid disintegration, other groups were not so lucky, and over the generations, scattered elements would become culturally adapted to, and in fact participate in, the definition of the Algonquin people.

[2] For example, the Iroquoians could offer corn, tobacco and fishing nets in return for dried meat, furs, etc.

[3] For strategic reasons, the Kichesipirini pitched their summer camp on Morrison's Island and not, as historians long believed, on Allumette Island.

[4] On the origin of the name Quebec, the reader may consult the article by Charles A. Martijn, 1991 : "Gepeg (Québec) : un toponyme d'origine micmaque", *Recherches amérindiennes au Québec* XXI (3) : 51-64.

[5] It is interesting to note here that Long Sault bore the name of "Quenechouan" and that a river named "Kinonge" was situated near present-day Montebello, which however was the site of the Weskarini.

[6] In the French period, these "peoples" were not part of the "Algonquins" as a specific entity, although some may have been covered by the general term "Anishnabe".

[7] With regard to the map that accompanies this article, we have taken the liberty of including under "Algonquin groups" three small groups which seem to us to partake of the definition of the Algonquin entity in this first half of the 17th century. These are chief Batiscan's group, the Sagaiguninini and the Sagnitaouigama.

ACKNOWLEDGMENTS

For their collaboration and comments, I wish to extend my thanks to Jacqueline Beaulieu, Alberto Poulin, Christian Couvrette and Gilles Vallée. Thanks to Nathalie Giroux and Pierre Morin for the cartography. Thanks as well to Daniel Clément and the editorial team of *Recherches amérindiennes au Québec*, especially Marcelle Roy.

BIBLIOGRAPHY

A) Archival sources

Archives nationales du Québec, Archives des Colonies, France :
  _ Series B, Letters sent
  _ Series $C^{11}A$, General Correspondance, Canada
  _ Series $C^{11}E$, Boundaries and Posts
  _ Series F^3, Moreau de Saint-Méry Collection
Archives of the Séminaire de Saint-Sulpice à Montréal.

B) Works cited

BAILEY, Alfred Goldsworthy, 1969 : *The Conflict of European and Eastern Algonkian Cultures 1504-1700 : A Study in Canadian Civilization*. 2d ed., Toronto, University of Toronto Press.

BEAULIEU, Alain, 1987 : "Réduire et instruire : deux aspects de la politique missionnaire des Jésuites face aux Amérindiens nomades (1632-1642)". *Recherches amérindiennes au Québec* V (1-2) : 139-154.

BIGGAR, H.P., 1922 : *The Works of Samuel de Champlain*. 6 vols. Toronto, The Champlain Society.

BURGER, Valérie, 1953 : "Indian Camp Sites on Kempt and Manouan Lakes in the Province of Québec". *Pennsylvania Archeologist Bulletin* XXIII (1) : 32-45.

CARTIER, Jacques, 1981 : *Voyages au Canada*. Paris, Maspéro, (Ch.-A. Julien, Ed.).

CHAPDELAINE, Claude, 1980 : "L'ascendance culturelle des Iroquoiens du Saint-Laurent". *Recherches amérindiennes au Québec* X (3) : 145-152.

CHARBONNEAU, Hubert, 1984 : "Trois siècles de dépopulation amérindienne", in Louise Normandeau and Victor Piché (eds.), *Les populations amérindiennes et inuit du Canada. Aperçu démographique*. Montréal, Les Presses de l'Université de Montréal : 28-48.

CHARLEVOIX, P.-F.-X., 1744 : *Histoire et description générale de la Nouvelle France avec le Journal historique d'un voyage fait par ordre du Roi dans l'Amérique Septentrionale*. Paris, Chez Nyon Fils, Libraire, 3 vols. (reprint 1976).

CLERMONT, Norman, 1974 : "L'hiver et les Indiens nomades du Québec à la fin de la Préhistoire". *La Revue de géographie de Montréal* XXVIII (4) : 447-452.

– , 1977 : "La Transformation historique des Systèmes économiques algonquiens", in William Cowan (ed.), *Actes du Huitième Congrès des Algonquinistes*. Ottawa, Carleton University : 182-187.

– , 1980 : "L'augmentation de la population chez les Iroquoiens préhistoriques". *Recherches amérindiennes au Québec* X (3) : 159-164.

– , 1982 : *Ma femme, ma hache, mon couteau croche : deux siècles d'histoire à Weymontachie*. Québec, ministère des Affaires culturelles, (c. 1977), Coll. Civilisation du Québec, Cultures amérindiennes No. 18.

– , 1987 : "La préhistoire du Québec". *L'Anthropologie* (Paris), 91 (4) : 847-858.

DAY, Gordon M., 1978 : "Nipissing", in Bruce G. Trigger (ed.), *Northeast*, Vol. 15, *Handbook of North American Indians*. Washington, Smithsonian Institution : 787-791.

DAY, Gordon M., and Bruce G. TRIGGER, 1978 : "Algonquin", in Bruce G. Trigger (ed.), *Northeast*, Vol. 15, *Handbook of North American Indians*. Washington, Smithsonian Institution : 792-797.

ETHNOSCOP, 1980 : *Étude de potentiel archéologique : axe Maniwaki - Témiscaming, secteur rivière Dumoine et Maniwaki*. Québec, ministère de l'Énergie et des Ressources, Service de la voirie forestière.

– , 1984 : *L'occupation amérindienne en Abitibi-Témiscamingue*. Québec, ministère des Affaires culturelles, Direction régionale de l'Abitibi-Témiscamingue.

GIGUÈRE, Georges-Émile, 1973: *Oeuvres de Champlain*. Montréal, Éditions du Jour, 3 vols.

GOUGER, Lina, 1987 : *L'acculturation des Algonquins au XVIIe siècle*. Master's thesis, Department of History, Université Laval, Québec.

Historical Atlas of Canada, 1987 : Toronto, University of Toronto Press, Vol. 1, *From the Beginning to 1800*.

HODGE, Frederick Webb, 1913 : *Handbook of Indians of Canada*. Ottawa, C.H. Parmelee.

J. R.= Thwaites, Reubens G., (ed.), 1896-1901 : *The Jesuit Relations and Allied Documents*. Cleveland, The Burrows Brothers Co, 73 vols.

JURY, Elsie McLeod, 1966 : "Batiscan (Batisquan) ". *Dictionary of Canadian Biography*. University of Toronto press and Les Presses de l'Université Laval, Vol. 1 : 80.

MAROIS, Roger J.-M., 1975 : *Les schèmes d'établissement à la fin de la préhistoire et au début de la période historique : le sud du Québec*. Ottawa, National Museum of Man, Archaeological Survey of Canada, Paper No. 17.

MARTIJN, Charles A., 1991 : "Gepèg (Québec) : un toponyme d'origine micmaque". *Recherches amérindiennes au Québec* XXI (3) : 51-64.

PARENT, Raynald, 1985 : *Histoire des Amérindiens du Saint-Maurice jusqu'au Labrador : de la préhistoire à 1760*. PhD dissertation, Department of History, Université Laval, Québec.

PENDERGAST, James F., and Bruce G. TRIGGER, 1978 : "Saint Lawrence Iroquoians", in Bruce G. Trigger (ed.), *Northeast*, Vol. 15, *Handbook of North American Indians*. Washington, Smithsonian Institution : 357-361.

PERROT, Nicolas, 1973 : *Mémoire sur les moeurs, coustumes et relligion des sauvages de l'Amérique septentrionale*. Montréal, Éditions Élysée.

PLOURDE, Michel, 1990 : "Un site iroquoien à la confluence du Saguenay et du Saint-Laurent au XIIIe siècle". *Recherches amérindiennes au Québec* XX (1) : 47-61.

RATELLE, Maurice, 1987 : *Contexte historique de la localisation des Attikameks et des Montagnais de 1760 à nos jours*. Québec, ministère de l'Énergie et des Ressources, 1 vol., 2 appendixes.

Relations des Jésuites. Montréal, Éditions du Jour, 1972, 6 vols.

SAGARD THÉODAT, Gabriel, 1866 : *Histoire du Canada et Voyages que les Frères Mineurs Récollects y ont faicts [...] depuis 1615*. Paris, Librairie Tross, 4 vols.

– , 1976 : *Le Grand Voyage Du pays des Hurons*. Montréal, Cahiers du Québec/Hurtubise HMH. Presentation by Marcel Trudel, Denys Moreau's edition.

SÉGUIN, Jocelyne, 1985 : "Réflexions sur les sociétés prédatrices : l'éloge de l'harmonie ou l'archéologie du rire". *Recherches amérindiennes au Québec* XV (3) : 58-76.

SIMARD, Jean-Paul, 1976 : "Le meeting de M8chau 8raganich". *Recherches amérindiennes au Québec* VI (2) : 2-16.

SPECK, Frank G., 1915 : *Family Hunting Territories and Social Life of Various Algonkian Bands of the Ottawa Valley*. Canada, Dept. of Mines, Memoir 70, no 8, Anthropological Series.

– , 1929 : "Boundaries and Hunting Groups of the River Desert Algonquin". *Indian Notes* VI (2) : 97-120.

SULTE, Benjamin, 1898 : "The Valley of the Grand River 1600-1650". *Transactions of Royal Society of Canada*, 2d series, IV (2) : 124.

– , 1911 : "Les Attikamègues et les Têtes-de-Boule". *Bulletin de la Société de géographie de Québec* 5 (2) : 121-130.

– , 1934 : "Les Têtes-de-boule", in G. Malchelosse, *Mélanges historiques/études éparses et inédites de Benjamin Sulte; compilées, annotées et publiées par Gérard Malchelosse*. Montréal, G. Ducharme, Vol. 20.

TESSIER, Albert, 1934 : *Jacques Buteux*. Trois-Rivières, Éditions du Bien public.

TOOKER, Elisabeth, 1964 : *An Ethnography of the Huron Indians, 1615-1649*. Bulletin 190, Bureau of American Ethnology, Washington, D.C.

TRIGGER, Bruce G., 1964 : *Native and Newcomers. Canada's "Heroic Age" Reconsidered*. Kingston and Montréal, McGill-Queen's University Press.

– , 1987 : *The Children of Aataentsic : A History of the Huron People to 1660*. Kingston and Montréal, McGill-Queen's University Press.

TRUDEL, Marcel, 1966 : *Histoire de la Nouvelle-France, II, Le comptoir*. Montréal, Fides.

– , 1974 : *Les débuts du régime seigneurial au Canada*. Montréal, Fides.

– , 1979 : *Histoire de la Nouvelle-France*, III, *La Seigneurie des Cent-Associés 1627-1663*, Vol. 1, *Les événements*. Montréal, Fides.

– , 1983 : *Histoire de la Nouvelle-France*, III, *La Seigneurie des Cent-Associés, 1627-1663*, Vol. 2, *La Société*. Montréal, Fides.

VIAU, Roland, 1986 : "Les dieux de la terre : contribution à l'ethnohistoire des Algonquins de l'Outaouais, 1600-1650". Report submitted to MRC Papineau in the context of the program "Amélioration de l'intervention régionale".

KITIGAN ZIBI ANISHINABEG
THE TERRITORY AND ECONOMIC ACTIVITIES OF THE RIVER DESERT (MANIWAKI) ALGONQUINS, 1850-1950

Jacques Frenette
Jacques Frenette Anthropologue Consultant Inc.

Translated by Michael J. Ustick

Not many ethnographic sources exist that cover the territory and economic activities of the members of the River Desert Algonquin Band, who live on the Maniwaki reserve. In fact, only Frank G. Speck has left a text on the subject (Speck 1929), in addition to collecting, within other publications, information on the material culture (Speck 1927; 1941) and divination rituals (Speck 1928) of this band and on the hunting territories of neighbouring bands (Speck 1915a and 1923).

Speck made three visits to Maniwaki in three consecutive years : 1927, 1928 and 1929 (Speck 1929 : 98). At a general meeting held in January 1929, he noted the distribution of some 30 families for the 1927-1928 hunting season on the band's territory, whose borders he also established. Map 1, taken from Speck's article, uses numbers and letters to locate the multifamily groups and families identified by the American ethnologist. Groups 1 to 5 are composed of the River Desert families whose names are provided in Table 1 (Speck 1929 : 98, 111-113). The band consisted of 78 families at the time (Speck 1929 : 108).

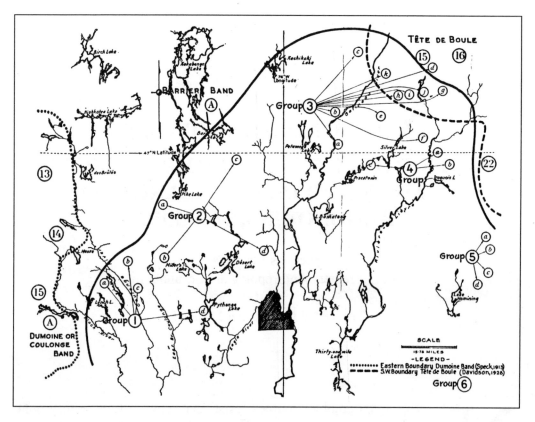

Map 1
Territory of the River Desert Band (1927-1928).
(Source : Speck 1929)

However, Speck does not succeed in delimiting the entire territory of the River Desert Band. And while he states that the family hunting territory system existed among these Algonquins as it did elsewhere in the continental northeast, he cannot locate a single family hunting territory. As he indicated at the time, the institution had disappeared : "The family group is the [basic] unit [of this band] with its now dissolved hunting territory institution" (Speck 1927 : 249). Only multifamily groups are associated with parts of the territory, or more precisely, parts of watersheds (Map 1, Table 1). Finally, Speck provides virtually no information on the hunting, fishing and trapping activities of the River Desert Algonquins. Rather he states that agriculture is playing an increasingly large economic role : "Farming has so developed among them that practically all are engaged in it." (Speck 1927 : 249-250)

Speck has no exact explanation for the advanced state of erosion of the family hunting territory system and the decline of hunting, fishing and trapping activities. He confines himself to saying that "the Maniwaki band [is] much affected, and that detrimentally, by social and economic Europeanization." (Speck 1929 : 97)

It is our intention in this article to provide new data on the territory and economic activities of the members of the River Desert Band. Surveys conducted with seven elders of the community in 1987,[1] archival research, and a review of historical and ethnological documentation on the region enable us to establish the extent of the band's territory and to analyse the changes to its boundaries and the causes of the disintegration of the family hunting territory system. Next we add the names of a few more families to the list compiled by Speck, and document the relative place of agriculture among the economic activities of the Maniwaki Algonquins from the reserve's creation in 1853 until the 1950s.

It should be noted that, for now, it is still not possible to sketch a complete picture of the occupation and use of the River Desert Band's territory up to the present day – and indeed, this will probably never be possible. As Speck has pointed out, this mode of territorial occupation and use suffered a very early and significant disruption. However, the work currently under way (summer 1992) on the reserve should allow us to ascertain more on this subject.

CREATION OF THE MANIWAKI RESERVE IN 1853

Let us first point out that the word "Maniwaki" means "land of Mary" (*Mani*: Mary; *wakan* : land) (Carrière 1962 : 76, note 6). Furthermore, the River Desert Algonquins call themselves "Kitigan Zibi Anishinabeg", as in our title, which means "the Algonquins of the river of gardens" (*kitigan* : garden; *zibi* : river; *Anishinabeg* : Algonquins). Interestingly enough, the Eurocanadian colonists used the term "desert" to refer to a plot of land that had been cleared for farming. Around the middle of the 19th century, a few Algonquins, including Pakinawatik, spokesman for the Gatineau River Algonquins, and his brothers Passenjewa and Pigiw, cleared land, built cabins and laid out gardens (or farms) near the mouth of the Desert River, where there was a little Hudson's Bay Company trading post. Apparently there were also gardens at Desert Lake

Table 1

Distribution of families on territory of the River Desert Band in the 1920s

According to Speck (1929)	*According to Deschênes and Frenette (1987a)*
Coulonge River basin	
1-A : Simon Cayer	
1-B : Jacko Michel Makatenine	Jacko Michel
1-C : Solomon Whiteduck	Daniel Whiteduck
1-D : J.B. Buckshot	
	Jos and Xavier Commandant (Corneille River)
	Sam and Michel Côté, César Paul (Lake Jim)
	Dick Tenasco (Corneille River)
Desert River basin	
2-A : Alonzo Commonda	Alonzo Commanda
2-B : Albert Jabot	
2-C : Abraham MacDougall	
2-D : J.B. Koko	
Gatineau River basin	
2-E : André Cayer	John Cayer
3-A : Peter Jacko	
3-B : Joseph Cesar	
3-C : Noe MacGregor	
3-K : Xavier Mactimonium	
Barrière Band A : Mathias Bernard	Mathias Bernard and John Jérôme
	Basil Smith (Lake Piscatosin)
	Carl family (Lake Baskatong)
	Tolé family (Lake Baskatong)
Lièvre River basin	
3-D : Pierre Clement	
3-E : J.B. Jabot	Jean-Baptiste Chabot
3-F : Jim Brascoupé	Jim Brascoupé
3-G : Noe Nouna	
3-H : Dominic Jabot	Dominique Chabot
3-I : Michel Pizendawatch (Côté)	
3-J : Frank Mungo and Frank Mungo Jr.	
3-L : Paddy Chaussé	
4-A : Antoine Jacko	
4-B : Joseph Jacko	
4-C : Xavier Toinish	
	Jos and Xavier Brascoupé (Rouge River)
Rouge River basin	
5-A : Xavier Amiconse	
5-B : Mathias Chichippe	
5-C : Abraham Chichippe	
5-D : Joseph Chawin	

(Carrière 1962 : 76, note 6). Hence both the Algonquins and the Eurocanadians of the time had given the same name, in their respective languages, to the same reality.

During the French regime, the Sulpician mission of Lake of Two Mountains housed mainly Algonquins, Nipissings and Mohawks. The Algonquins and Nipissings usually spent the summer there, returning for the rest of the year to their hunting ground, which was the Ottawa River basin as far as the Mattawa. After the Conquest, in 1763 and 1772 the Algonquins and Nipissings asked the colonial authorities to protect these lands from invasion by the colonists (St. Louis 1951 : 7, 9). Nonetheless, Loyalists began settling there in 1783, in what was then known as Upper Canada. In that year and the following one, treaties were signed with the Mississauga which the colonial leaders viewed as extinguishing Indian title even to the Algonquin and Nipissing territories. On several occasions in the 1790s, these two nations demanded compensation for the territories they had lost (St. Louis 1951 : 7).

In the 19th century, colonization and the logging industry began to advance in the Ottawa valley, and wildlife resources diminished at an alarming rate. From 1820 to 1836 the Algonquins and Nipissings tried many times to draw the attention of the government authorities to their situation. The merit of the Algonquin and Nipissing claims was acknowledged (Francis 1983 : 14, 26; St. Louis 1951 : 7, 8-9, 15-19, 21). For example, a committee of the Executive Council indicated in 1837 that the Algonquins and Nipissings were "the most helpless and destitute of the Indians of Lower Canada" (quoted in Francis 1983 : 27; St. Louis 1951 : 22). The committee recommended that these nomadic hunting populations be converted to sedentary, self-sufficient farmers living on one reserve :

> . . . that a sufficient tract of land should be set apart in the rear of the present range of townships on the Ottawa River, and that such of them as may from time to time be disposed to settle on land should be located there, and that both they and the rest of these tribes should continue to receive such support, encouragement and assistance as may supply the place of their former means of subsistence, and at the same time prepare and lead them to a state of independence of further aid. (Canada 1905-1912, Vol. 2 : 16)

The Algonquins and Nipissings continued to complain of the invasion of their hunting grounds, but to no effect : in fact, the situation worsened.

Dan Whiteduck, one of the elders interviewed in 1987. (Photo by the Kitigan Zibi Anishinabeg Band Council, 1992)

To a request of March 9, 1840 for monetary compensation for the appropriated territories, the Governor General replied on July 19, 1841 that no compensation would be forthcoming to the Algonquins and Nipissings, since the government was bound by no treaty (St. Louis 1951: 24). Again, at a council held on September 4, 1841 at Lake of Two Mountains in the presence of Indian Agent James Hughes, the Algonquins and Nipissings demanded that their remaining hunting territories be protected, that they receive financial assistance, and that they be granted a settlement on Allumette Island in the Ottawa River (St. Louis 1951 : 22). Here too they received no satisfaction.

Their situation continued to deteriorate. A sad picture was painted in 1847 by the same Indian Affairs agent, James Hughes :

> They were once the richest and most independent tribes of this continent, but are now the reverse. Great parts of their hunting grounds have been assumed by Government, and laid out into townships : a vast extent has been taken possession of by Squatters, and the rest almost entirely ruined by lumbermen. Their deer have disappeared, this [*sic*] beaver and other furs annihilated, caused by continual and annual fires made in their forests by lumber men. (quoted in Francis 1983 : 27)

In a report filed in 1844, the assistant commissioner of Crown Lands, T. Bouthillier, indicated that the Algonquins and Nipissings still wanted to move their settlement further up the Ottawa River so as to distance themselves from the colonization areas. A few Algonquins had already begun clearing parcels of land on the Gatineau River. Supported by the Bishop of Bytown, they wanted to obtain 60,000 acres of land at the confluence of the Desert River (Ratelle 1987 : 175-176). In 1845, an initial petition to this effect bearing 60 signatures was sent to the Governor General of Canada. When there was no response, it was sent again to Lord Elgin on October 10, 1848, accompanied by a supporting letter from the Bishop of Bytown, Mgr. Eugène Guigues (Carrière 1962 : 85-88).[2]

In 1849, Mgr. Guigues visited Desert River in person (see Barbezieux 1897 : 434-441). There he talked with, among others, Pakinawatik, spokesman for the Gatineau Algonquins. The Monsignor returned from his journey with a new petition from these Algonquins, signed by 60 men (Barbezieux 1897 : 445). Renewing his support for the petition, Mgr. Guigues (Barbezieux 1897 : 446) asked that missionaries be established on the future reserve (Carrière 1962 : 77, 88). On August 5, 1849 Father Clément, missionary to the Algonquins, brought back a final petition, this one bearing 41 signatures (Carrière 1962 : 78). Finally, the efforts of the Algonquins and the clergy bore fruit. On August 17, 1849, Mgr. Guigues was informed (Barbezieux 1897 : 446-447) that the commissioner of Crown Lands had received authorization to reserve the land on the Gatineau requested by the Algonquins (Carrière 1962 : 90). The plan was acted upon in 1850. The future reserve was situated in the very middle of numerous lumber concessions which had already been granted to entrepreneurs (Aumond, Gilmour, Hamilton, Masse, McGoey and Paterson).

Mgr. Guigues would have preferred to see the Oblates named as proprietors of the Maniwaki reserve. However, his wishes were opposed by the member for Bytown, Thomas MacKay (Barbezieux 1897 : 447-454). The Oblates had to be content with a plot of 600 arpents within the reserve, which some Attikameks who had arrived in May 1849 had cleared but then left behind after their departure a few weeks later (Carrière 1962 : 91-96). In 1906 these Attikameks were finally granted a reserve at Manouan on Kempt Lake.

In 1851 Parliament passed the *Act to Authorize the setting apart of Lands for the use of certain Indian Tribes in Lower Canada*. This law paved the way for the creation of the Maniwaki reserve in 1853. The authorities intended the reserve to accommodate not only the Algonquins and Nipissings, but also Attikameks – in short, all hunters whose territories used to lie between the Ottawa and St-Maurice rivers and who were in the habit of gathering in the summer at Lake of Two Mountains (Francis 1983 : 32-34; Ratelle 1987 : 176; Savard and Proulx 1982 : 66-67). At the time, the size of the reserve was 45,750 acres.

In addition to the Algonquins with whom Mgr. Guigues had met on Desert River in 1849, other Algonquin and Nipissing families withdrew to Maniwaki to remove themselves from another increasingly tense situation involving the Sulpicians and Mohawks at Lake of Two Mountains (Day 1978 : 790; Day and

Trigger 1978 : 795; Hessel 1987 : 93; Marinier 1980 : 31; Pariseau 1974 : 83-84). According to a census done in 1873, there were only 66 Algonquins and 35 Nipissings left at Lake of Two Mountains. The majority went to Maniwaki and Lake Timiskaming, where another reserve had been created in 1853, and to Mattawa, Fort William and Fort Coulonge along the Ottawa River, where it was possible to obtain the same services as at Lake of Two Mountains, yet closer to the hunting grounds (National Archives of Canada 1873a and 1873b). However, Lake of Two Mountains was still visited on occasion (Moore 1982 : 6-9).

Also, between 1870 and 1927 a small village of Algonquins, Métis and Eurocanadians was established on Lake Baskatong, the source of the Gatineau River. This small community disappeared in 1929 when the Mercier dam went into operation, to eventually form the present Baskatong Reservoir (Bouchard 1980 : 86-88). At that time, the Algonquin families who assembled there in the summer – the Smiths, Tolés and Carls – joined the River Desert band, of which they considered themselves a subgroup (Couture 1983 : 121; Deschênes and Frenette 1987a : 53-54, 79-80).

TERRITORIAL LIMITS OF THE RIVER DESERT BAND

A band's territory is never set in stone, any more than people's membership in the band. Thus its size will vary from one band to another, depending on the movements of individuals. This phenomenon was described by Davidson in the early 20th century, with reference to the Algonquins of Grand-Lac-Victoria.

> The boundaries of a band . . . include all the territory owned by its members. The band itself, it must be emphasized, is not a land owning unit and therefore its limits cannot be indicated as being permanently fixed, for they may fluctuate slightly from time to time, according to the ownership of the various districts and the affiliation of the owners, as they succeed each other, with one band or another. (Davidson 1926 : 80)

In addition to movements of families between bands, a band's territory could also be modified as a result of encroachment caused by colonization, the lumber industry, communication routes, and so on.

The way to establish the territorial limits of the River Desert Band is to combine all hunting grounds used by its members. As we shall see, this band's

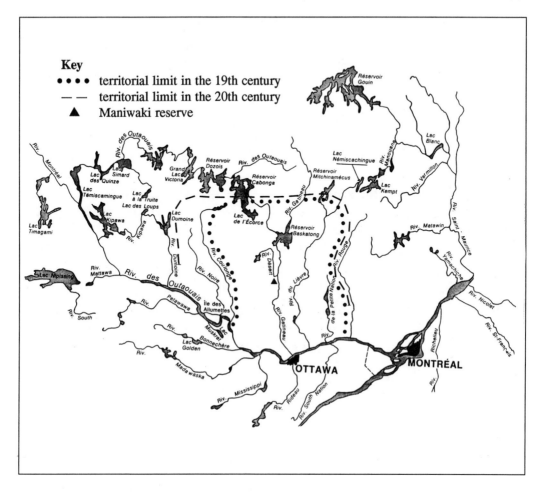

Map 2
Territory of the River Desert Band in the 19th and 20th centuries.
(Source : Deschênes and Frenette 1987b : 14)

territory has changed since the reserve was created (Map 2). Neighbouring bands have dissolved and their members have joined the River Desert Band (Deschênes and Frenette 1987a : 40-41). Colonization and lumbering have also brought about significant changes.

In the 19th century, the band's territory on the west side probably stopped around the Coulonge River. One Algonquin band was in fact affiliated with this river, and with the Noire (= "Black River", Speck 1929 : 97). It frequented Fort Coulonge, situated at the confluence of the river of the same name and the Ottawa. In the early 20th century, the Coulonge River band broke up, with most of its members joining the River Desert Band. Even today, the elders consulted consider that the territory of the River Desert Band extends to Dumoine River, where Kipawa Algonquins may be encountered (Deschênes and Frenette 1987a : 19-20, 27, 75; Moore 1982 : 51; Speck 1929 : 113-114).

The northern border of the territory of the River Desert Band seems to have always been situated between Lac à l'Écorce (= "Bark Lake", Speck 1929 : 97) and the Cabonga Reservoir. In this region the Algonquins from Maniwaki met with those from Lac-Rapide (Deschênes and Frenette 1987a : 9, 18; Johnson 1930 : 29-30; Speck 1927 : 240).

In the northeast, in the 19th through to the 20th century, the headwaters of the Gatineau, Lièvre and Rouge rivers formed a shared boundary with the territory of the Attikameks of Manouan (Davidson 1928 : 46; Deschênes and Frenette 1987a : 6; Speck 1927 : 240). In the early 1880s, Indian Affairs agents reported that the Attikamek lands lay north of Lakes Baskatong and Argent (="Silver Lake", Speck 1929 : 97) and along the Gens de Terre River (Canada, Annual Reports 1881 : 34; 1884 : 27). In the same period, Father Guinard also mentioned that Lake "Masamegous" ('Lac à la Truite', now Lake Mitchinamécus), situated at the head of the Lièvre River, marked the limit of Algonquin territory (Archives Deschâtelets HEB 6964 .E83C : 32). The Algonquins who frequented the Lièvre River were sometimes considered a distinct band in the early 20th century (Petrullo 1929 : 225-242). If this was the case, they are now part of the River Desert Band. The eastern boundary of River Desert territory seems to have followed the Rouge River (Deschênes and Frenette 1987a : 7, 26). According to Speck (1923 : 221-222; 1929 : 113), the Mohawks hunted as far as the Rouge River in the 19th century, sharing the territory with the Algonquins. In the 1920s, a group of Algonquin hunters not affiliated with the River Desert Band were still hunting on the Rouge.

As to the southern limit, the territories south of the reserve as far as the Ottawa River were still frequented by the Algonquins in the 19th century. But the advance of colonization in the Gatineau valley gradually dislodged the hunters from this region. In the 20th century, the Algonquins progressively ceased to visit the territories south of Maniwaki (Deschênes and Frenette 1987a : 89-90).

The rivers were the Algonquins' normal traffic routes, allowing them to penetrate the territory, and hence their families were distributed along the waterways. In the mid-19th century, River Desert Algonquins travelled the Gatineau, Desert and Lièvre rivers (Archives Deschâtelets JC 3301 .C21R : 86). In the 20th century they were still using these rivers, as well as the Noire and Coulonge (Speck 1927 : 240).

FAMILY HUNTING TERRITORIES
OF THE RIVER DESERT ALGONQUINS

In 1761, an explorer reported on the main characteristics of the mode of territorial occupation of the Lake of Two Mountains Algonquins :

> . . . these lands are subdivided, between their several families, upon whom they have devolved by inheritance. I was also informed, that they are exceedingly strict, as to the rights of property, in this regard, accounting an invasion of them an offence, sufficiently great to warrant the death of the invader. (Henry 1969 : 23)

While it is possible to identify elements of the family hunting territory system in this description, such as a close link between families and territories inherited from their ancestors, as well as respect for the borders of these territories, the information provided nonetheless remains insufficient to conclude that this mode of territorial occupation and use did indeed exist at the time. In any case, it is not our intention to discuss the origin of family hunting territories among the Algonquins of Maniwaki. We shall simply mention that our investigations have shown that, one or two generations ago, this system still existed among the members of the River Desert Band (Deschênes and Frenette 1987a: 4-5, 6, 9, 18, 30-41, 52-53, 60, 61, 68-69, 77-81, 98).[3] Using data collected in the field, from archives and in the literature, we aim rather to discuss the distribution of families throughout the territory, and above all, to analyse the causes of the disappearance of family hunting territories in the territory of the River Desert Band.

Essentially, as documented by Davidson (1926 : 82-88) for the Algonquins of Grand-Lac-Victoria, the size of the family hunting territories was connected with the abundance of game. The limits of these hunting territories corresponded with specific geographical features (rivers, lakes and mountains). They were well known and respected by the other Algonquin hunters, but could be crossed in case of need. It was thus possible to hunt moose on another family's territory if one's survival was at stake, although trapping fur-bearing game was prohibited.

Various methods for conserving animal species were practised, such as selective hunting. Finally, family hunting territories were normally bequeathed from father to son.

During our stay in Maniwaki in 1987, it was of course not possible for us to trace and map all of the family hunting territories of the Maniwaki Algonquins. Had it been possible, this operation would have required much more time than we had at our disposal. In fact, of the seven elders questioned, only two were able to precisely outline the limits of their family's hunting territory. While the others were able to indicate the sector where their family hunting territory was located and the places where the portages were and where the camps had been built, they were unable to delimit them with any precision. Their families had been removed from their hunting grounds when they were still very young. After that, they had simply experienced a succession of moves within the band's territory. Finally, even if the elders were able to identify and locate the waterways and lakes visited every year by other families, they could not trace the borders of those hunting territories, which had been broken up too long ago.

The still incomplete list of hunting grounds that we were able to collect from our informants (Deschênes and Frenette, 1987a : 10, 14-16, 25, 49, 51-52, 68-69, 74, 88) nonetheless corresponds substantially with the one compiled by Speck in the late 1920s (1929 : 111-117). We were also able to add to it some new family hunting territories (see Table 1).

As to the causes of the erosion of the family hunting territory system of the River Desert Algonquins, it must be realized that even before the Maniwaki reserve was created in 1853, colonization and the logging industry were threatening the continuation of the Algonquins' traditional activities (Deschênes and Frenette, 1987b : 26). The petition of October 10, 1848 is eloquent testimony to this fact :

> When you see us travelling here and there on the rivers and lakes in our frail canoes, you find us to be quite impoverished. That is indeed the truth : we acknowledge it, we are destitute – since every day we are stripped of what we used to own. Our lands move quickly into the hands of the white men . . . Before, we were rich, and we lacked for nothing : the forests were populated with animals of all species, whose hides we would sell at high prices to the eager merchant; this gave us the means to provide for our needs and those of our children, but that is not the way it is now. The whites are settling everywhere on our lands; where there is no farming, the lumbermen wreak their destruction and drive off what animals remain on what little land has not yet been taken from us. Our families have no means to provide for themselves and we know not

where to seek our subsistence. We are reduced to the greatest distress. (Archives of the Archdiocese of Ottawa 1847-1850 : 91-92)

Agriculture was causing major changes to the ecosystems. Logging drove off various species of game, such as the marten. The colonists and lumbermen also went into competition with the Algonquin hunters for the trapping of furbearing animals, and sometimes even stole catches and traps (Deschênes and Frenette 1987a : 94-95).

Development of the network of logging roads opened the territory to more and more Eurocanadian hunters and trappers (Deschênes and Frenette 1987a : 15). For instance, in the middle of the Depression in the 1930s, many Euro-canadians found sometimes considerable extra income in the trapping of fur animals. Seeing their territory plundered, the Maniwaki Algonquins caught as much game as they could rather than leave it for others, as William Commanda relates:

> The Indian returned home and began to talk with his brothers [about the presence of the white men hunting on their territory] : "We will bring our dogs, we will clear out the beaver, then we will clear out everything." . . . Their hearts broken, the Indians killed everything . . . Some days, 12 beaver were taken, hunting with a good dog . . . Why did they do this? . . . They were taking vengeance on someone who was there and who had no business being there. (Deschênes and Frenette 1987a : 60)

The pressure on the fur animals was so severe that certain species, including beaver, became endangered (Deschênes and Frenette 1987a : 20, 62, 66).

Albert Tenasco, band councillor, our assistant during the 1987 interviews.
(Photo by the Band Council, 1992)

Starting in 1899, the introduction of private hunting and fishing clubs was to strike a fatal blow to the family hunting territories of the Maniwaki Algonquins. From then on, families were denied access to their traditional hunting territories if they lay within the bounds of a private club (Deschênes and Frenette 1987a : 41, 94). Three hunting and fishing clubs were established in the Maniwaki region in 1899; some 20 more followed between 1900 and 1915 (Black 1980 : 23; Roy 1933 : 151-155). The list subsequently grew steadily longer, and the number of Algonquin families shut out from their hunting grounds increased at the same rate (Deschênes and Frenette 1987a : 75-76). For the majority of River Desert Algonquins, travel was increasingly necessary if they were to continue to hunt, fish and trap. Only certain portions of territory between the hunting and fishing clubs remained accessible. In such conditions, the usual rules of territorial occupation and use could no longer apply. This was no doubt the situation that Frank G. Speck witnessed in the late 1920s.

The family hunting territory system continued to disintegrate, from west to east, until the late 1940s (Deschênes and Frenette 1987a : 29-31). Albert Brascoupé tells how his family was one of the last to be dislodged from its hunting territory during World War II. He was not yet 20 years old at the time, and was hunting with his father :

> The territory was leased in 1938 [to a Montréal businessman] . . . he held hunting and fishing rights, [but] he trapped as well. The first four or five years, he told us : "You can hunt here, but you have to take good care of my territory . . . ". During the war, one of his sons, instead of going off to fight, . . . went into the woods . . . I think he spent two winters with us . . . His father told us : "Show him the entire territory so that he gets to know it well. [Show him] the location of the camps, where you hunt, where you trap . . . ". His son stayed with us, and after he had learned everything about our territory, he told us : "We're sorry, but now that we know all of your territory, you can no longer go hunting there . . . ". We had to go away . . . We have never gone back. We couldn't. We would have been driven out. (Deschênes and Frenette 1987a : 3-4)

In 1947, reorganization of the registered trapline system led to the final break-up of the family hunting territory structure of the River Desert Algonquins. The government's wildlife management system in fact never took into account the presence and activities of the Algonquin hunters. To gain access to the territory, the Algonquins now had to lease a trapline from the Government of Quebec. The unlucky ones whose names did not come up in the draw had to wait until the next year to make a new application. The others were often to be found scattered over lands assigned to them without consideration for the traditional organization of the family hunting territories. The Algonquins also complained of problems of proximity with Eurocanadians and regulatory annoyances. Today, the traplines that are leased are so small that they cannot afford a suitable livelihood for the Algonquin trappers. (Deschênes and Frenette 1987a : 13-14, 28, 52, 72-79).[4]

In this context, which is unfavourable to say the least, some River Desert Algonquins still continue to frequent the territory by trying to obtain a trapline and/or by adapting, more or less successfully, to federal and provincial legislation (Deschênes and Frenette 1987a : 28). Up until the end of the period of interest to us here (1850-1950), even when game was very scarce and fur prices were down considerably, a majority of Maniwaki Algonquins continued their traditional activities (hunting, fishing, trapping and gathering), combining them regularly with other follow-up activities. Contrary to what Speck has suggested on this point (Speck 1927 : 249-250), establishment of agriculture on the reserve's land has remained a difficult proposition, as we shall see when we examine the economic activities of the River Desert Algonquins.

ECONOMIC ACTIVITIES OF THE RIVER DESERT ALGONQUINS

Until the beginning of the 20th century, Algonquin families used to leave the Maniwaki reserve in September and October (Archives Deschâtelets JC 3301.C21R : 86; Deschênes and Frenette 1987a : 88-89). Later, as a result of the invasion of the territory and Amerindian settlement policies – such as education – only the men visited the territories. The women and children remained on the reserve (Deschênes and Frenette 1987a : 8, 39).

Autumn was devoted mainly to trapping beaver and otter. In fact, trapping took precedence over subsistence hunting, which did not bring in enough money to pay for the goods and services now available on the reserve (Deschênes and Frenette 1987a : 44). Moose were occasionally killed to lay in new provisions of fresh meat (Deschênes and Frenette 1987a : 83-84).[5] Fish (walleye, pike, lake trout, brook trout) was also an important part of the diet, for it could be found everywhere and in every season (Deschênes and Frenette 1987a : 33-34, 43-44, 87).

Some people returned to Maniwaki for the Christmas period (Deschênes and Frenette 1987a : 71-72). In January, only fisher and marten could still be trapped, for the other species rarely emerged during the coldest months of winter (Deschênes and Frenette 1987a : 85). Trapping was in full swing from March until May 10, after which the fur of moulting animals lost its commercial value (Deschênes and Frenette 1987a : 6-7). Today, the trapping season ends in March, except for muskrat; this leaves the trappers insufficient time to make profitable harvests (Deschênes and Frenette 1987a : 85).

When the price of furs was low and hunting and fishing did not yield the expected return, or when salaries were high, the men would go off to work in the logging camps. In winter, therefore, the Maniwaki Algonquins divided their time between the pursuit of traditional activities and salaried work. For example, for a period of about ten years in the late 19th century, the price of furs was constantly on the rise, and trapping took precedence over other activities. An Indian Affairs agent reported that in 1888 a majority of individuals (75% of band members) were engaged in trapping fur animals. Ten years later in 1899 this activity was still generating nearly a quarter (23%) of the band's total revenue, but in 1910 it had sunk to 14.4%. Salaried work at that time accounted for almost half (49.6%) of the total revenue of the Maniwaki Algonquins. The price of furs was then in free fall, and the same number of pelts could bring in much less from one year to the next. Wages were also on the decline, but a decline that was less rapid.[6]

In spring, the return to Maniwaki began in May and June. Smoked meat and fish were brought back to family members and friends on the reserve (Deschênes and Frenette 1987a : 42). The hunters went to negotiate for their furs with the highest-bidding merchants. The Hudson's Bay Company and other merchants from Maniwaki would do business with the Algonquins. Buyers also came from Montréal and Ottawa to meet with the hunters (Deschênes and Frenette 1987a : 44-46).

In spring and summer, many worked on the timber drives on the Gatineau. In the late 19th century, salaries seem to have been attractive ($1.25 per day).[7] Algonquins also worked as forest wardens or guides. Tourism in the region provided a new market outlet for Algonquin crafts. The elders and women chiefly engaged in the manufacture of canoes, snowshoes, mitts and moccasins (Black 1980 : 39-40; Bouchard 1980 : 71).[8] Others made use of the summer months to visit relatives and friends and plan for the next hunting season. Finally, some families did a little hunting, fishing, and gathering of wild fruit on or near the reserve territory (Deschênes and Frenette 1987a : 31-32).

On the other hand, agriculture never met with the expected success, even though the Maniwaki reserve had been created for the purpose of promoting its development. This had been the goal of the Department of Indian Affairs and the Oblate Fathers, as well as the wish expressed by the Algonquins in their petitions to secure a reserve in Maniwaki. However, the Algonquins always regarded agriculture as a last-resort solution to the reduction of resources on their hunting grounds.

In 1867, part of the reserve had even been subdivided into farming lots. But only a few Algonquins worked the soil during the summer, even though the Indian Affairs agent hoped that the decline of resources on the hunting grounds of the Maniwaki Algonquins might one day induce them to take up agriculture :

> With a few exceptions, they have hitherto principally depended on fishing and hunting to make a livelihood; but, as the fur bearing animals are rapidly decreasing, they will necessarily be compelled at an early date to devote their time and attention to the soil as a means of obtaining support for themselves and their families. (Canada, Annual Reports, 1880 : 35-36)

The Department of Indian Affairs provided financial assistance to the families on the basis of the amount of reserve land that they placed under cultivation (Archives Deschâtelets JC 3341 .C211 : 3). The agent reported that a few Algonquins, such as the chief and councillors, made a success of it. The others encountered a major obstacle : they often lacked the capital to purchase draught animals (Canada, Annual Reports, 1880 : 35-36).

In the early 1880s, there was a substantial decline of fur-bearing game and moose. At last, certain Algonquins intensified their agricultural efforts. For example, in 1885 about 50 families cultivated the land, and almost half relied on it exclusively. These 50 families made up a little over half the total population of the Maniwaki reserve, which then stood at 410 (Canada, Annual Reports 1881 : 33; 1882 : 17-18; 1883 : 19; 1884 : 26; 1885 : 3; 1886 : 27; 1888 : 32; Deschênes and Frenette 1987a : 104-105). In 1896, although 57 families were still living on plots of land, only about 30 were cultivating them. At the end of the century, their income accounted for only 12% of the total revenue of band members. In 1907, 26 families were still engaged in some cultivation, and their income represented 20.9% of total band revenue (Black 1980 : 23, 39-40; Bouchard 1980 : 71, 77-78).[9]

With the onset of World War I, the price of furs and salaries both dropped (Canada, Annual Reports 1915 : 23; 1916 : 24; 1917 : 24-25), a fact which may explain why agriculture started up again for a time. As Frank G. Speck found on his visits to Maniwaki, everyone seemed to be engaged in farming to various degrees (1927 : 249-250). Toward the end of the period with which we are concerned, however, the wage economy became the main source of revenue for the River Desert Algonquins. Agriculture and hunting, fishing and trapping went into decline. For example, in 1937, the income of band members was distributed as follows : salaries 67.6%, agriculture 12.6%, hunting 7.2% (Black 1980 : 23).

Shortly after World War II, in addition to paid work in the lumber camps and on timber drives, many Algonquins went to the United States to find seasonal work, for example, in pipeline construction or on mink farms. In the Maniwaki region, the last family hunting territories suffered the effects of the expansion of logging and colonization, but above all of the creation of new private hunting and fishing clubs. Agriculture was gradually abandoned (Beck 1947 : 259; Black 1980 : 23-24; Deschênes and Frenette 1987a : 12). It must be admitted that work in the lumber camps, on timber drives or in the United States, as well as hunting, fishing and trapping activities, were not very compatible with the demands of farm work. Indeed, the Algonquins were rarely in Maniwaki at the proper time to plough or sow the fields, or to take in the harvest.

CONCLUSION

As the Algonquins see it, and as William Commanda often repeated to us,[10] the objective of creating a reserve at Maniwaki was never to restrict their movements on the territory. The reserve has always been perceived as a final bulwark against Eurocanadian society. Since the reserve was established in 1853 until the late 1940s, the Algonquins of the River Desert Band continued to occupy their ancestral lands, despite increasing difficulties. The Department of Indian Affairs and the Oblate missionaries never succeeded in converting them into a sedentary farming population.

John Lambert-Cayer, another elder interviewed in 1987.
(Photo by the Band Council, 1992)

However, as the result of certain unfortunate actions by the Department of Indian Affairs, part of the Maniwaki reserve has been carved up since its creation for the benefit of the Oblate fathers, the town of Maniwaki, Eurocanadian colonists and the regional road system (Beaulieu 1986 : 20-23). Furthermore, from the very beginning of the British regime, the ancestral hunting grounds of the Algonquins have been progressively invaded, despite the opposition which has been many times expressed. The available area has gradually diminished under the impetus of the forest industry, colonization and recreational sports. The mode of territorial use and occupation based on the family hunting territory system was disrupted at the end of the late 19th century, and disappeared completely in the late 1940s. Since then, more and more families have come to reside permanently on the reserve.

Unlike developments elsewhere in Quebec, in the Maniwaki region the Algonquins have been unable to enjoy the protection, however fragile, of the beaver reserve system, which guarantees exclusive exploitation of fur-bearing animals by the Amerindians based on the former existence of family hunting territories. Only registered traplines exist in the Maniwaki region. Available to the entire population, these are allocated by the Quebec Department of Recreation, Fish and Game by means of a draw. However, the reduced area of these traplines does not enable Algonquin trappers to derive sufficient income from them.

The present band council is making numerous efforts to preserve what is left of the Algonquin culture in Maniwaki. However, the River Desert Band, like the Algonquin nation as a whole (apart from the Pikogan Band, the only one to sign Treaty No. 9 in 1906, a treaty that applies to northeastern Ontario), has never ceded its rights to its ancestral lands. The Maniwaki band council is quite aware that a more equitable division of the resources on those lands might promote not only the resumption and continuation of traditional activities, but also the development of other sectors of economic activity favourable to the growth of the community.

NOTES

[1] Our informants were : Albert Brascoupé, William Commanda, Angus Dancey, John Lambert-Cayer, Bazil Smith, Dick Tenasco and Daniel Whiteduck. We were assisted by Albert Tenasco, band councillor.

[2] The text of the petition of 1845 and 1848 as well as the letter of support from Mgr. Guigues have been reproduced in Barbezieux (1897 : 442-445). A transcription of the original petition of 1845 and 1848 may be found in the Archives of the Archdiocese of Ottawa (1847-1850 : 91-92).

[3] The issue of the origin of family hunting territories is still very controversial (Bishop and Morantz 1986). The principal characteristics of the system as it relates to the Algonquins have been treated extensively in the literature (Beck 1947; Cooper 1939; Davidson 1926; Jenkins 1939; McGee 1951; McPherson 1930; Moore 1982; Speck 1915a and 1915b).

[4] The creation of controlled harvesting zones (ZECs) in 1978 confirmed the dispossession of the River Desert Band Algonquins. Territorially, the ZECs are so vast that they cover all areas formerly left free between the hunting and fishing clubs. Unlike these clubs, the ZECs are open to the general public, thus drawing even more sport hunters and fishermen to the territory. These new organisms prescribe regulations and additional fees (Deschênes and Frenette 1987a : 29-30, 65).

[5] Deer moving north gradually replaced moose on the territory (Deschênes and Frenette 1987a: 42, 43, 84).

[6] See : Archives Deschâtelets JC 3301 .C21R : 25; National Archives of Canada, Archives of the Hudson's Bay Company, D.5/10 : 182-183, 382-384; Black 1980 : 23; Bouchard 1980 : 77-78; Canada, Annual Reports 1876 : 20; 1877 : 25; 1879 : 35; 1881 : 33; 1882 : 17-18; 1883 : 19; 1884 : 26; 1885 : 3; 1886 : 27; 1888 : 32; 1889 : 27-28; 1890 : 34-35; 1891 : 22; 1892 : 30-31; 1895 : 32; 1897 : 39-40; 1898 : 41; 1899 : 42; 1908 : 40; 1909 : 44-45; 1910 : 45-46; 1911 : 43; 1912 : 44-45; 1913 : 46; 1914 : 43; 1915 : 23; 1916 : 24; 1917 : 24-25; Deschênes and Frenette 1987a : 29, 39, 104-107.

[7] See : Canada, Annual Reports 1881 : 33; 1882 : 17-18; 1883 : 19; 1884 : 26; 1885 : 3; 1886 : 27; 1888 : 32; Deschênes and Frenette 1987a : 37-38, 104-105.

[8] See also : Canada, Annual Reports 1889 : 27-28; 1890 : 34-35; 1891 : 22; 1892 : 30-31; 1895 : 32; 1897 : 39-40; 1898 : 41; 1899 : 42; 1901 : 47; 1903 : 47; 1904 : 44-45; 1905 : 43; 1906 : 40-41; 1907 : 41-43; Deschênes and Frenette 1987a : 65, 70, 98.

[9] See also : Canada, Annual Reports 1889 : 27-28; 1890 : 34-35; 1891 : 22; 1892 : 30-31; 1895 : 32; 1897 : 39-40; 1898 : 41; 1899 : 42; 1901 : 47; 1903 : 47; 1904 : 44-45; 1905 : 43; 1906 : 40-41; 1907 : 41-43; 1908 : 40; 1909 : 44-45; 1910 : 45-46; 1911 : 43; 1912 : 44-45; 1913 : 46; 1914 : 43; Deschênes and Frenette 1987a : 65, 70, 98.

[10] William Commanda is the great-grandson of Pakinawatik, first chief of the Maniwaki reserve. Commanda was himself chief of the band for many years. He is still regarded as an important spiritual leader, and is also a craftsman renowned for his bark canoes.

ACKNOWLEDGEMENTS

We wish to thank Jean-Guy Whiteduck, Chief of the River Desert Band in Maniwaki, as well as the firm of ssDcc Inc. of Montréal, for their permission to use the content of reports prepared for them a few years ago (Deschênes and Frenette 1987a and 1987b, Frenette 1988). We also wish to thank Daniel Clément of the Canadian Museum of Civilization and Daniel Chevrier of the Archéotec company for their comments on the preliminary versions of this article.

WORKS CITED

ARCHIVES OF THE ARCHDIOCESE OF OTTAWA, 1847-1850 : Register of letters, Vol 1.

ARCHIVES DESCHÂTELETS, HEB 6964 .E83C : Guinard Collection.

– , JC 3301 .C21R : Maniwaki Collection.

– , JC 3341 .C21I : Maniwaki Collection

BARBEZIEUX, Alexis de, 1897 : *Histoire de la Province ecclésiastique d'Ottawa et de la colonisation dans la vallée de l'Ottawa*. Ottawa, La Cie d'Imprimerie d'Ottawa, 2 vols.

BEAULIEU, Jacqueline, 1986 : *Localisation des nations autochtones au Québec. Historique foncier*. Québec, Les Publications du Québec.

BECK, H. P., 1947 : "Algonquin Folklore from Maniwaki". *Journal of American Folklore* 60 : 259-264.

BISHOP, Charles A., and Toby Morantz (eds.), 1986 : "À qui appartient le castor? Les régimes fonciers algonquins du Nord remis en cause". *Anthropologica* 18 (1-2).

BLACK, Meredith J., 1980 : *Algonquin Ethnobotany : An Interpretation of Aboriginal Adaption in Southwestern Québec*. Ottawa, National Museum of Man, Canadian Ethnology Service, Mercure Series No. 65.

BOUCHARD, Serge, 1980 : *Mémoires d'un simple missionnaire, le père Joseph-Étienne Guinard, o.m.i. 1864-1965*. Québec, ministère des Affaires culturelles.

CANADA, 1905-1912 : *Indian Treaties and Surrenders from 1680 to 1890*. Ottawa, King's Printer, 3 vols.

CANADA, Parliament, House of Commons, 1876-1917 : "Annual Reports of the Department of Indian Affairs". *Sessional Papers*. Ottawa, King's or Queen's Printer.

CARRIÈRE, Gaston, 1962 : *Histoire documentaire de la Congrégation des Missionnaires Oblats de Marie-Immaculée dans l'est du Canada*. First Part : *De l'arrivée au Canada à la mort du fondateur (1841-1861)*. Vol. IV. Ottawa, University of Ottawa.

COOPER, John M., 1939 : "Is the Algonquian Family Hunting-Ground System Pre-Columbian?" *American Anthropologist* 41 : 66-90.

COUTURE, Yvon, 1983 : *Les Algonquins*. Val-d'Or, Éditions Hyperborée.

DAVIDSON, D. S., 1926 : "The Family Hunting Territories of the Grand Lake Victoria Indians". *International Congress of Americanists, Proceedings* 22 (2) : 69-95.

– , 1928 : "Notes on Tête de Boule Ethnology". *American Anthropologist* 30 : 18-46.

DAY, Gordon M., 1978 : "Nipissing", *in* B. G. Trigger (ed.), *Handbook of North American Indians*. Vol. 15: *Northeast*. Washington, Smithsonian Institution, pp. 787-791.

DAY, Gordon M., and Bruce G. TRIGGER, 1978 : "Algonquin", *in* B. G. Trigger (ed.), *Handbook of North American Indians*. Vol. 15 : *Northeast*. Washington, Smithsonian Institution, pp. 792-797.

DESCHÊNES, Jean-Guy, and Jacques FRENETTE, 1987a : *Maniwaki, transcription des entrevues réalisées les 10 et 12 mars 1987. Document de travail.* Québec, ssDcc, Report submitted to the River Desert Band Council.

– , 1987b : *Les Algonquins de la Rivière Désert : le territoire de la bande et son occupation depuis 1850.* Québec, ssDcc, Report submitted to the Band Council.

FRANCIS, Daniel, 1983 : *A History of the Native Peoples of Québec, 1760-1867.* Ottawa, Department of Indian and Northern Affairs.

FRENETTE, Jacques, 1988 : *Le pays des ANICENABE. La revendication territoriale globale de la nation algonquine.* Sainte-Foy, Jacques Frenette Anthropologue Consultant Inc., Report submitted to the River Desert Band Council.

HENRY, Alexander, 1969 : *Travels and Adventures in Canada and the Indian Territories Between the Years 1760 and 1776.* Edmonton, M.G. Hurtig Ltd.

HESSEL, Peter, 1987 : *The Algonkin Tribe. The Algonkins of the Ottawa Valley : An Historical Outline.* Arnprior (Ontario), Kichesippi Books.

JENKINS, William H., 1939 : *Notes on the Hunting Economy of the Abitibi Indians.* Washington, Catholic University of America Press, Anthropological Series 9.

JOHNSON, Frederick, 1930 : "An Algonkian Band at Lake Barrière, Province of Québec". *Indian Notes* 7 (1) : 27-39.

MARINIER, R., 1980 : "La mission du lac des Deux-Montagnes". *Cahiers d'histoire des Deux-Montagnes* 3 (4) : 27-39.

McGEE, John T., 1951 : "Family Hunting Grounds in the Kippewa Area, Quebec". *Primitive man* 24 (3) : 47-53.

McPHERSON, J. T., 1930 : *An Ethnological Study of the Abitibi Indians*. Canadian Museum of Civilization, Library, Ethnology III-G-38M.

MOORE, Kermet A., 1982 : *Kipawa : Portrait of a People*. Ontario, Highway Book Shop.

NATIONAL ARCHIVES OF CANADA, 1873a : Indian Affairs, Red Series, RG 10, Volume 1913, File 2567 : "Oka Reserve - Census of the Algonquin, Nipissing and Iroquois Indians of the Lake of Two Mountains, 1873".

– , 1873b : Indian Affairs, Red Series, RG 10, Volume 1915, File 2633 : "Oka Reserve - Agent J.E.R. Pinsonneault Forwarding the Census Return for the Iroquois and Algonquins, 1873".

– , Archives of the Hudson's Bay Company, George Simpson, Correspondence Inward, D.5/10.

PARISEAU, Claude-L., 1974 : *Les troubles de 1860-1880 à Oka: Choc de deux cultures*. Master's thesis, Department of History, McGill University.

PETRULLO, V. M., 1929 : "Decorative Art on Birch-Bark from the Algonquin River du Lièvre Band". *Indian Notes* 6 : 225-242.

RATELLE, Maurice, 1987 : *Contexte historique de la localisation des Attikameks et des Montagnais de 1760 à nos jours*. Québec, ministère de l'Énergie et des Ressources.

ROY, Anastase, 1933 : *Maniwaki et la vallée de la Gatineau*. Ottawa, Imprimeur du Droit.

SAVARD, Rémi, and Jean-René Proulx, 1982 : *Canada : derrière l'épopée, les autochtones*. Montréal, Éditions de l'Hexagone.

SPECK, F. G., 1915a : "Family Hunting Territories and Social Life of Various Algonkian Bands of the Ottawa Valley". Ottawa, Geological Survey of Canada, Memoir 70, Anthropological Series 8.

– , 1915b : "The Family Hunting Band as the Basis of Algonkian Social Organization". *American Anthropologist* 17 (20) : 289-305.

– , 1923 : "Algonkian Influence on Iroquois Social Organization". *American Anthropologist* 25 (2) : 219-227.

– , 1927 : "River Desert Indians of Québec". *Indian Notes* 4 : 240-252.

– , 1928 : "Divination by Scapulimancy among the Algonquin of River Desert". *Indian Notes* 5 : 167-173.

– , 1929 : "Boundaries and Hunting Groups of the River Desert Algonquin". *Indian Notes* 6 (2) : 97-120.

– , 1941 : "Art Process in Birchbark of the River Desert Algonquin". *Bulletin of the U.S. Bureau of American Ethnology* 128 : 229-274.

ST. LOUIS, A. E., 1951 : *Ancient Hunting Grounds of the Algonquin and Nipissing Indians Comprising the Watersheds of the Ottawa & Madawaska Rivers*. Ottawa, Report deposited in the Claims and Historical Research Centre, Department of Indian and Northern Affairs Canada.

OF WAMPUM AND LITTLE PEOPLE :
HISTORICAL NARRATIVES REGARDING
THE ALGONQUIN WAMPUM RECORD[1]

Pauline Joly de Lotbinière
Department of Anthropology and Sociology
University of British Columbia

In March, 1987, elders from the Algonquin communities of River Desert and Barriere Lake, Quebec, stood before delegates at the final First Ministers' Conference on Aboriginal Constitutional Matters. There they gave a reading of wampum belts, testifying to the sacredness of historic compacts between aboriginal and european nations. Amidst the opulence of the Ottawa Conference Center, with its high vaulted ceilings, ornate glass windows and plush carpets, surrounded by politicians and bureaucrats in business suits and silk ties, the elders struck a curious note.

On the morning of the first day, an elderly man, clothed in buckskin, his long grey hair held back with a leather band, made his way to the front row of speakers. Looking tired and aged, the Wampum Keeper seemed disoriented, though deeply absorbed in the task of presenting the belts to his audience. Gently, with his left hand he gathered at its center a long beaded belt and began in a tone of recitation a wampum reading.

The presentation caused an awkward hiatus in the flow of speeches. It was not a strong performance. Pale and fragile looking, the Wampum Keeper seemed to represent the last gasp of a vanishing people. His speech was sometimes unclear, the meaning diffuse. Yet amidst the power and privilege displayed so conspicuously by the government, there was something in the presence of the Keeper which demanded attention. It was unsettling, full of contradictions.

Armed with questions regarding the presentation in Ottawa, I made a trip in 1989 to Maniwaki, Quebec, to interview the Keeper, William Commanda. Focusing my inquiry on the belts, I hoped to document a tradition about which there is little mention in the literature on Algonquin culture. The Keeper, however, appeared to have his own agenda for our meeting. When asked for details regarding the wampum's history, Commanda launched into the narration of a story about the encounter between one of his ancestors, Peter Tenesco, and spirit beings known as the "Little People". His account, given here as it was recorded in English, began in this way :

> My great-grandfather on my grandmother's side was the one Paganowatik. He was the holder of the belts. When he died, and he died suddenly on his feet – he must have had heart trouble, and he didn't wake up anyway – and his son-in-law, who was married to one of his daughters, he gets these belts from 1873 to 1890 and, as he was trapping up there at Serpent Lake and Oldwoman's Lake, something happened to him : he was visited by the Little People. (Commanda, April 1989)

The Keeper then recounted how Paganowatik's son-in-law, Peter Tenesco, challenged the Little People and in fear shot one of them. War between the Algonquin of River Desert (Maniwaki) and the Little People was only narrowly averted when the community rallied to hold a mass, followed by a religious procession, which drove the spirits away.

During a second interview, I questioned Commanda again about the belts and their history, and again he repeated the story of the Little People, almost verbatim. Obviously, this narrative was important for the Keeper to record as part of his account of the wampum's history. His approach was very different from my own and raised questions about the ways people from different cultures go about documenting history.

Commanda's narrative presented a singular problem when it came to mapping out a history of the belts for the purposes of my research. The story of the Little People brought another dimension to the ethnographic process, one which did not appear to correlate in space or time with Western documentary traditions. Rather than contributing to the interpretation process between two cultures, the Keeper's narrative only served to further distance his world from that of the ethnographer's.

Recent concerns in anthropology about the representation of divergent voices in the ethnographic encounter address this problem of perspectives (Marcus and

Fischer 1986; Clifford 1988). George E. Marcus and Michael M.J. Fischer point to developments in anthropology since the second World War which attempt to include the voice of those marginalized by dominant trends in Western ethnography. One such development is the incorporation of indigenous notions of time and history within an ethnography, which the authors of *Anthropology as Cultural Critique* illustrate with works by Rosaldo (1980) and Price (1983), among others.

These two examples come closest to suggesting frameworks within which to consider the language, style and content of such non-Western forms of historical discourse as that of the Algonquin elder, William Commanda. Rosaldo and Price address the problem of how to represent alternative notions of history by translating and reproducing the oral tradition, correlating indigenous accounts with the more conventional Western historical narrative. Price (1983), for example, included the textual translations of historical narratives elicited in conversation with Saramaka elders. His book has the appearance of a collage : Saramaka narratives are interspersed with the ethnographer's own commentaries, which provide a Western-style perspective on historical events described by the elders. Rather than considering the indigenous form as representative of a "primitive mentality," a mentality without a sense of history, such forms of analysis suggest that there are alternative ways of representing history which are no less valid than the Western historical tradition.

The following account of the Algonquin wampum legacy is structured in such a way as to represent the very different perspectives on the wampum tradition which Western and Algonquin narrative styles offer. Rather than shaping our study of Algonquin wampum in a way that reflects Western knowledge regarding the tradition, the analysis is shaped by Commanda's own understanding of events, his narrative featured as a balance to Western documentary sources. Thus, in accordance with Commanda's own perspective on the wampum's history, our account begins with the origin of the Maniwaki wampum belts in Oka, Quebec, at the Lake of Two Mountains mission. The narrative focuses on a period in the wampum's history in the early 1890s when the belts were transferred to Barriere Lake following the adoption of the electoral system under the *Indian Act*. This is the time during which Commanda situates the story of Peter Tenesco's encounter with the Little People.

Our analysis of the story of the Little People occupies a central place in this account of the Algonquin wampum tradition, for it is in examining the oral tradition that one gets a sense of the importance of wampum to the Algonquin today. As we will see, the Maniwaki wampum belts have appeared intermittently throughout this last century as the focus for the telling of powerful stories relating to the history of the Algonquin people. Analysis of the Wampum Keeper's narrative will show that the concept of self-government, as it was discussed at the constitutional round table, is linked in the Algonquin oral tradition to the people's sense of their relationship to the land; and that the wampum belts consecrate that relationship, through their association with historic treaties implicitly recognizing the principle of aboriginal self-government.

WAMPUM

According to the *Handbook of Indians of Canada*, "wampum" is "the contracted form of [the] New England Algonquian *wampumpeak*, *wampumpeage*, or *wampompeag*", "wamp" being a derivative of a word expressing the concept of "being white"; "umpe" or "ompe" describing a string (of shell beads); and "ak" or "ag" indicating the animate plural (Hewitt 1913 : 503). The term was shortened to "wampum" by the New England colonists who traded the shell beads obtained from the coastal Algonquians for furs with the interior tribes, notably the Iroquois. The latter came to employ the term "wampum" in their dealings with colonial governments, though amongst themselves, as among the speakers of various Algonquian dialects, they employed a varied terminology to describe the strings and belts.

The shell beads used in wampum belts and strings are cylindrical in shape, and according to Hewitt, "from about one eighth to three sixteenths of an inch in diameter; and from one eighth to seven sixteenths of an inch in length" (1913 : 503). They were strung on strands of sinew or, later on, thread, and these were used in a variety of capacities, namely bunched and tied together at one end as bundles or sheaves of wampum; and tied or woven together with additional strands to form belts, scarfs or sashes.

When strung the beads conveyed a range of ideas, depending on the proportion and sequence of colors. Thus, the width, length and proportion of white to purple beads on a belt conveyed the importance of an occasion, and designs such as diamonds, hexagons, lines, diagonals, trees, human figures and longhouses suggested the events and ideas with which the belt was associated.

In the 17th and 18th centuries Indian and European nations throughout the Northeast came to adopt Iroquois protocol in diplomacy, and in particular the use of wampum. Wampum belts, designed to express certain ideas mnemonically, were exchanged in a diplomatic process which began with the recitation of the terms of proposals, alliances and treaties, and ended with the exchange of wampum, signifying the commitment of both parties to the negotiated settlement.

ORIGIN OF THE ALGONQUIN WAMPUM BELTS

You see : from the very beginning, when we live in early 1800s in Oka ... (Oka is our Indian locality; we used to live at Quebec City itself. Then we came up through the St. Lawrence, and – first Sillery – we came to the fork of Ottawa River and St. Lawrence, and...) ... some of these belts were made in that part. (Commanda, April 1989)

Information regarding the origin of the Algonquin wampum belts under the present Wampum Keeper's care is missing from the literature. When asked from whom Paganowatik, his great-grandfather, had obtained the belts Commanda replied simply :

That's a mystery to me. He died in 1873, and how many years he had them before ... nobody knows. I don't know. But he was the holder of the belts. And he was also hereditary chief – for life. (Commanda, May 1989)

Historical and ethnographic data suggest that the use of wampum was widespread among the Algonquin by the early 1600s. Some of the earliest references to Algonquin wampum appear as a result of the travels of Samuel de Champlain along the Ottawa River in the early sixteen hundreds. Vachon notes that the *Oeuvres de Champlain* mention an occasion in 1616 when the "Island Algonquins [the Kichesipirini of Morrison's Island on the Ottawa River] buy peace by paying the Huron nation of the Bear [the Attignawantan of the Penetanguishene Peninsula] 50 belts and 100 fathoms of beads" (Vachon 1970 : 254)[2].

Detailed study of the archives of the Jesuit fathers and of other religious orders which documented such diplomatic encounters is needed in order to trace the development of an Algonquin tradition of wampum diplomacy. In another article (1971) which relies heavily on Thwaites' translation of the *Jesuit Relations*, André Vachon indicates that the "Algonquins" did indeed use wampum in diplomacy. However, the fact that Vachon opposes the "Algonquins" to the "famille huronne-iroquoise" – after having refered to the "race algonquine" in the previous sentence – suggests that the author is refering not to the Algonquin nation specifically, but to the Algonquian linguistic family. Nevertheless, the quote is worth mentioning despite these problems (noting also that the comparison with the Iroquoians is phrased in a way which is somewhat diminishing to the Algonquians) since it does indicate that Algonquians in general were using wampum in diplomacy :

> In general, if the Algonquin, for the most part nomads, never attained the institutional stability of the Huron-Iroquois family, nor the decorum which characterized the latter's political life, they did not differ fundamentally from these in their diplomatic behavior, in the usage they made of oratory and the importance they gave to wampum. (Vachon 1971 : 182)

In a study of the "Grande Paix de Montréal" of 1701[3], historian Gilles Havard (1992) mentions the participation of Algonquin in treaty protocol dominated by Iroquois traditions of wampum diplomacy.

The existence of an Algonquin wampum tradition in diplomacy is further suggested by the association of Algonquin chiefs at the Lake of Two Mountains mission with efforts by the Kanesatake (Oka) Mohawk to receive title to lands granted to the Sulpicians. Traditionally, the Algonquin have been classified with the group of bands which inhabited the lower Ottawa River region and the north shore of the St. Lawrence east to and beyond Montréal, in the first half of the 17th century (Speck 1929; Day and Trigger 1978). In the late 1600s, following extensive contact and conflict with the Iroquois during the fur trade, a number of Algonquin Christian converts took refuge with the French Sulpician order. They were among a "motley group of Huron, Algonquin, Pawnee, Iroquois, Foxes and even several Sioux from the western territories" (Stanley 1950 : 205) who settled at the Mission of the Mountain in Montréal (founded in 1677). The "evils of intemperance" (1950 : 206) were apparently the reasons for which the mission was removed first to a site near the sault aux Récollets in 1698, and then to a new site on Lake of Two Mountains in 1721. Consideration was also given to the strategic advantages afforded by the presence of an Indian village near Montréal, namely protection from the "insults of other savages in the event of war" (National Archives of Canada, C 1A, 106 : 422-424 as cited in Stanley 1950 : 206).

At the Lake of Two Mountains mission there were two separate communities, one – the village of Kanesatake – of Iroquois and the other of Algonquin and Nipissing Christian converts. According to Black, "the 19th Century Algonkian community at Oka normally included individuals of at least five different ethnic groups : Algonquin, Nipissing, 'Tête-de-Boule', Ottawa, and Abenaki" (1988 : 5). The Iroquois generally practiced subsistence agriculture, hunting, and were employed as voyagers in the fur trade (and later as raftmen in the lumber industry). The Algonquians were principally involved in the fur trade as hunters and trappers who, aside from the "women and aged men, who are unable to follow the chase", actually only lived at the Lake of Two Mountains Mission for two months out of the whole year (Canada, Indian Department 1845 : 20 as cited in Black 1980 : 20).

When the decision was made to move the mission at sault aux Récollets to the site at Lake of Two Mountains the Sulpicians had argued that, since the Indians "are not capable of keeping the things which are the most necessary to them", title to the lands should be granted to the Sulpician Seminary of Paris (Stanley 1950 : 206). In 1718, the land concession was granted by the King of France, on condition that should the Indians leave the mission the lands would revert back to the King.

It was in the final years of the French regime in Canada that conflicts over land tenure began to surface at Lake of Two Mountains. In his account of the problems at the mission (1930), the Superior of the Externat Classique de St-Sulpice, Olivier Maurault, mentions that in 1763 one of the mission resident's sale of land to an English merchant was broken by the governor of Montréal under the new regime, with the stipulation that lands abandoned by the residents should revert to the Seminary. Similar conflicts erupted over the cutting of wood and leasing of land to non-Indian farmers.

In 1781 began the first of several petitions to colonial officials, in which the chiefs at Lake of Two Mountains sought recognition of title to the property. Authors who have studied the archives of the Seminary of St-Sulpice report that in 1781 "several chiefs" delivered an address to the officer in charge of Indian Affairs, the Colonel Campbell, presenting as they concluded their argument a belt of wampum.

A summary of the speech, translated by the Chevalier Delorimier, is contained within the writings of Urgel Lafontaine, missionary with the Sulpician order of Montréal[4]. The chiefs noted first that they had always believed that they were occupying ancestral lands, and gave detail for several instances where missionaries had prevented residents from using the land as they sought fit. Presenting a wampum belt, they then outlined the essence of the contract which they believed to exist between the Seminary and its inhabitants :

> Here is our contract : the white line that you see on this belt, shows the length of our land : the figures, which hold hands near the cross, represent our fidelity to our religion; the two dogs, placed at the extremities guard the boundaries of our land. And if someone wants to trouble us in our possession; they have to warn us by barking : and that is what they have been doing for three years. (Lafontaine, 1781, underlining and punctuation that of Lafontaine)

The presentation ended with the Colonel Campbell returning the belt, having concluded that "such an object could not serve as a property title to the seigneury in question" (ibid.). Lafontaine lists the names of those chiefs present at the reading, noting that the belt in question had been at the mission for some time, and that it "was made uniquely for the purpose of representing the union which must exist between the two catholic villages at the Lake mision (Iroquois village in the south west, and Algonquin village, in the north east)" (ibid.). Iroquoians and Algonquians might dispute the assumption that there is a "unique" message to every belt (the context of its interpretation being perhaps more significant). Nevertheless, these documents from the archives of the Sulpician Seminary do suggest that both Iroquois and Algonquin participated in the tradition of wampum diplomacy at Lake of Two Mountains.

Seven years later the same belt was presented to the Chevalier Johnson, director of Indian Affairs, in a reading which sought to remind the Chevalier both of promises he had made in the King's name to confirm Indian title, and of the Chevalier's presentation of the belt in question to the chiefs on that occasion. According to Pariseau, Algonquin, Nipissing, as well as Iroquois were present at this later reading (1974 : 61n.). Subsequent petitions confirm that the Algonquin often acted separately or in concert with the Nipissing and Iroquois in pushing for the recognition of their claims.

Though the belts in Commanda's care cannot be tied specifically to the petitions of the Oka chiefs, their interpretation by Algonquin elders today suggests that they did indeed originate with the association between Iroquois and Algonquin groups at Lake of Two Mountains. Three belts were presented at the 1987 Conference on Aboriginal Constitutional Matters. Solomon Matchewan, an elder and traditional chief from the Algonquin community of Barriere Lake, read the first belt – the Agreement Wampum – in Algonquin. His reading was interpreted in English by a younger member of the Barriere Lake community. This was followed by Commanda's readings of the Seven Fire Wampum Belt and of the Jay Treaty Belt. The Keeper has indicated subsequently that there were originally four belts in the care of the River Desert Algonquin, but that one was lost when the belts were transferred out of Maniwaki in the late eighteen hundreds (Commanda, April 1989)[5].

In an "attempt to decode the meaning" of the belts and to "draw a bit closer to the truth", Arthur Einhorn has offered an interpretation of all three belts, based on a comparison with similar belts among the Iroquois and Eastern Algonquians (1974 : 80-83). The Agreement Wampum (which the author describes as the "Human Figure Belt", 1974 : 80), suggested to Einhorn the union between the three main cultural groups at Lake of Two Mountains, namely, the Nipissings, Iroquois and Algonquins. The Seven Fire Wampum (or "Multi-Diamond Belt", 1974 : 81), according to the author, might have come into the possession of the Algonquin by way of their participation in the Seven Nations Confederacy. The double diamond in the center

Patricia Lee, 03:20 PM 3/19/99 , Address? (fwd)
_____

Date: Fri, 19 Mar 1999 15:20:34 -0800 (PST)
From: Patricia Lee <patlee@interchange.ubc.ca>
To: Ken Bassett <bassett@powerline.chspr.ubc.ca>
Subject: Address? (fwd)

Hi Ken,
Could you please pass this on to Pauline. Patricia

---------- Forwarded message ----------
Date: Fri, 12 Mar 1999 14:42:55 -0500
From: THOMAS ABLER <tsabler@WATARTS.UWATERLOO.CA>
Reply-To: Canadian Anthropology Society/Societe canadienne <CASCA@YorkU.CA>
To: CASCA@YorkU.CA
Subject: Address?

Arthur Einhorn (Box 286, Lowville, N.Y. 13367) who has done field work at
Maniwaki (see his 1974 article in _Man in the Northeast_, 7:71-86) would
like to contact Pauline Joly de Lotbiniere who has published on the same
(in 1993, _Recherches Amerindiennes au Quebec_, 23(2-3):53-68. Could she
(or someone who knows a current address for her) contact Einhorn by mail or
pass the address to me <tsabler@watarts.uwaterloo.ca> by e-mail?

Thank you.

Thomas S. Abler
Department of Anthropology
University of Waterloo

would have represented the council fire at Caughnawaga. The Jay Treaty Belt, which Einhorn describes simply as the "Single Row Belt," suggested two possible interpretations : the first being that the central row of white beads, commonly interpreted as signifying a path or link between nations, records an overture of friendship on the part of the Iroquois towards the Algonquin; the second possible interpretation was that the use of glass instead of shell beads in the center row, common in Wabanaki belts, represented an overture of friendship from the Wabanaki Confederacy. Einhorn concluded his analysis with the proviso that :

> ... any one of the belts could well have multiple meanings inherent in them (but unrecorded) from the time they were utilized as mnemonic devices and political documents ... Lacking a consensus of the oral tradition or written historical documents, we are left with only question marks. (1974 : 83)

In the years since Einhorn's analysis William Commanda has come to offer his own interpretation of the wampum record, one which sees no difficulty in the fact that there is little consensus as to the "true" meaning of the belts. What is significant about the Keeper's reading of the belts is that it addresses issues which are of concern to the Algonquin today.

While familiar with the literature in anthropology on the origins of wampum, the Keeper indicates that the origin of the Algonquin belts, and in particular the 1796 Jay Treaty Belt, was revealed to him in a ceremony :

> We were all making ceremonies through the shamans, and then the head shamans, they started to begin the ... Some of these would come into a trance, you know, when they're doing the ceremonies. But their words, when they're talking, the Creator will be talking through them. What they say they don't even remember when they wake up.

> And they said : "These belts were made between these two big rivers [between the Ottawa and St. Lawrence rivers]. One particular belt, ... it took three years to make the belt, and it took three years to negotiate the boundaries [between the United States and Great Britain]." (Commanda, April 1989)

The significance of the Jay Treaty to Commanda is that it recognizes the special status of aboriginal peoples respecting their relationship with the British Crown; and in particular, enshrines in European law respect for aboriginal rights. It was this relationship which the Keeper saw as being threatened by the move to repatriate the

Constitution. Thus the origin of the belts is tied to their significance as records of treaty relationships between European and Indian nations.

The representatives from Barriere Lake who read the first of the three belts at the Constitutional Conferences described the Human Figure Belt as the "Agreement Wampum" (Canada 1987 : 16), referring to the "Three Figure Wampum Belt Agreement". This reading of the belt was reiterated in Jean-Maurice Matchewan's outline of the history of relations between the Barriere Lake Algonquin and the federal and provincial governments (Matchewan 1989). Essentially, the Agreement Wampum is said by the Algonquin to represent an historic agreement which took place between the French, the English and Indian nations, in which the Europeans engaged to seek consent from aboriginal groups on matters pertaining to land and sovereignty, thus implicitely recognizing the authority of Native governments. On the belt the agreement is symbolized by three figures, representing Indian nations in the middle and European powers on either side. To one side a cross symbolizes the presence of a priest witness to the proceedings.

While such is the interpretation given the Agreement Wampum by the people of Barriere Lake, Commanda has spoken of this belt in other terms, describing it as the "Prophecy Belt." In the course of discussions regarding the impact of Christianity on the belief system of aboriginal peoples, Commanda detailed an apocalyptic vision of the future he experienced while in a sudden trance induced by the presence of the Agreement Wampum in his hands (Commanda, May 1989). Such forewarnings of things to come have also appeared to him while holding the Seven Fire Wampum Belt. In such a vision Commanda learnt that eventually the many churches which competed for their congregations would become unified under one church, thus creating a unifying force amongst aboriginal peoples (ibid.).

There is obviously a very strong political message to this vision. A similar interpretation was given by the Keeper in his reading of the belt at the Constitutional Conferences, where he expressed what he saw as the future of aboriginal political development, one drawing strength from concerted action by all First Nations. Referring to a conference of chiefs and elders held in Lethbridge, Alberta, that year, the Keeper spoke of the council fires which historically brought together various Indian nations in the formation of alliances, and pointed to an end diamond on the Seven Fire Belt :

> These belts was [sic] over out West, and we rekindled the fire that we see on my far left, and it [sic] [the council fire] going to come towards this way. And I believe ... our Western

brothers will be responsible for what we will achieve, from that visit. (Archives of the National Film Board 1987, transcription by the author)

FROM OKA TO MANIWAKI

Paganowatik was my great-grandfather. He died in 1874 – 1873-74, around there – and he was the first chief of this reserve. He came up here – that was his trapping ground anyway – in 1822, and a lot of Indians came with him. They made this settlement between these two rivers – Gatineau and Desert. He work out with some missionaries that first arrive here to missionize the Indians and also to convert them, and the missionaries worked with Paganowatik – they went to Upper Canada – to try to obtain Indian lands. (Commanda, April 1989)

The move to the Gatineau region at River Desert was precipitated by a number of factors. In the 18th century, lumbering and farming in the St. Lawrence valley had led to extensive deforestation and the destruction of wildlife, forcing trappers to travel greater distances and leading to competition and conflict between the neighboring Algonquin and Iroquois. According to Bouchette (1831, as recorded by Black 1980), the Algonquin and the Iroquois were afraid of the same thing happening in the Ottawa valley. Indeed, in 1800 a white settlement was established on the north shore of the Ottawa River at the mouth of the Gatineau on lands "purchased from Iroquois and Algonquin chiefs from Oka for the sum of thirty dollars" (Bouchette 1831; Hughson and Bond 1965 : 4, in Black 1980 : 20).

From that time on white settlement increased in response to a boom in the logging industry spurred on by the War of 1812. The entire region of the Gatineau and Desert rivers was absorbed into the boom and by the 1840s it was becoming increasingly difficult for the Algonquin to pursue their traditional pattern of subsistence. The Indian Report for 1844-1845 describes the situation for the Algonquin as "deplorable" :

> ... their hunting grounds on the Ottawa, ... which their ancestors had enjoyed from time immemorial, have been destroyed by the chase ... The operations of the lumber-men have either destroyed or scared away the game throughout a still more extensive region ... Their case has been often brought before the Government and demands early attention. (Canada, Department of Indian Affairs, Report 1845 : 20-21 as cited in Black 1980 : 21-22)

According to Meredith Jean Black, the area in which the Maniwaki reserve was established had been part of the trapping territory for the Oka and non-Christian Algonquin throughout the 19th Century (1988 : 4), and since 1832 a Hudson's Bay

Company post had been operating at the confluence of the Gatineau and Desert rivers to serve the trappers in the area. Conflicts at the Lake of Two Mountains mission led to several Algonquin families moving to the area, and a few years later, in 1853, the government formally granted a reserve (Maniwaki) of 45,000 acres. It is William Commanda's great-grandfather Antoine Paganowatik, a "second chief" (Gidmark 1980 : 17) at Oka, who is credited with having obtained the settlement due to his efforts in petitioning the government of Upper Canada. In 1869 the majority of Algonquin associated with the Lake of Two Mountains mission relocated to the Desert-Gatineau region.

In 1851 an Oblate mission was established at the present site of Maniwaki (Algonquian for "Land of Mary") to serve both the Algonquin and the increasing number of white settlers in the region. By 1900 there was a population of 800 non-Indians at Maniwaki, located within the limits of the River Desert reserve, and three-fourths of the reserve lands were being occupied by timber companies (Black 1980 : 22-23).

Throughout the later half of the 19th century, the Algonquin at River Desert were involved in the lumbering and later the pulp industry, although, according to the Indian Agent writing in 1908, "A large number of them [the Algonquin] still adhere to the old system of hunting" (Canada, Department of Indian Affairs Report, 1908 : 40 as cited in Black 1980 : 23). Finally, in the early part of the present century a number of Algonquin found employment as guides with the increasing number of fish and game clubs which had become popular with southerners. Employment away from the reserve also became important as a source of income on a seasonal basis, men heading to the United States to work on projects such as gas pipeline construction.

The River Desert Band people call themselves today the *Kitigansibiwiniwag* – meaning "People of the Garden River" – after their own name for the River Desert, *Kitigan-Sibi* (River of Gardens or Farms) (Hessel 1987 : 93-94). The band is apparently one of the largest of the Algonquin communities in southwestern Quebec (Black 1988 : 3), numbering 1617 members according to Statistics Canada, of which one third live off the reserve (Bouchard, Vincent and Mailhot 1989 : 359). The community of River Desert is located now on the edge of the town of Maniwaki, approximately one hundred and fifty kilometers north of Ottawa. Today, a large lumber mill sits in the middle of the reserve and logging trucks can be heard coming and going outside the Commandas' house. The area leading up to the reserve is one of second growth forest and rocky pasture clinging to a thin layer of soil covering the Canadian shield. Its lakes and streams are prized by sports fishermen, canoe enthusiasts and summer cottagers, who migrate from the cities of Ottawa and Hull at the first sign of spring. On one of the days when I met with Commanda the highway was clogged with the traffic of Ottawans heading north to go fishing over the May long weekend.

THE MANIWAKI WAMPUM NARRATIVE

My great-grandfather on my grandmother's side was the one Paganowatik. He was the holder of the belts. When he died, and he died suddenly on his feet – he must have had heart trouble and he didn't wake up, anyway – and his son-in-law [Peter Tenesco], who was married to one of his daughters, he gets these belts from 1873 to 1890... (Commanda, April 1989)

In the second interview Commanda went into detail regarding events which took place between 1873 and 1890.

One of [Paganowatik's] daughters [Manian] had married Pete Indécis ["undecided". French translation for *Tena'sko* (Speck 1929 : 118)] – who you call Pete Tenesco. Then, in turn, Pete Tenesco – with this wife – had two daughters. And one of my grandfathers, Louis Commanda, married one of his daughters. Her name was Marianne. The other one, Shanoud [Charlotte] had married Pete Dubé. He was from Manouane, way back above Three Rivers, up there. There's a big lake we call Manouane ... Well, back there. It's very far in the bush. They have the road there now. And, that's where he's from.

Anyway, one of my grandfathers, Peter Tenesco – who had married the daughter of Paganowatik – he used to go by with the Indian Agent because he had become band chief then – not hereditary chief. He was the one that accepted the *Indian Act*; he was the first one accepting the *Indian Act* here, and ever since that time we're having trouble. (Commanda, May 1989)

I then asked William Commanda how this was related to the wampum belts :

Well, he [Peter Tenesco] brought them up to Barriere Post, because something happened to him. I don't know the reason why that he had accepted the *Indian Act* here, the reason he had seen what we call these Little People. He was trapping up there in the bush and he had never encountered any of them before.

So, one evening, he was boiling his tea, and as the tea was just about to boil he seen the water moving in the water over there. It was very calm, coming on evening. He thought it was a beaver swimming out there. Them days they had muzzle loaders – you put the black powder in there and some pellets. Then, after that, you could push some moss to hold them down; there's a lot of moss in the bush. So, he took his gun, pushed his tea aside because it was just ready to boil, and went down, walking slowly – he thought he was going to see this beaver swimming by the shore. Then, all at once, he seen this figure coming up – probably two feet high; a little man – coming up, smiling at him. He just stand there – stop there – and this figure keep coming towards him. He said : "Who are you?" I believe the answer never came. It never said a word – just kept on coming up the hill and smiling at him. He says : "Answer me or I'm going to shoot!" He had already pointed his gun at it, and still he was coming, smiling at him, never saying a word. He fired, and hit him in the breast I believe. After this figure fell he seen that five others came up to pick up their friend, put him in the canoe and start paddling away. The canoe disappeared fifty feet off the shore, and all you could see was the water moving. They disappeared. Afterwards, he came down through the night – he was scared. These small people followed.

The next day, my grandfather [Louis Commanda], who was living down the track, down there a couple of miles, was pulling out his net, five o'clock in the morning. All at once he seen this water moving, and he heard the paddles but he couldn't see nothing. He looked out there – the water was coming like that [William Commanda demonstrates, making thrusting motions with his hands pointed together in a "V", in imitation of a canoe's movement across still water] – and it came right beside the canoe. When it grabbed his canoe – that's the only time he seen the fingers or the hands – they appeared.

"We want to deal with him according to our laws", they said. Then he said : "I have to find out who the man is; then I'm going to look for him." When he came home he told his wife. His wife was the daughter of that man that shot : Peter Tenesco's daughter. You see, my grandfather had married one of the daughters. The first thing he asks her is : "Where's your father supposed to be going?" "I don't know. Out there" she said, "out there somewhere."

And he went over, out early in the morning. As he got out there, the old lady [Peter Tenesco's wife, Manian] was cooking some breakfast, I suppose, and he said : "The old man home?" She says : "Yes, he just came home there, not long ago. He went to bed. He's tired; he's sleeping." He says : "Where'd he come from?" Then she told my grandfather the story her husband [Peter Tenesco] had told her. She said : "Something happened to him out there, last night, just before dark. He shot somebody – one of these little men, the spirits – and ran away from there. All night he paddled down and he just arrived here." He must've paddled hard because it's quite a ways : that's Oldwoman's Lake – we pass across that; and then generally we portage a height of land – the other water runs towards Gens de Terre; towards Baskatong – and that's where it happened. They call that Serpent Lake, and on one of these little islands – I wouldn't know which ones; there's two, three little islands there; I often look when I pass – on one of these three islands it happened.

They had said "We will be back tomorrow." So they woke him up and were talking about it. He told his story the way it was; and my grandfather told him that they were going to be back tomorrow ... "So they told me. And I'm supposed to give them an answer."

Well, they said : "What are we going to do?" So they had a meeting that day. "The only thing we going to do" they said, "is go and find the missionary." So, to the missionary they explained what was happening, and they made a parade : the priest would sing mass, and put holy water all over. And they never heard from them again. That was the end. They never came back. So, up to date, that's what happened. (Commanda, May 1989)[6]

Throughout the interviews Commanda made no distinction between "fact" and "fiction", between history and folklore. This served to illustrate the differences of perspective which separated Native elders from First Ministers at the Constitutional Conferences. Evoking the supernatural while discussing constitutional matters, Commanda made one wonder whether he was not going off on tangents. Writer Hugh Brody put into words this sense of unease which is often experienced by the non-Native observer when confronted by the unfamiliarity of a cultural other's discourse. In his account of research with the Beaver Indians of Northeast British Columbia he pondered the significance of the elderly Joseph Patsah's story of his people's history :

> As an elder, he had spoken beyond us, addressing the richness of another culture, another spiritual domain, even another time altogether. Perhaps he had not sought to understand the work ... Old-timers are sources of wisdom – but old men? Who knows? (1981 : 11)

It is only by becoming familiar with the oral tradition of elders such as Joseph Patsah that questions like these can be answered.

According to anthropologist Jacques Leroux (pers. comm.), the Algonquin of Grand-Lac-Victoria tell stories about "little Indians", in a narrative framework which blends historical events with personal experiences and beliefs inherited from mythology. This is very much the manner in which Commanda spoke about the Little People. In the first interview, the Keeper began his story of the belts with Tenesco taking possession of them following Paganowatik's sudden death. In the same sentence the narrative addressed the subject of Tenesco's encounter with the Little People. Similarly, in the second interview, having wondered out loud why it was that Peter Tenesco endorsed the *Indian Act*, in the same breath Commanda also wondered why Tenesco was visited by the Little People. Following the story of the encounter, Commanda indicated that the Maniwaki Wampum belts were brought to

William Commanda, Wampum Keeper, at the Conference on Aboriginal Constitutional Matters.
(Source : "Dancing Around the Table", Dir. Maurice Bulbulian, National Film Board of Canada)

Barriere Post for safekeeping by Tenesco because he was "scared, because there was something ... why these little men were after him" (Commanda, April 1989).

It became apparent from the above that the story of the Little People was very much part of the framework in which Commanda structured his interpretation of the belts and of their historical significance. Commanda's narrative of Tenesco's encounter with the Little People was obviously important to record as part of his history, and thus the first step in analysis was to make sense of the context in which the Keeper historically situated the story of the Little People.

Throughout the narrative Commanda appeared to make an association between, on the one hand, Tenesco's taking possession of the belts following Paganowatik's sudden death, and his responsibility for instituting the *Indian Act* at River Desert; and, on the other hand, the visit by the Little People and subsequent removal of the wampum belts to Barriere Post. Both actions with respect to the *Indian Act* and to the role of Wampum Keeper had serious implications. In the first instance, Commanda appeared to suggest that it was Tenesco's role in bringing the *Indian Act* to Maniwaki which led to his being visited by the Little People. "He used to go by with the Indian Agent," Commanda explains, "because he had become band chief then – not hereditary chief" (Commanda, May 1989). The use of the expression "he used to go by" to describe the connection with the Indian Agent – suggesting an association of an unsavory character – conveys the light in which Commanda viewed this relationship. According to Speck (1929), Peter Tenesco would have been chief of the Kitiganzibiwiniwag anyway had the hereditary system of chieftainship been maintained, so Commanda was obviously not disputing Tenesco's right to the position. It was Tenesco's association with the Department of Indian Affairs which constituted the main source of contention[7].

As mentioned previously, it was following the acceptance of the *Indian Act* that the Maniwaki wampum belts were transferred to Barriere Lake. Arthur Einhorn situates this time as "just prior to 1893" when "some significant changes in the administration of the reservation" took place (1974 : 76). This was at a time when aboriginal cultures were under pressure from the provisions of the *Indian Act*, which was being used by government agents and missionaries to combat Native practices such as the Potlatch by confiscating traditional regalia. In 1886 an amendment to the *Indian Act* had been passed which made it illegal to participate in a potlatch feast or tamanawas dance. There were several highly publicized trials and convictions in the early 1900s, including an incident on the Six Nations reserve, in 1924, when the Royal Mounted Police arrived to enforce the electoral system, confiscating the Six Nations wampum (ibid.). It was only in 1951 that the amendment was repealed. Thus, rather than reflecting the demise of the traditional political system among the Algonquin, as suggested by Einhorn, the move may well have reflected the desire by the River Desert people to maintain the traditional system intact, away from the incursions of the R.C.M.P. This forms the historical context in which we need to situate the story of the Little People.

An additional element comes to complicate the picture, however. Commanda began narrating the history of the Algonquin wampum belts by refering to Peter Tenesco taking possession of the wampum belts following Paganowatik's death. The passage is quoted here again as it appears in the introduction to this article :

> My great-grandfather on my grandmother's side was the one Paganowatik. He was the holder of the belts. When he died, and he died suddenly on his feet – he must have had heart trouble, and he didn't wake up anyway – and his son-in-law, who was married to one of his daughters, he gets these belts from 1873 to 1890 and, as he was trapping up there at Serpent Lake and Oldwoman's Lake, something happened to him : he was visited by the Little People. (Commanda, April 1989)

In this narrative Commanda links the appearance of the Little People with Tenesco's claim to the role of Wampum Keeper. Peter Tenesco assumed the role of Wampum Keeper without having been appointed by the original Keeper, Paganowatik. This, according to Commanda, was contrary to tradition.

Thus a relationship is established between tradition as implicit in the role of Wampum Keeper, history in the relationship of the Algonquin people to the *Indian Act*, and world view as expressed in the story of the Little People. We will now turn to examining the significance of Little People in the Algonquin oral tradition and, specifically, in the Wampum Keeper's narrative.

Four years after the interviews in Maniwaki Commanda and I had a telephone conversation about the nature of the Little People. He began by explaining that there are two kinds of Little People. One of these is associated with mischievous sorts of behavior, in reference to a reputation for bothering horses at night while they sleep. Commanda indicated that some people use the term "volontins" to describe them in French[8]. The other kind of Little People are those spirits to which Commanda attributes certain powers giving them the ability, for example, to disappear from sight. Along with powerful natural elements such as lightning and thunder, they are associated with the works of the Creator and are often mentioned because of this in the morning pipe ceremony. Commanda indicated that the Algonquin term for these spirits was *Eninisak*.

According to the linguist Yves Goddard (1978), the Algonquin word *inini* signifies "man". Writing in 1886, the Abbé Cuoq made reference to something similar in his dictionary of the Algonquin spoken at the Lake of Two Mountains : "*inini, ... wak*, homme"; "*ininins*, petit homme"; "*Pakwatc-ininins*, le petit homme des bois" (1886 : 128). Somewhat later, in a brief ethnographic account of the culture of the Algonquin of River Desert, the anthropologist Frank G. Speck mentions a number of "minor semi-supernatural beings" in Algonquin mythology, including the *Pakwadjé.winini* (1927 : 251).

Many questions remain regarding the origin and nature of the *Eninisak*, or Little People, about which William Commanda spoke in his interviews with me. The work of anthropologist Jacques Leroux among the people of Grand-Lac confirms the existence of little spirits in the oral tradition of Grand-Lac-Victoria, for the people there "speak of them readily, often and abundantly" (pers. comm.). They are called *Anicinabececic* (pl., *Anicinabececik*) or again *Nadowececic* (pl., *Nadowececik*) by the people in this community. These terms are translated by the Algonquin there as "petits Indiens" (little Indians), and are said to resemble the Algonquin in that they speak an Algonquian language, have a similar way of life, as well as similar customs and beliefs[9]. They are said to reward those who defend tradition and the well-being of the community, particularly with regards to political and social issues affecting its future. This is, of course, very suggestive of the manner in which we might interpret the significance of Peter Tenesco's encounter with the Little People.

The information from Grand-Lac-Victoria would indeed suggest that the *Eninisak* and the *Anicinabececik/Nadowececik* are one and the same. However, they differ in that the latter are said to enjoy playing a variety of tricks on human beings who express doubts as to their powers or their existence, whereas Commanda associates this kind of behavior specifically with the "volontins". He stressed that such Little People are very different from the ones encountered by Peter Tenesco.

Commmanda's version of the Little People may in fact reflect a syncretic historical tradition, one drawing its inspiration from written sources (documenting, for example, the shaking tent ceremony), as well as from the contacts with other Algonquian oral traditions in addition to the oral tradition exemplified by the people of Grand-Lac-Victoria[10]. The term "Little People" as employed by Commanda reflects the plasticity and creative nature of the oral tradition. We must examine, therefore, the context in which the term is employed in order to understand the particular significance of the Little People for the history of the Maniwaki wampum belts.

In an article on the structural analysis of American Indian folktales, Alan Dundes (1965) suggests a method of interpretation which lends itself well to the story under consideration. The author has isolated a four-part structure of interdiction, violation, consequence and attempted escape which provides a point of reference with which to analyse Commanda's version of the Maniwaki wampum narrative. We have to deduce, therefore, what is the nature of the interdiction implied in the violation which constitutes the shooting of the spirit Tenesco encounters at the lake shore. Commanda indicates on both occasions of the interviews that he did not know why Tenesco had this encounter with the Little People. But, as mentioned previously, he appears to associate this encounter both with the adoption of the provisions of the *Indian Act* and Tenesco's claim to the title of Wampum Keeper.

As also indicated previously, Commanda is very critical of the association between Tenesco and the Department of Indian Affairs. Prior to the electoral system which was adopted under the *Indian Act*, Peter Tenesco would have held his position as chief based on the hereditary system of political leadership. He would have been answerable for his actions only to the people he represented. However, under the provisions of the *Indian Act* that power was now lost to Indian Affairs.

As we saw earlier, Tenesco had assumed the function of Wampum Keeper even though Paganowatik had died before indicating who should be the next Keeper. This ambiguity regarding the belt's transfer led to "these belts having trouble," namely contesting claims to the belts' possession by the Barriere Lake Algonquin (and to the medal which they maintain in their possession) (Commanda, May 1989). Furthermore, Tenesco's claim to the role of Wampum Keeper was in the same course of events which led to the encounter with the Little People. We thus have to look to the implications of the adoption of the electoral system under the *Indian Act* and the ambiguity connected with Tenesco's role as Wampum Keeper in order to explain his encounter with the Little People.

One of the effects of the *Indian Act* was to deny the authority of Native governments and thus to undermine the principles upon which these governments negotiated access by non-Natives to the land. But more importantly, Tenesco's actions on the *Indian Act* – instituting the federally sanctioned electoral system – compromised the principles upon which aboriginal parties entered into the treaty-making process with European representatives. According to Michael Jackson (1984), the early treaties were understood by aboriginal parties as an expression and confirmation of the status of Indian nations as sovereign entities. These treaties involved certain provisions such as the payment annually of small sums of money to tribal members and of, in particular, medals and larger sums of money to chiefs. According to the same author, such provisions were interpreted very differently by European and Indian parties to the treaties :

> To the Indians, in the context of negotiations in which their tribal governments negotiated with the Government of the Queen, these provisions affirmed the authority of their tribal

governments and provided a diplomatic protocol for the annual review of treaty agreements (1984 : 263).

The terms of such agreements recognizing the authority of tribal governments were symbolized by the wampum belt, having been "read into" the belts upon concluding the agreement. Tenesco's actions on the *Indian Act*, effectively abrogating the sovereign nature of aboriginal governments, constituted a violation of those principles embodied by the wampum belts.

In Commanda's narrative, the Little People, described as "defenders of tradition" by the people of Grand-Lac-Victoria (Jacques Leroux, pers. comm.), are defenders of those values associated with the authority of tribal governments. "We would deal with him according to our laws" were the words of the Little People in reference to Peter Tenesco (Commanda, April 1989). Slipping quietly accross open water towards their encounter with "the other", these creatures appear as mirror images of all that the Algonquin hold true. As a consequence of his failure to uphold the principles embodied by the belts, Tenesco was challenged by the spirits of the land and forced to relinquish his title as Wampum Keeper.

William Commanda's version of the Tenesco story thus establishes the relation between the traditional form of government and the wampum symbol. The story of the Little People situates the wampum record within the historical tradition of the Kitiganzibiwiniwag, suggesting the symbolic nature of wampum not simply as a document recognizing specific rights, but as a living entity embodying the principles according to which the first treaties were signed. The tradition remains alive as recorded by the belts and as narrated by the Wampum Keeper.

WAMPUM AND ABORIGINAL RIGHTS

Commanda concluded the Maniwaki wampum narrative in the following way :

> Then, once he got this experience, he brought the belts up to Barriere Post. Them days the hereditary chief was Harry Nottaway – the life chief who was there. So he give them to them. But there were four belts; four belts, plus this big medal that Queen Victoria had given to my great-grandfather Paganowatik. Harry Nottaway died. And, in 1927, Clinton Rickard was going around here trying to defend the border-crossing of the Indians. They had this crossing every year, in July ... In 1927, then, the three belts [the fourth one has never been located] went down to the border-crossing to be used.

Rickard died. Just before he died, two days before, he wrote a letter – his wife was writing, but according to his words. He says : "I'm going to give these belts to ..." – that's when he mentioned me, in his letter. Because, when he seen this spirit – this vision – I suppose he must have understood it. Mrs. Frank Meness – who brought the belts up here – they know very well the Clinton Rickard family. She brought the letter with her and she read it – we were having a meeting at Bitobi Lake. All the Indians – including the Akwesasne people, Kahnawake, and some Onondagas from United States – were all present there when these belts were handed to me, in my hands. They came after these belts. Since they were in the United States, probably they were trying to claim them as Iroquois. Anyway, when he read these belts he said : "I'm going to send them back to the original holders of these belts." And they handed them to me. So, I'm still holding them. (Interview No. 2, Maniwaki, Quebec, May 19, 1989)

Rather than disappearing into oblivion when they were transferred to Barriere Lake, the Maniwaki wampum belts continued to provide the focus for concerted action by aboriginal organizations against provincial and federal governments. When he spoke of Clinton Rickard's fight for border-crossing rights Commanda was referring to the Six Nations movement which led to the Algonquin rallying again behind the wampum symbol. This was an action begun in the early 1920s, whereby representatives from the Iroquois communities in New York State and the province of Ontario petitioned the Mohawk, Huron, Abenakis and Algonquin in Quebec for funds to launch a law suit against the state for neglecting the terms of agreements made between representatives of aboriginal nations and the British Crown. A missionary described the scene when strangers arrived in the community of Obedjiwan to speak of the movement :

I... hurried towards the house where the meeting was being held. The men were so interested in the affair that very few saw me enter.

Squatting on their heels, they were listening to a stranger speak who, sitting in a chair, held in his hand *an old band of beads and was giving lengthy explanations of its value and significance*. At his feet, a chest held belts, collars, helmets, calumets, eagle feathers, documents and badges. All of this did not bode well and I intervened without delay, ordering my Indians to leave the room immediately because the cause described was not good for them. A heavy silence followed my intervention, during which the Indians looked at me with sadness, but without obeying my order. After a few minutes, they decided at last to leave one by one, slowly, and to regain their homes. They did not say a word, in such a way that I never knew if they approved of my gesture or not. I could be sure of nothing because never had I seen a movement interest them to such an extent (in Bouchard, Vincent and Mailhot 1989 : 277-278, italics mine).

The Six Nations movement did not end there, however :

> In Maniwaki, [the Indians] invaded the hotels, drinking, eating and occupying the rooms
> while refusing to pay one cent, since it all came back to, they said, the "old deed" which
> none understood too well, one way or another, what it was exactly. Basing themselves on
> this "old deed", they claimed nothing less than all the forests of Canada. (Bouchard,
> Vincent et Mailhot 1989 : 278-279).

The chiefs of the River Desert Band and leaders of the Six Nations movement were eventually imprisoned. However, in 1969, the River Desert Band of Maniwaki joined the Six Nations Confederacy, and that year Mrs. Frank Meness retrieved the belts from the Tuscarora Reservation in New York and returned them to Maniwaki.

The significance of wampum to the political life of the Algonquin did not end there. Today, the Seven Fire Wampum Belt has come to symbolize unity between aboriginal nations, a unity prophesied by the Keeper in his presentation to the Prime Minister and Premiers at the Constitutional Conferences. The wampum record serves to remind the federal government of its responsibilities in ensuring that aboriginal peoples are not alienated from the land, responsibilities enshrined in the Royal Proclamation of 1763, which many leaders including William Commanda see as an ersatz "Charter of Indian Rights". Commanda saw the repatriation process as potentially undermining the spirit of this document, were the Canadian government not to assume in the new Constitution the responsibilities taken on by the British Crown in 1763. Thus it was that following repatriation he took upon himself the responsibility of reminding the leaders present at the Constitutional Conferences of this historic relationship, saying : "It had to be brought out and it had to be told" (Commanda, April 1989). The wampum belts had to be brought out, and history recounted, so that it would not repeat itself.

CONCLUSION

This article is the result of a line of questionning which began with the intention of making sense of the presence of elders at the First Ministers' Conferences on Aboriginal Constitutional Matters. What was intriguing about the elders' presence was their role in performing various ceremonies which included giving voice to Native grievances according to the oral tradition. Amidst politicians and bureaucrats concerned about power and privilege, the elders struck a curious note, one emphasizing the distance that truly separates the non-Native observer from understanding the aboriginal point of view.

Analysis of the oral tradition respecting the Maniwaki wampum belts brought depth to our understanding of the wampum reading ceremony, and a perspective on history as yet unrecognized in the literature based on Western-European forms of historical documentation. Commanda's narrative provided an interpretation of the wampum record which established the relationship between the people and their land, as well as the basis whereby this relationship was built into the historic accords. It suggested that attention must be given to such non-Western forms of historical documentation as the wampum record in encounters between the dominant majority and aboriginal peoples.

Central to this discussion was the problem of representation, or how to include within an analysis of the encounter between aboriginal peoples and the state the voice of cultural others. William Commanda's interpretation of the wampum's history, focusing as it did on the story of the Little People, made it difficult to include the oral tradition within the framework of ethnographic narrative based on Western-European forms of documentation.

Historian James Clifford has suggested that such discrepancies between narrative traditions should be represented in ethnographies, as a challenge to the audience/readership to confront its own partial location. Thus it was that this project set out to include two very different perspectives on the wampum tradition : one based on Western-European documentary sources (which don't normally include stories about Little People); and the other based on the analysis of the oral tradition as exemplified by William Commanda's narrative.

There are many parallels, here, between William Commanda's interpretation of the Algonquin wampum tradition and the encounter between Tlingit elders and museum curators described in a recent article about Clifford's work (Wallis 1989). In describing the encounter, Clifford noted that the Tlingit elders appeared to have their own agenda for the meeting. Similarly, without explicitly contesting the meanings given the wampum belt tradition by historians and anthropologists, Commanda acknowledged the literature – much of which he had obtained for his *own* collection – and, in the same breath, moved on to record the oral tradition. In a sense, it was a process of reappropriating the power of the word, and specifically the power to interpret and to give meaning to local practices.

The issues addressed in this paper, and the approach taken to the presentation of material on the Algonquin wampum tradition, mirror in many ways Clifford's concern both to have audiences confront their own partial location, and to decenter the power to represent cultural others. This paper has sought to represent that discrepancy between contexts – between the meaning given the wampum tradition in the context of Commanda's narrative, and the meaning given to the tradition by Western styles of historical documentation focusing on the written word.

Commanda's record of the oral tradition, therefore, must stand as a challenge to Western-European forms of documentation – including the ethnographic enterprise – in their bid to interpret cultural practices. Perhaps one might view the presence of the elders at the Constitutional Conferences as a form of contestation, their presence unsettling because of their capacity to put into question the limited vision with which Western society has sought to encompass relations with aboriginal peoples.

NOTES

[1] This article is based on my Master's thesis entitled "Western Perspectives and Algonquin Narratives : Divergent Interpretations of the Wampum Tradition", University of Montréal, Department of Anthropology, 1991.

[2] Hostilities had erupted between the Huron and Algonquin, for in their bid to maintain their position as middlemen between the French and interior populations the Algonquin were harassing Huron traders passing through their territory.

[3] The "Grande Paix" refers to a negotiated settlement between representatives of New France, of the Five Nations Iroquois and of thirty or more Indian nations allied with the French, which brought peace to the region after almost a century of war.

[4] Portions of the text of these two petitions as recorded by Urgel Lafontaine have been published in *Recherches Amérindiennes au Québec* XXI (1-2) : 93-94.

[5] Records from the archives of the American Museum of Natural History and the Peabody Museum of Archeology and Ethnology indicate that two and maybe even three wampum belts in their possession may have originated with the Algonquin in the 16th century. Furthermore, in an article entitled "The Peace Tomahawk Algonkian Wampum" (1929) author Joseph Keppler describes a fourth belt in his museum which was given to the Algonquin in a peace treaty following their defeat by the Five Nations Iroquois in the mid-sixteen hundreds. All four belts in question were purchased by Mrs. Harriet Maxwell Converse from an Algonquin Mohawk chief at Caughnawaga, Quebec, in 1901, before being turned over to the museums described above.

[6] The conclusion that William Commanda brings to the narrative reflects a history of Catholicism amongst the Algonquin of Maniwaki, beginning with the first mission recorded to have included

Algonquin converts in the late 1700s at Mount Royal (Stanley 1950 : 205) and ending with the move from the Lake of Two Mountains mission to the Notre-Dame-du-Rosaire mission in Maniwaki in the mid-1800s. Tradition has it that it was William Commanda's great-grandfather, Paganowatik, who led Algonquin Christian converts to the lands at the confluence of the Gatineau and Desert rivers.

[7] When the *Indian Act* was first written, in 1876, hereditary chiefs were still allowed to hold office so long as the federal government approved of them. It wasn't until 1880 that the federal government reserved the right under the *Indian Act* to enforce the electoral system.

[8] Among the Micmac, similar creatures are known to ride the horses at night and then to leave them with their manes and tails tightly braided (Bock 1978).

[9] This connection between the spirits and tradition is taken up in another version of the Tenesco story featured in a collection of tales entitled *Sagana : contes fantastiques du pays algonkin* (1972), narrated by Bernard Assiniwi (a Cri from Lac Tapini, north-east of Mont-Laurier). In "Aji-ji-wa-t'chig Manito-akki : la dernière fois" the protagonist Tenascon is accused of neglecting tradition respecting man's relationship to the land. Strange creatures dressed in the ancient way of the Algonquin appear to him. Tenascon fails to deal with the strangers in the customary manner, and challenges these powerful beings from another world. His actions reflect a loss of traditional knowledge. Assiniwi first heard the story of Tenesco's encounter with the spirits from William Commanda's father, Alonzo Commanda. William Commanda also narrated to Assiniwi his own version of the story. Assiniwi's version appears to reflect both its sources with the Commandas and the poetic licence of the author himself.

[10] Commanda is very much an innovator, one comfortable in the idiom of many cultures, both Native and non-Native. He is very aware of the ethnographic literature pertaining to the Algonquin people, and may have drawn on these sources in constructing his own narratives of Algonquin history. In addition, as Wampum Keeper, Commanda maintains contacts with Native healers throughout North America, and no doubt draws much inspiration from this work for his own practice.

ACKNOWLEDGEMENTS

I would like to thank William Commanda for taking the time to sit down with me and tell me the story of the Little People. I would also like to thank Daniel Clément, curator of ethnology at the Canadian Museum of Civilization, for his patience and encouragement during the task of commenting numerous drafts of this paper. Further thanks go to Jacques Leroux and José Mailhot for additional comments and insights. Finally, I would like to thank Professors Rémi Savard and John Leavitt at the University of Montréal for sending me off to meet with William Commanda in the first place, as well as for their comments and encouragement throughout the time of my involvement in researching and writing on the Algonquin oral tradition.

WORKS CITED

ASSINIWI, B., 1972 : *Sagana : contes fantastiques du pays algonkin*. Ottawa, Éditions Leméac.

BLACK, M. J., 1980 : *Algonquin Ethnobotany : an Interpretation of Aboriginal Adaptation in Southwestern Québec*. National Museum of Man, Canadian Ethnology Service, Mercury Series No. 45, Ottawa.

– , 1988 : "Nineteenth Century Algonquin Culture Change". Paper presented at the Twentieth Algonquian Conference, Hull, Quebec, October. Manuscript.

BOCK, P., 1978 : "Micmac", in B. Trigger (ed.), *Northeast*, Vol. 15, *Handbook of North American Indians*. Washington, D.C., Smithsonian Institution, pp. 109-122.

BOUCHARD, S., S. VINCENT et J. MAILHOT (eds.), 1989: *Peuples autochtones de l'Amérique du Nord. De la réduction à la coexistence*. Sainte-Foy, Quebec, Télé-Université.

BRODY, H., 1981 : *Maps and Dreams : Indians and the British Columbia Frontier*. Middlesex, England, Penguin Books.

CANADA, Canadian Intergovernmental Conference Secretariat, March 26-27, 1987 : *First Ministers' Conference on Aboriginal Constitutional Matters*. Verbatim Transcript (unrevised). Intergovernmental Document Centre, Ottawa.

CLIFFORD, J., 1988 : *The Predicament of Culture : Twentieth Century Ethnography, Literature and Art*. Cambridge, Massachusetts and London, England, Harvard University Press.

COMMANDA, William, Wampum Keeper : Interview by author, April 14 1989, Maniwaki, Quebec. Tape recording.

– , 1989 : Interview by author, May 19 1989, Maniwaki, Quebec. Tape recording.

CUOQ, J.A., 1886 : *Lexique de la langue algonquine*. Montréal, J. Chapleau & Fils.

DAY, G., and B. Trigger, 1978 : "Algonquin", in B. Trigger (ed.), *Northeast*, Vol. 15, *Handbook of North American Indians*. Washington, D.C., Smithsonian Institution, pp. 792-797.

DUNDES, A., 1965 : "Structural Typology in North American Indian Folktales", in Alan Dundes (ed.), *The Study of Folklore*. Englewood Cliffs, N. J., Prentice-Hall Inc., pp. 206-215.

EINHORN, A., 1974 : "Iroquois-Algonquin Wampum Exchanges and Preservation in the Twentieth Century : A Case for In Situ Preservation". *Man in the Northeast* 7 : 71-86.

GIDMARK, D., 1980 : *The Indian Crafts of William and Mary Commanda*. Toronto, McGraw-Hill Ryerson.

GODDARD, Y., 1978 : "Central Algonquin Languages", in B. Trigger (ed.), *Northeast*, Vol. 15, *Handbook of North American Indians*. Washington, D.C., Smithsonian Institution, pp. 583-587.

HAVARD, G., 1992 : *La Grande Paix de Montréal de 1701: Les voies de la diplomatie franco-amérindienne*. Montréal, Recherches amérindiennes au Québec.

HESSEL, P., 1987 : *The Algonquin Tribe*. Arnprior, Ontario, Kichesippi Books.

HEWITT, J. N. B., 1913 : "Wampum". *Handbook of Indians of Canada*. Ottawa, The King's Printer, 1913; reprint, Toronto, Coles Publishing Co., 1971, pp. 503-508.

JACKSON, M., 1984 : "The Articulation of Native Rights in Canadian Law", *UBC Law Review* 18 (2) : 255-287.

KEPPLER, J., 1929 : "The Peace Tomahawk Algonkian Wampum". *Indian Notes* 6 (2) : 130-138.

LAFONTAINE, U., 1781 : *Droits du Séminaire: documents relatifs aux Droits du Séminaire et aux prétentions des Indiens sur la Seigneurie des Deux Montagnes. Copiés et interprétés par Urgel Lafontaine, p.s.s. Cahier écrit de la main d'Urgel Lafontaine prêtre missionnaire et auxiliaire de cure*. Archives of the Séminaire de Saint-Sulpice de Montréal. Cahiers Lafontaine, 9, pp. 1-12. Ottawa, National Archives of Canada, [microfilm M-1648].

MARCUS, G. E., and M. M. J. FISCHER, 1986 : *Anthropology as Cultural Critique : An Experimental Moment in the Human Sciences*. Chicago and London, The University of Chicago Press.

MATCHEWAN, Chief J.-M., 1989 : "Mitchikanibikonginik Algonquins of Barriere Lake : Our Long Battle to Create a Sustainable Future", in B. Richardson (ed.), *Drumbeat : Anger and Renewal in Indian Country*, Toronto, Summerhill Press, pp. 139-166.

MAURAULT, O., 1930 : "Les vicissitudes d'une mission sauvage". *Revue trimestrielle canadienne*, 16 (juin) : 121-149.

NATIONAL FILM BOARD OF CANADA, 1987 : *Archives (on video) of the Fourth Constitutional Conference, Ottawa, March 26-27, 1987*. [3/4 in., "U Matique"].

PARISEAU, C., 1974 : *Les troubles de 1860-1880 à Oka: choc de deux cultures*. Master's thesis. Montréal, McGill University, Department of History.

PRICE, R., 1983 : *First-time : The Historical Vision of an Afro-American People*. Baltimore, The John Hopkins University Press.

ROSALDO, R., 1980 : *Ilongot Headhunting, 1883-1974 : A study in Society and History*. Stanford, Stanford University Press.

SPECK, F. G., 1927 : "River Desert Indians of Québec". *Indian Notes* 4 (1) : 240-252.

– , 1929 : "Boundaries and Hunting Groups of the River Desert Algonquin". *Indian Notes* 6 (2) : 97-120.

STANLEY, G. F. G., 1950 : "The First Indian 'Reserves' in Canada". *Revue d'histoire de l'Amérique française* : 178-210.

VACHON, A., 1970 : "Colliers et ceintures de porcelaine chez les Indiens de la Nouvelle-France". *Cahiers des Dix* 35 : 251-278.

– , 1971: "Colliers et ceintures de porcelaine dans la diplomatie indienne". *Cahiers des Dix* 36: 179-192.

WALLIS, B., July 1989 : "The Global Issue: A Symposium", Interview with James Clifford. *Art in America* 86-87 : 152-153.

ALGONQUIN LEGENDS AND CUSTOMS FROM AN UNPUBLISHED MANUSCRIPT BY JULIETTE GAULTIER DE LA VÉRENDRYE

Daniel Clément and Noeline Martin
Canadian Ethnology Service
Canadian Museum of Civilization

Among the archival documents preserved at the Canadian Museum of Civilization, formerly known as the National Museum of Man, there exists an unpublished collection of Algonquin customs and legends collected in the 1940s by Juliette Gaultier de la Vérendrye. The very name of this person is intriguing. Juliette Gaultier de la Vérendrye, whose real name was Juliette Gauthier, was probably not related to the famous explorer Pierre Gaultier de Varennes et de la Vérendrye (1685-1749) although she claimed to be his descendant (Turbide 1986 : 11).

JULIETTE GAUTHIER

Originally from Ottawa, Juliette Gauthier (1888-1972), like her sister Eva, enjoyed a certain musical success during the first half of the 20th century. A professional singer, she first studied the violin at McGill University Conservatory of Music in Montréal, and the folk music of the gypsies at the Royal Academy of Budapest in Hungary; she then studied opera in Italy under the direction of Vincenso Lombardi. After her debut with the Boston Opera her true career took her on a rather different course. Over the years, Juliette Gauthier became a renowned folksinger and her repertoire included Indian and Inuit songs as well as songs from Québec and Acadia.

She enjoyed the patronage of several eminent figures of the time such as Lady Laurier and Mackenzie King and of ethnologists such as Marius Barbeau, Edward Sapir and Diamond Jenness[1]. Juliette Gauthier sang songs that she, herself, had collected as well as songs that had been collected by others (by Jenness and Sapir for example; see the Château Frontenac 1927 music program)[2]. In a short biography published in a book on music in Canada (Kallmann et al. 1981 : 368) one author states that Juliette Gauthier knew several Native languages but this is the only time this fact is mentioned. In public performances she usually accompanied herself with musical instruments of the same origin as the songs she sang and she dressed accordingly (fig.1), a fact that probably made her appear to be a rather exotic character :

> Her work in collecting the folk music of the French-Canadians, Acadians, Eskimos, and Indians, and presenting the songs in costume recitals [...] is under the patronage of the National Museum of Canada, and has been endorsed by the American Museum of Natural History, the Archaeological Institute of America, and many distinguished anthropologists as well as musicians, owing to the care and accuracy with which the music has been transcribed and the authenticity of the presentation – free from false harmonizations, and accompanied only by such instruments as the native musicians themsel-ves use. The songs [...] are sung to the unelaborated taps of the tom-tom, in the case of the Eskimo and Indian songs, or simple chords on the harp cithare in the Acadian music. (Darrell 1930 : 366)

It is probably in part due to her exotic appearance that Juliette Gauthier was able to travel throughout North America, from Alaska to Acadia, in the first half of this century. In 1920, she went to Vancouver Island and a film called *Totem Land* shows her learning the motions to a Native song. Perhaps it is also her alleged exoticism that enabled her to present several illustrations made from birch bark at the 1937 Paris Exposition; because of their unique character she was awarded a medal by the French government.

Fig. 1
Juliette Gauthier in Inuit costume. (Photo CMC III-L-64M)

THE GAUTHIER COLLECTION

The Canadian Museum of Civilization owns several birch bark objects obtained by Juliette Gauthier, some of which are of Algonquin origin. The Gauthier Collection owned by the Juliette Gauthier Estate was bought by the Museum on March 19th 1975; it contains birch bark baskets, wooden ladles, pendants, photographs, etc. as well as one manuscript already mentioned in the introduction. This manuscript, written in English, is classified among other miscellaneous material (III-L-64M) in the archives; it consists of eight series of typed leaflets entitled "Around the Birch Bark Wigwam". Each series also features a sub-title given by Juliette Gauthier indicating the theme predominant in the writings :

I.   Legends and Songs of the Onigoke Agonkian Indians of Canada
II.   Songs and Legends of the Sky-World, Onigoke (Algonkian Indians Upper Gatineau Valley, Quebec)
III.   Primitive Medicinal Cures Among the Onigoke – Algonkian Indians of Canada, Upper Gatineau Valley
IV.   Ancient Customs, and the Different Uses of Birch Bark – *Wig-Was-Gwi-Gwa* – The Algonkian Indians of the Upper Gatineau Valley
V.   Legends, Songs, and the Animal-Calendar Stories of the Onigoke (Algonkian Indians of the Upper Gatineau Valley)
VI.   The Preservation of Foods Among the Algonkian Indians of the Upper Gatineau Valley
VII.   Legends, Songs, Animal Calendar Stories and Pictorial Birch Bark Illustrations
VIII   Legends and Songs – The Dream-Men and Women Pygmies, The Fish-World, and the Music-Spirit World – Onigoke Algonkian Indians of the Upper Gatineau Valley

The first set contains only drawings but all the others feature texts - one hundred and eighty five in all, as well as a Table of Contents. Series III and V are respectively dedicated to the Pasteur Institute of France, to the Boy Scouts of Canada and to their late president. Although undated, it is possible that this manuscript was offered to publishers such as MacMillan House Co. (HBCA, A.104/119) but with little success. It seems that only *The Evening Citizen*, a local newspaper, published a legend excerpted from the manuscript, (this legend "The Little White Caribou Child Meets Dwarfs In Sugar Bush", April 24 1943, is not presented here), as well as a few articles on various subjects such as the porcupine and the Algonquin (June 3rd 1943), the way the Algonquin tan hides

(March 27 1943) and the clothing of Native people in Canada (February 27 1943). These articles were written for children.

JULIETTE GAUTHIER'S INFORMANTS

A quick look through the manuscript preserved at the Canadian Museum of Civilization reveals musical scores, press clippings, photographs, drawings and some information on the origin of all these materials as well as ethnographic texts and legends. Thus we learn that two Algonquin women were Juliette Gauthier's main informants. They were born at Lake Baskatong (spelled Piskatang and Baskatang in the texts). In the manuscript, only their Algonquin name or its English equivalent is given : "Wa Ba Dic Kwe" (White Caribou Woman) and "Mka Di Mik Kwe" (Two Black Beaver Women). The two women were probably first cousins, descendants of Paginawatik, founder of Maniwaki, and their husbands were probably in the Armed Forces during the First World War. White Caribou Woman's children are named, especially her daughter "Wa Ba Dic Uis" and one son "Caponicin" to whom we owe several of the drawings accompanying the manuscript.

In addition, enquiries made from several Maniwaki residents enabled us to identify these main figures. Several families originally from Lake Baskatong moved to Maniwaki in 1929 after the construction of the Mercier dam and the creation of a reservoir. White Caribou Woman was thus identified as Angélique Caponicin (1884-1979) and Two Black Beaver Woman as Madeleine Jacko Clément (?); Caponicin is Frank Caponicin Maheu (1906-1961). The daughter of Angélique Caponicin referred to in the manuscript is probably Bertha Caponicin who, like her brother Frank, was a Second World War veteran. Moreover, Madeleine Jacko Clément was renowned for her fine birch bark objects. She was one of Speck's (1941) main informants whose article on birch bark objects from Maniwaki includes a photograph in which one can easily recognize Two Black Beaver Woman, in addition to numerous references to the artistry of "Madenine Cesar (Mrs Pierre Clement)" (Speck 1941 : 250). A photograph of the latter is also included with Juliette Gauthier's manuscript at the Canadian Museum of Civilization (fig.2).

As the reader will see in the following legends and texts concerning Algonquin customs, other informants are mentioned such as Sun Woman, Mated Beaver Woman, etc., but we have not tried to identify them all. It is sufficient to remind the reader of the origin of some of them so that he can understand the texts better. Thus, "White Duck, chief of the Little Nation of the North" probably used the territory around Lake Simon at the head of the Petite Nation River. Speck (1929) gives us these precisions about certain Algonquin families residing in Oka but who hunted in the vicinity of Lake Simon :

> Some families besides those mentioned are still hunting out from the Lake of Two Mountains reserve (Oka) on North Nation river and about Lake Simon. Detailed information, however, is lacking. They would form the residue of the Algonquin of the Lake of Two Mountains divisions after the movement of 1854, with which should also be affiliated those comprising Group 5, just mentioned, who are not enrolled with the Maniwaki band. (Speck 1929 : 116-117)

Speck (1929) refers to a certain Aimable Whiteduck from this group, possibly a relative of White Duck whom Juliette Gauthier met about ten years later. We indeed believe that it is towards the 1940s that her interest in the Algonquin awakened, resulting in the writing of the manuscript. Thus, a letter found in the Hudson's Bay Company Archives (HBCA, A.104/119) indicates that in 1942, Juliette Gauthier went to Barriere Lake, north of Maniwaki; there are also legends brought back from this trip or from former trips in the manuscript. These legends carry the signature "The Bush-Men Indians" and in at least one text, these Bush-Men are also called "*Têtes de Boule*". This text, dating from 1940, is entitled "The Bush-Indian (or *Les Barrières*)" and begins in this manner: "The Bush-Indian, Men and Women Indians, were named *Les Têtes de Boules* (Round-Heads)". However, Juliette Gauthier and her informants are not the only ones to have used the name Bush-Men or *Têtes de Boule* for the Barriere Lake Algonquin (see Lee Rue III 1961) but in general, this appellation is more often associated with the Atikamekw living in the Mauricie region.

OTHER INFORMATION ABOUT THE MANUSCRIPT

Archival sources, and others, hardly offer any other information about the manuscript. For example, most sources reveal nothing about Juliette Gauthier's methods for collecting the legends and beliefs of the Algonquins. We therefore know nothing about their origin (the stories from Madeleine Clément and Angélique Caponicin probably come from Lake

Baskatong, those of White Duck from Lake Simon and those of the Bush-Men from Barriere Lake). We also do not know the language in which they were originally written down (possibly in Algonquin, English or even French), nor whether these are verbatim transcriptions or just summaries. Juliette Gauthier was not an ethnographer and she had other concerns. She wanted to learn about the Upper Gatineau valley Algonquin and then pass this information on to children. At the present, we can only say that we now have a manuscript containing narratives in English, presumably collected as found in the manuscript and most probably collected in the different locations they are identified with.

THE MANUSCRIPT ARRANGEMENT

The forty eight short texts presented here were chosen because they represent all the series from the manuscript, with the exception of the first one which virtually contains only drawings. The following table shows the proportion of texts chosen in relation to the total number of texts in each set :

Set No.	Number of texts chosen	Number of original titles
I	-	-
II	6	20
III	10	30
IV	19	40
V	1	6
VI	6	34
VII	1	3
VIII	5	21
Total	48	185

The proportion of texts chosen from each series is not always the same. Various reasons explain this disparity : certain texts were repetitive, others were unduly lengthy and others again did not correspond to our objective of making the most interesting and original texts publicly available while providing a general ethnography of the Algonquin as shown through this manuscript.

The order of presentation of the ethnographic texts and legends is the same as in the manuscript and respects, in general, the classification used at the Canadian Museum of Civilization. The original sub-titles for each section were maintained. Character and informant names are also indicated as they are in the manuscript. Thus, when informants' names are mentioned, we are enabled to better identify the origin of a text (Lake Baskatong, Barriere Lake or Petite Nation).

THE IMPORTANCE OF THE MANUSCRIPT

The analysis of the manuscript constitutes a different sort of task than a mere presentation. However, some comments emphasizing its importance are in order. First of all, let us remind the reader of the relative paucity of ethnographic works specifically concerning this region : nothing about Baskatong and Petite Nation; and in the case of Barriere Lake, at the most some unpublished manuscripts (Bechmann-Khera 1961, 1962 and 1964), a recent dissertation (Merveille 1987) and a few articles (Johnson 1930; Lee Rue III 1961). Concerning mythology, there is nothing, with the exception of the legends inherited from Juliette Gauthier; these provide a complement to the very few works concerning Algonquin mythology, the most easily available and famous being those of Speck (1915) for Témiscamingue, Davidson (1928) for Grand-Lac-Victoria and Beck 1947 for Maniwaki.

Second, we wish to draw attention to the originality of the written legends. Among the 48 texts presented here, nine are legends but only one of them ("The Pike Fish, the Pickerel and the Sturgeon") reminds us of related Algonquin narratives (Davidson 1928 : 281-2) while two others ("The Thunder Cloud and the Leaping Deer" and "The Indian Boy and the Serpent") evoke legends from neighbouring people such as the Montagnais, the Cree and others. The other legends are apparently unpublished, at least if one relies on the classic ethnographers mentioned above who were more concerned about publishing legends featuring famous characters of the Algonquin mythology (for example, Tcaka-besh and Meso, in Davidson 1928; and Wiske.jak in Speck 1915 and Beck 1947).

In third and last place, the customs and legends collected by Juliette Gauthier are fascinating in themselves. By bringing together legends and customs within the bounds of a single work, Juliette Gauthier follows in the footsteps of at least two of the authors quoted above (Speck 1915 and Beck 1947) In doing so, she is able to offer a general picture of Algonquin culture through ethnographic anecdotes taken from daily life : activities such as hunting, fishing, agriculture, gathering sap from maples are evoked, and the mythological realm is presented as well. Juliette Gauthier's concern that her data be transmitted to children has thus led her to note certain details which might have otherwise been neglected, namely, certain stories featuring children (for example, "The Colors of the Sunset", "The Black Eagle and the Indian Boy", etc.). But we are also and perhaps especially thinking of all the details told to Juliette Gauthier by her informants concerning their own childhood (remedies used, children's clothing, toys, etc.). Thus, this ethnography is valid for the end of the last century. On the other hand, Juliette Gauthier's main concern for children perhaps explains a certain lack of ethnographic methodology in the collecting of her data. We have already mentioned the lack of information about her methods and we could

Fig. 2
Madeleine Clément (Two Black Beaver Woman) and her son.
(Photo : J. Alex Castonguay, CMC III-L-64M)

probably draw attention to a number of inaccuracies in properly identifying animal and plant species (Juliette Gauthier only uses vernacular names, thus causing some problems) and to the fact that she showed little interest for certain details that are today deemed essential (the notation of Algonquin terms for stars, plants, animals, objects of material culture, etc.); these imprecisions are nevertheless minor and should not impede recognition of the manuscript's value. If anyone reading the following texts acquires a global understanding of the Upper Gatineau valley Algonquin of a certain period, we will have reached our objective. Juliette Gauthier's goal and that of her informants will no doubt also have been reached.

II. Songs and Legends of the Sky-World, Onigoke (Algonkian Indians Upper Gatineau Valley, Quebec)[*]

The Sun Woman Kisisokwe

My Grandmother, the Sun-Woman Kisisokwe, never ate until the sun had touched a certain plant, then she would eat, said White Caribou Woman. She told me that when the Bear-head was in the sky, it kept turning all the time, and that is how she could tell the different seasons. The Bear-head was in the form of seven stars, and from the Bear-head she could tell if it was going to be a cold, or warm winter.

The Thunder and Wind

My mother was afraid of thunder and wind. Great-Grandfather, Great-Knife, took a handful of tobacco and threw it out of the wigwam opening. "Here is your tobacco," he said to the storm. Soon after the storm was appeased.

(White Caribou Woman)

The Colors of the Sunset

There was once an Indian boy, who supposedly was very good natured, only every day at sunset time he would start to cry and cry, and his parents could not

---

[*] In general, the grammatical errors and word order have been retained as they appear in Gauthier's original manuscript.

stop him. They called upon all the Indians of their tribe to come and see him, asking them, each in turn, if they knew what ailed their child.

Among the many Indians present was an old Medicine Woman, who's name was Kisisokwe, the Sun Woman. "It is the colors of the sunset your child craves for," said the Medicine-Woman witch. "You must go to a certain place and there, at the bottom of a large lake, you will find all the colors of the sunset."

The child's father consented to go in search of the colors. "The lake is very far," the Witch Woman warned him. After many days, travelling by canoe, the father finally reached the lake of the sun. He saw many strange looking people guarding the lakeshore, and among them was an enormous fish, a polly-wog, who's name was Podonch[3], who had a great big belly and a small puckered up mouth. The chief caught the polly-wog, and glued his mouth with sturgeon glue, so as the other fish on the shore would not hear him calling for help. He stunned the polly-wog and pushed him into the water, then, in one leap, the Indian dived to the bottom of the lake, and started to search for the colors of the sunset. After much searching the chief found the beautiful colors, and he brought them back to his child.

And ever after, at sunset time, the father would give his son the powdered colors of the sun to play with, and never more did he cry when the sun was setting.

Podonch was severely punished by the other fish, for not having guarded the lakeshore, and allowing the chief to carry away the secret colors of the sun. And, for his punishment, they left him his gills to breath from. And, ever since, all the polly-wogs have been born with small puckered up mouths [...].

The Black Eagle and the Indian Boy

Once a black eagle stole a small Indian boy, and took him away to her nest, high above in a cliff, to live. The eagle had three young ones. One morning, the mother eagle went out in search of food, the boy killed one of the baby eaglets (ospreys), took out its entrails, crawled inside, and rolled himself down the cliff, to earth.

The Wild Duck and the Loon

Once a wild duck was playing with a loon. The duck went to sleep, and he dreamed of a loon, who had a long beak with an arrow on the end of it. When the duck woke up, he told the loon about his dream. "You had a fine dream", said the loon, "for my beak is well worth an arrow". "Just because of your dream I will spear you with my beak". "I'll eat you up, and that will be your finish". "And that was the end of the little wild duck," said Two Black Beaver Woman.

Three Loons Swimming Among the Water Lily Pods

The cry of the loon serves as a mate call, for the Indians. When they hear the loons calling, to one another, and uttering a certain cry, a plaintive one, they know there is a moose, or deer nearby. "It is always a sure warning," said Two Black Beaver Woman, "the loon hardly ever fails us. Otherwise, we have to use the hunter's horn to call the moose, or deer to us".

III. Primitive Medicinal Cures Among the Onigoke
– Algonkian Indians of Canada,
Upper Gatineau Valley

A Rattlesnake[4] for Toothache

When we were children, said White Caribou Woman, my great-grandmother, the Sun Woman Paginawatik[5], would catch a rattlesnake, and when we suffered from toothache, she would make us bite into the snake's body several times, and when she would let the snake loose, this would cure our toothache. It also preserved our teeth from decay.

I would never consent to bite into the rattlesnake, and today my teeth are all gone. If only I had listened to my great-grandmother the Sun Woman, I would still have my teeth. My sisters and brothers all have good teeth. My great-grandmother believed in all snake cures.

––––––––––

The Indians made their own false teeth from hardwood, and inserted the tooth in the cavity. Mostly cedarwood was used.

Water Lily Roots

Once, when I was a child, I took very ill, and had the chills. "I'll cure your child," an old Medicine Witch told my mother. It was wintertime and all the lakes and rivers were frozen over. Notwithstanding, the Witch broke the ice with a chisel, and at the water's edge, she found some water lily roots. She knew exactly where they grew, and brought them to our camp.

She boiled the lily roots, I drank the water, and in no time I was better, and the chills had left me. My mother was very happy. Although my mother knew many cures, it is best for other people to heal, said White Caribou Woman.

Skunkroot Plant[6]

Cut the root, use the main root, dry it in the sun, it becomes as hard as a bone. Scrape the root into powder form, and infuse for coughs.

It is also used to sniff, in powder form, and used as a charm. If you see a boy you like, get a mesh of his hair, put it in a birch bark box, and add some of the powdered skunkroot. As long as you will retain the box you will keep the boy's love.

Bleeding the Indian Way

My grandmother believed in bleeding for headaches. She would pull the hair in the back of our heads until it caused a blood blister. Then, with a sharp crude stone instrument, she drew the blood. The blood fell into a birch bark cornucopia shaped container.

White Caribou Woman relates, she attended a bleeding done by an old Indian Medicine man, blood being drawn from the head, the heel and wrist.

Charcoal Cures

The Indians of Piskatang Lake would burn different sorts of wood, in the form of small sticks, and would give it to the children to chew. This purified the blood. The charcoal sticks were also used red hot, and put into a cup of water. This also served as medicine.

Charcoal was used in great quantities by the Indians of the Upper Gatineau valley. We always used it in the case of illness, said White Caribou Woman. We also rolled our own charcoal pills. Charcoal was also injected in the temples for high blood pressure among the Indians of Canada. A small incision was made with a sharp stone implement, and the charcoal inserted. This explains why so many Indians have retained the black markings on their temples.

Alder Bark

In summertime, when we were walking long distances, it was very warm with our buckskin clothing, and often we got scalded. An old Indian told us to go in search of alder bark, and to apply it, freshly gathered, to the bruised parts. It smarted at first, said White Caribou Woman, but was it healing.

The Pickerel Fish Oil

The pickerel fish carries a small sack of oil, which the Indians gather when fishing. The oil is used for medicinal purposes, for tanning leather, or making soap.

Blood Poisoning

Once an Indian had blood poisoning in his arm. Mated Beaver Woman gathered some cedar boughs, mashed them into a paste, and applied the paste directly on the sore. The cedar draws the poison out, or drains the infection. It is an excellent cure.

Mad Dog

White Caribou Woman relates that an Indian was badly bitten by a mad dog. Mated Beaver Woman, her grandmother, sucked the blood from the Indian's arm, taking away several mouthfuls of blood; no infection followed. She then bandaged the arm with birch bark. "The Indians and the bears heal their injuries almost in the same way," said White Caribou Woman, "they suck the poison from their sores."

Surgery

Two Mated Beaver Woman always carried a needle fastened to her buckskin tunic. Once, when she was walking through the bush, she met a small child, whose name was Jocko, who had met with an accident, his upper lip was split, and bleeding badly.

Mated Beaver Woman took the small boy, held him over her knee, stopped the flow of blood with certain herbs. Then she drew from her tunic the concealed needle. She pulled one of her long black hairs from her head, threaded it, and sewed the boy's lip. She was then seventy-eight years old, and this took place almost sixty-five years ago, said White Caribou Woman, in the Upper Gatineau valley. Generally, the Indians did not apply stitches to a cut, but Mated Beaver Woman always did.

To this day one can plainly see the black stitches which remained concealed under the skin. There was not even a scar left.

IV. Ancient Customs, and the Different Uses of Birch Bark – *Wig-Was-Gwi-Gwa* – The Algonkian Indians of the Upper Gatineau Valley

Head Gear Worn for Hunting White or Grey Partridge

The women wear a bark headgear dress, trimmed with partridge wings, for hunting partridge. A bark headband is also worn with feathers.

There used to be white partridge in the Upper Gatineau valley. Therefore the women wore this headdress of partridge wings to hunt both white and grey partridge. Headdress is also made of the tail feathers of the partridge, and worn also for hunting, and for the partridge dance. [...] The dance brings good luck, and the wings keep away the evil spirits such as the eagle feathers.

The partridge wings are also worn in the hair as an ornament. The headband made of bark undulated to imitate the mountains.

La Nouvelle-France La Fleur de Lys[7]

The Algonkian Indians always depict *La Fleur de Lys* (The Lily of France) on their basketry, as a symbol of friendship.

Many of the older Indians are named Louis, in memory of the Kings of France, said White Duck, chief of the Little Nation of the North.

Indian Children's Clothing

All the children's clothing was made of young deer hide, smoked, or washed. In case of illness, the children were dressed in pure white deerskins and unsmoked. White chased the evil spirit away. A newborn child was also dressed in pure white deerskins.

Ancient Customs

All our utensils were made of birch bark, clay, or dugout wood, said White Caribou Woman. Many fragments of our ancient pottery has been found at Piskatang. Wherever we found skulls, or bones, we would find pieces of clay dishes.

Double curved lines were burned into the wood, in the Upper Gatineau valley, as an ornamentation. An old Indian used to carve small images of birds and human faces, when I was a child. The Indians would stick these small images in the ground, around their wigwams, or log houses. Pine, cedar, or birch was used for carving.

Our dolls were made from corn husks, pine needles, inner birch bark, pine wood, or buckskin stuffed with milkweed gloss, cattail, or birch tree moss[8].

Many animal figures were cut from tree bark, and served the Indian children as toys [...].

The Indian Hammock

Hammocks were hung high in the tree for a young child. [...] Both large and small hammocks were used by the Indians. They were made of birch, ash[9], or basswood. The basswood hammock was the best, it did not break so easily.

The hammocks were dampened, every now and then, to keep them pliable, they were good and strong and long lasting.

The hammocks were woven, basket weave (interlaced), cut in long thin strips of wood, tied at both ends with *Watap* (roots), and attached to two tree posts.

(White Caribou Woman)

Toboggans

To hunt the beaver, the Indians would use a toboggan made of either birch bark or cedarwood, laced with babiches or thick moose sinew. The toboggan was entirely outfitted for hunting beaver.

Spears, paddles, nets, the different traps, were all placed in the front part of the toboggan. A space was left at the back for the food containers.

The toboggan was either drawn by harnessed dogs, or by hand.

Elm Bark Mats

The bark of an entire elm tree was used in making a ground mat. The bark comes off easily in summer. These mats were used, in summer, when sleeping in the bark habitations. They were rolled, when not in use.

The Bark of Trees

The trees only grow once a year, and in springtime. When the tree is growing, the bark is loose around the tree. The marrow[10] of the tree is good to eat in springtime, and only certain trees are edible such as balsam, spruce, yellow birch, or white birch. The outer bark is cut in strips like ribbon. The older trees are best, and richer in marrow. The marrow comes off by scraping it with a knife, or stone scraper.

Sap from the Maple Tree, Canoes, Fuel, etc.

When the sap oozes from the maple tree, it is time for the Indians to gather their bark, for making their canoes and birch bark containers and pictorials. The bark is then the right color, a brick red.

Canoes are also made of elm bark.

It was an ancient custom for the Indian woman to gather birch bark fuel, for hunter's fires.
(Nomak. White Feather Woman)

Tooth designs (fig. 3) were also made from leaves and used as a pattern, for making designs on moccasins or buckskin clothing.

Long strands of maple leaves, fastened together with a thorn, or stem, was used by the Indian children as headgear, or game transparencies. When the garland was exposed to sunlight, it formed

Fig. 3. NA-SA-MA – Tobacco Plant. Bitten birch bark pattern by Madeleine Clément. (Photo CMC III-L-64M)

a pattern.

Patterns were bitten in thin sheets of birch bark, and used for porcupine embroidery designs, for basketry, or moccasins. In each dent a porcupine quill was inserted.

Bracelets, rings, headgear, belts, anklets, earrings all were made of birch bark. Pictorial designs either floral, or geometrical, or animal pictures were worn by the Indians of the Upper Gatineau valley.

Match Holders, Walking Sticks etc.

[...]
Match holders are made of narrow strips of birch bark coiled around a rounded stick, flat pieces of wood are inserted for the cork and bottom part of the holder, then the stick is removed. Should the match holder fall into the water, it floats, and keeps the matches dry.

Walking sticks were also made of birch bark, and coiled around a stick. The stick was not removed.

"The Indians claim the beaver was the inventor of apartment houses."

(Caponicin)

Rattles are made of birch bark, and filled with small pebbles. Pictorial designs cover the rattles.
[...]

Indian Caches

The Indian caches were built on stilts, the branches of the tree were cut to a certain length, and served as steps to climb to the roof of the cache. The cache was covered with birch bark and sewn together with spruce roots.

The food was hidden under the bark and was packed in sealed containers also made of birch bark. Long birch trees were best for the cache posts, as they showed from a far distance.

Birch Bark Torches

There are different kinds of torches used by the Indians, some are rolled on a stick, others are made of pieces of rough outer bark, and attached to a cleft stick.

Green bark does not flare, the dry bark makes a nice bright fire. Large and small torches are used when traveling through the bush at night. Birch bark is perfumed and has a very pleasant odor when burning.

Smudge Torches

Tree fungus, inserted in a short wedged stick, and worn on the headdress, or hat, is used by the Indians, when walking through the bush, against black flies or mosquitoes. The fungus are used green, and there is no danger of fire. The smaller kind is used.

Masimin Dyes

Blue, black, and red were the most difficult dyes or colors to obtain among the Indians. They were kept most preciously, and were used only on special occasions such as ceremonial feasts.

The Indians would paint their faces and their bodies, using these colored dyes for their secret markings. The women were entrusted with this form of decoration, working at times an entire day on one single body. Red and yellow ochres were also used.

The dyes were kept, some of them in small birch bark envelope-shaped containers; others were kept in powdered form in small buckskin pouches. The paint brushes were made of moose or deer hair, and fastened to a small stick. Small twigs were also used to apply the paint.

A slight coat of grease was first applied to the skin. Few mordants were used as a fixative for the skin, grindstone[11] being the favorite mordant used among the Indians, or certain astringent barks, infused. Many vegetable dyes, or mineral, have their own mordants. Wood ashes were often used.

The woman always went in search of dye plants, or minerals, never the men. No one was ever told where the dyes had been found. "Only an Indian can keep a secret," said Two Black Beaver Woman [...].

Wasp Nest Shaped Carriers

The ancient papoose carriers were made in the shape of the wasp nests, pointed at one end, and made of deerskin. The carriers were carried with the aid of a tumpline attached to the forehead. These carriers were also hung on tree branches, such as the wooden carriers, when the mother worked in the bush.

The carriers were lined with maple or ash moss, some of the same moss was applied to the child's chest for warmth, or for medicinal purposes.

Burden Baskets

The burden basket was large, and cumbersome, therefore it was carried on the Indian's back, and attached to a tumpline. The baskets were made of a different shape, so as to fit the person's back; more of a flat shaped basket, and longer. These baskets are made of birch bark, and are very beautiful in construction.

Sun Transparencies

Transparencies are bitten in a sort of long leaf, which resembles corn husks. The indented part showed green, and the under part silver. These transparencies were not long lasting, and were done more for pleasure or as a game. The birch bark bitten designs were more useful.

Our Sledge Dogs

In summer we could let our dogs loose in the bush. We could not care for some hundred dogs, dog food being scarce. In the fall, when the first snow fell, we would set traps in the bush to catch the dogs; they had almost become wild. We would pad the traps with soft feathers, so they would not get wounded. We fed them, and harnessed them all winter.

(White Caribou Man)

Corn Planting

White Caribou Woman relates how the Algonkian Indians of Baskatang would sow their corn first in clay. A large bag was made, the clay inserted, and the corn kernels were planted in the clay, and in a few days the corn would germinate, and then it was planted in the ground. The bag must have been made of untanned leather, so as to hold the humidity. I would think the raw skin better, such as [the one] used for holding the sap. The winter corn was braided and hung to dry, and used when needed, steeped in water overnight.

V. Legends, Songs, and the Animal-Calendar Stories of the Onigoke (Algonkian Indians of the Upper Gatineau Valley)

Big Chief Paginawatik, Tree Struck by Thunder

Big chief Paginawatik (fig. 4), the second chief of Oga, the Lake of the Two Mountains, had come to search for a place to settle. Travelling in a small birch bark canoe he finally settled in Rivière Désert, in the Upper Gatineau valley, because the Hudson Bay Fur Co. was settled there, said White Caribou Woman.

There were only three white people living at the Post, including one Indian, Old Tobacco-Man. Thomas Mowatt was in charge of the Post in 1839, and Louis Desert was the interpreter assigned to the company. Paginawatik got all his tribe together, and formed the present town of Maniwaki (Mary land) in 1848, and he became the Chief of the Algonkian Indians. When Paginawatik was no more, the Pale-face drove the Indians away from the village. They were then allowed four square miles to live on, and were placed on a government reserve. 1854- [12]

VI. The Preservation of Foods Among the Algonkian Indians of the Upper Gatineau Valley

Gathering the Maple Sap in the Upper Gatineau Valley

The Indians would make a wood frame, and attached a green and undressed deerskin hide, tied loose around the frame, to gather the sap-water, taken from the birch bark containers. One large buckskin (deer) container would hold forty pails of sap. We never used a dressed skin, said White Caribou Woman, because the sap would penetrate. We never left the sap, for fear some twigs, or dirt, would fall into the containers. Green bark was sometimes used to make our containers.

Our moulds were sculpted in cedar, with mostly the beaver design. To make the maple sugar, we would boil the sap until thick, and then beat it into sugar, and

Fig. 4
Sculpture of Paginawatik, founder of
Maniwaki, carved by Caponicin.
(Photo CMC III-L-64M)

pour it into the moulds. We would add some grease into the syrup, and in one spot only, where one pours. The sugar was thrown into either the wooden moulds or in the green bark *casseaux*[13] (containers).

We boiled the sap in green bark, or copper kettles. The containers were covered over with birch bark and left either in the caches or taken back to our encampments. The sugar bush caches were never robbed by us Indians, and were never left bare, so as to protect another hunter who would be lost in the forest. Our caches were built on four trees, a sort of platform. There are very different kinds of caches used among Indians.

The Indians would sing certain songs and dances, when boiling the maple sap.

Ladles

Ladles for lifting hot stones were made of green wood, with a square hole pierced in the center such as the flat (*palette*) for testing maple syrup, only smaller. Our platters were made of dugout wood.

Heated stones were sometimes used to boil the sap.

Bone Tallow

Tallow was made from the bones of deer, or moose, or any animal bones. The bones were boiled for many hours, and from the substance, which came to the surface, they made their tallow for sealing the birch bark containers. The tallow was skimmed, and poured hot over the food in the bark containers, which formed a sort of wax.

No seams whatever were used on the containers, and if seams were used, pine or spruce gum was applied, partly heated, to the open spaces or seams and pressed with the thumb or a flat slab of wood.

(White Caribou Woman)

How to Prepare Porcupine Meat

First you throw the dead porcupine into the bonfire, to remove the quills. Then you skin it the same as you would a small milk pig. The meat is then roasted over the bonfire. The porcupine meat is very fat, and not palatable to the white people.

The brush, which grows under the porcupine belly[14], the Indians use as a clothes brush, attached to a slab of wood.

The quills of the porcupine are very valuable to the Indians, and should not be wasted. These are used to decorate the birch bark baskets, or the buckskins, moccasins, or tunics. The quills are used either natural colour, or dyed with vegetable dyes, or mineral. The dye is prepared, and the quills put to soak in the cold dye, otherwise the heat would destroy them. The Indian often barters the quills for food.

Porcupine quills are used for medicine, infused. The meat of the porcupine is one of the favorite foods of the Indians including moose, deer and bear meat. (One must never approach a porcupine at night; they roam around).

Fishing in Wintertime

We would fish in wintertime by drilling holes in the ice. To attract the fish, we would throw bones of deer or moose in the hole. It seemed the fat from the bones would rise to the surface, and attract the fish. We always had a better catch, when we used bones, said White Caribou Woman. The old bones were the best. We would make our chisels out of bone, and in later years the Indians used the steel chisel.

Fishnets were made from willow bark, interlaced. The teeth were used in bending the bark, and splicing it.

Fish eggs, the spawn of the carp, is used as food by the Indians. We would gather the spawn on the tenth of May.

Turtle eggs, birds, sea gull were also eaten by the Indians.

Blueberries

To preserve blueberries you boil them one hour, or more, until they are very thick, and with little heat, no sugar, little water, and add a little at a time. When the berries have come to a paste, you put them in an envelope shaped birch bark container and dry them in the sun. When they are dried you transfer the paste to another covered container, also made of bark. The containers are then put in the ground. Sometimes the berries were smoked.

How to prepare for eating : you cut large pieces of the dried paste and soak in cold water overnight; add maple sugar or cane sugar, to taste, and reboil in water to the thickness wanted. All berries can be preserved, apart from strawberries. The blueberry paste keeps for years and never looses its flavor or colour, it is also used as a dye.

VII. Legends, Songs, Animal Calendar Stories and Pictorial Birch Bark Illustrations

The Thunder Cloud and the Leaping Deer

There was once a leaping deer which the Thunder Cloud had put on earth. There was a pond of grease, which looked like a lake. There was a moose, a bear, an elk, a rabbit, a porcupine and an otter, a muskrat, a fox, a skunk, many ducks, and a leaping deer. All but one of the animals, the leaping deer, had jumped in the grease pond. The different animals were trying to catch the deer, but he ran too fast, and jumped so high, they could never catch him. That is the reason the deer has so little grease on his back, and very little on his belly[15].

The leaping deer can jump forty feet in the air[16]. The deer is fattest in summer, and in the fall, in November, the hunting season.

VIII. Legends and Songs – The Dream-Men and Women Pygmies, The Fish-World, and the Music-Spirit World – Onigoke Algonkian Indians of the Upper Gatineau Valley

Bizan and the Dream People

Long ago, an Indian man, whose name was Bizan, was married to an Algonkian Indian girl, who did not believe in the Dream-Men and Women (Pygmies).

Bizan always seemed to be haunted by the Dream People, and every time he would fall asleep they would come and steal his birch bark headdress. Although he could never see the Dream-Men, they fled too fast into the bush.

Once he killed a moose, and he hung all of the meat out to dry, close by the birch bark wigwam. "I'll have to sit up all of the night to watch the meat", he told his life mate. She laughed at him so Bizan decided to sleep in his wigwam. "I hear faint voices", said Bizan. They both looked out from the opening of the wigwam, they saw the tiny prancing Dream-Men and Women carrying away all of the moose meat. So ever after Bizan's life mate believed in the Dream-Men and Women.

Canulah, the Fox and the Bear

In spring time, in thawing season, Canulah, an Indian fisherman, was fishing through the ice. The fish he caught he put on his sled, and started for home. There was a fox, who had crossed his trail, ahead of him. The fox lay on the ground, as if he were dead, so the fisherman, when passing by, grabbed the fox by the tail, and put him on his sled.

But the fox came to, and spied the fish, so he jumped off the sled, and fled into the woods, carrying away all of the fish. On his way the fox met with a bear. The bear, on seeing the fox with the fish, asked him where he got it. "I just sat on the edge of a hole, on the ice, and when the fish would nibble at my tail, I would quickly jump away, and the fish would cling to the end of it".

So the clumsy bear thought he could do the same. But he sat on the edge of the ice, and he put all of his tail into the hole. He sat too long, and froze most of his tail off. And ever since all the bears have been born with very short tails.

"In the olden days, and in another world," said Canulah (Nadawesi-Iroquois Bird) "all the bears had big long tails".

(Legends of the Bush-Men Indians)

The Pike Fish, the Pickerel and the Sturgeon

Once there lived a pike fish who had two sons-in-law. The pike had never cared for either of them, and he always wanted to have them devoured by the sea gulls. Each time the pike would swim around the islands, he would try to capture the pickerel and the sturgeon. One day he tried to trick them by forcing the fish to jump over the rapids and a big mountain of rocks. The old pike could never catch up to them because they swam too fast.

Then all three of them made a bet. "Let us see who can jump the farthest, and the best", the pike told his two enemies. Instead, the shrewd pickerel, and the sturgeon, urged the pike to jump the first.

The pike jumped first and broke his skull and ever since all the pike have been born with crushed in skulls.[...]

(Bush-Indian, The Pond-Man, Cabonga Lake)

The Indian Boy and the Serpent[17]

Once an Indian widow had married an Indian chief, who's name was Black Bear Man. The widow had two children, a girl and a boy. The stepfather was very fond of the girl, but he did not care for the boy. One morning he took the boy away to live on a far off island, which stood in the middle of a lake. The island was large and very flat, and built of solid rock. "Now we will cross to the opposite island", the stepfather told his son, "and search for sea gull eggs". So they crossed over to the opposite shore, in their bark canoe. No sooner had they reached the island the stepfather stole away, and left the boy by himself. He called to his father, and started to cry, but the father took no heed.

Then there appeared a huge green and yellow serpent, who had a deep hollow on her back. "Why do you weep" hissed the kind old Mother-serpent? "I have been left here all by myself", answered the frightened boy. "Weep no more my little one". "Go and fetch me a great big rock, you will place the rock in the hollow of my back", said the serpent. The boy obeyed the serpent's orders, and together they started to swim accross the lake. The lake was a very wide one. "If ever the lightning strikes us you must quickly jump from my back into the lake", the serpent told the boy.

"Do you see a big black cloud overhead, one which follows all the other clouds", asked the serpent? "Yes I do and it is getting very dark," answered the child. They had almost reached the lakeshore when a bright streak of lightning struck close by, followed by a loud clash of thunder. "Jump into the water", said the serpent. The boy dived into the lake, and everything around him turned to a pool of bright red blood then the Mother-serpent disappeared.

The Indian boy swam to shore, and started to walk on earth in search of his mother and his sister.

"The serpent always fears thunder and lightning," said White Cloud Woman, "and goes to hide beneath the earth."

(Legends of the Bush-Men and Women Indians)

Hiwatha[18]

When Hiwatha was a small boy, he lived with his grandmother Nokomis. He always wanted to sing. "You must go to the forest and listen to the birds and copy them", said Nokomis. Each morning, at sunrise, Hiwatha would go to the forest, and listen to the birds singing, but he never could retain their songs. "You must try once more", said his grandmother. The following morning Hiwatha went back to the forest, he listened and listened to the birds, and tried to imitate their songs. Suddenly he heard some beautiful music, and it came from afar. Walking slowly, he followed the echo. Then he came upon a high waterfall, it was a waterfall that gave forth music. At once Hiwatha started to sing, and he called his song the laughing waters (fig. 5). Out of the wood of alder he carved a flute, and played his song. Ever after, when Hiwatha went to the forest, he would take his flute along, and would play and sing the song of the laughing waters to the warbling of the birds. "And that is how the Indians obtained their music", said White Caribou Woman.[...][19]

Fig. 5
Copy of a musical score ("Song of the Laughing Waters") accompanying the legend of Hiwatha.

CONCLUSION

Through these excerpts from Juliette Gauthier's manuscript, the words of some Algonquin men and women from the Upper Gatineau valley were brought to life. Stories from their own childhood, about their material culture, beliefs and legends would probably have remained hidden for some time had this publication not been possible. Specialists from several disciplines will benefit from it : mythologists will discover new stories; ethnographers will discover some rich descriptions concerning maize culture in clayish soil, sap collecting – rather poorly documented in general – berry smoking, etc; those studying material culture will discover less well known objects such as wasp nest shaped baby-carriers; finally, ethnoscientists will find numerous references to plants and animals and their Algonquin usage. This publication will perhaps stimulate further interest in the manuscript itself as well as for the complete collection of objects collected by Juliette Gauthier and kept at the Museum.

NOTES

[1] According to our sources, neither Barbeau, nor Jenness, nor Speck played a role in financing the collecting and treatment of Juliette Gauthier's Algonquin material although, on the other hand, they had supported her at the beginning of her career as a singer of Native songs.

[2] In the bibliography one can find a complete list of known sources, whether archival or other (correspondance, recital programs, etc.) which are relevant to Juliette Gauthier. These sources are the object of an ongoing research project conducted during the last three years by Noeline Martin. The latter works as a volunteer at the Canadian Museum of Civilization; she has also completed recently a Master's degree at Carleton University, Ottawa.

[3] In a footnote, the author identifies Podonch as follows : "Podonch. Oga. Pike Fish".

[4] There exists several species of rattlesnakes in southwestern Ontario. The massasauga (*Sistrurus catenatus*) is found most frequently. None are reported for Quebec.

[5] In other texts, Sun Woman is the informant's grandmother rather than her great-grandmother. Furthermore, the name of Paginawatik, Maniwaki's founding chief, means "tree which has been struck by lightning" (McGregor n.d. : 305), rather than "Sun Woman".

[6] In her work on Algonquin ethnobotany, Black (1980 : 135) refers to this plant : "At River Desert a medicine plant which is unavailable locally and which has not been identified is known as skunk

plant (*sigawusk*). This plant has been obtained in the past from locations farther south, especially Golden Lake, Ontario, and New York State. No one could describe the plant to me nor could they identify it from pictures shown to them of various species. The odor is the one characteristic about which they knew and which supports a tentative identification of *Symplocarpus foetidus*. [...] The specific application was never learned but it is considered to be quite strong." According to Marie-Victorin (1964 : 844), *Symplocarpus foetidus* grows everywhere in Quebec but it is relatively rare in the West.

[7] The whole title is in French in the manuscript.

[8] The last three plants are *Asclepias syriaca*, also known as wild cotton, Virginia silk, etc., *Typha* spp., or cattail, and probably *Betula papyfera* or white birch.

[9] The name ash could also refer to the mountain-ash.

[10] *Moelle* (marrow) : "Soft matter (medullary parenchyma) contained at the center of the stem and of the root of dicotyledons" (Robert 1984 : 1213). Is it surprising then that Mohawks called the Algonquins *atirq.taks*, which literally means "tree-eaters" (Day and Trigger 1978 : 797)?

[11] Probably "sandstone".

[12] According to a letter sent by the Hudson's Bay Company to Juliette Gauthier on April 21 1943, (HBCA, A.104/119), it appears that certain information contained in this text is inaccurate. In this letter, it is said that Thomas Mowatt was responsible for the trading post in 1863-1864 whereas Louis Desert was an interpreter in 1845-1846.

[13] In French in the manuscript.

[14] We have not been able to identify what the author calls a "brush". She could have confused this with an Algonquin comb cleaner made from porcupine tail.

[15] One Montagnais legend features a similar scene where all the animals are led to soak themselves in a huge lake of liquid fat. The scene explains in more detail how the different species came to have the fat distributed differently in their bodies : "The seal immerged himself completely [...], the beaver [...] dipped only his chest [...]. For his part, the caribou only had a drink [...]." (Savard 1979 : 14)

[16] One zoologist reports jumps 9 metres long (30 feet) and 2,7 metres high (9 feet) (Wooding 1982: 52).

[17] This story is well known and exists in Montagnais, Cree and Ojibwa, etc. versions.

[18] Hiwatha is the name of an Iroquois hero. We have included this legend here as an example of Iroquoian influence on the Algonquin.

[19] We owe many thanks to Nicole Beaudry who recopied the score of the song "The Laughing Waters" and to Benoît Thériault from the Canadian Museum of Civilization who made Juliette Gauthier's manuscript available to us. Many thanks also to Sue Roark-Calnek and to Jacques Frenette who provided information enabling us to identify several male and female informants of Juliette Gauthier.

BIBLIOGRAPHY

A) Archival sources

NATIONAL ARCHIVES OF CANADA
Eva Gauthier Collection (MG30, D145).
William Lyon Mackenzie King Collection (MG30, D50).
William Lyon Mackenzie King Collection, Programs (MG26, J15).
A-Leo Leymarie, writer and journalist (MG30, D56, Vol. 17).
International Council of Women : Arts & Letters & Press, 1923-33 (MG28, I245, Vol. 19, File 288).
Juliette Gaultier de la Vérendrye, correspondence to William Lyon Mackenzie King (MG26, J3, Vol. 49).
Gatineau Park Museum (RG34, Vol. 275, File 190S [1]).

AMERICAN MUSEUM OF NATURAL HISTORY
Correspondence between Juliette Gaultier and Dr. Wissler.

NATIONAL LIBRARY OF CANADA
(Music Division)   - Eva Gauthier Collection (1977-2).
                        - Harold D. Smith Collection (1979.39, I,25).

HUDSON'S BAY COMPANY ARCHIVES
Sir Patrick Ashley Cooper Correspondence (HBCA, A.104/119).

LIBRARY OF CONGRESS, AMERICAN FOLKLIFE CENTER
Juliette Gaultier Correspondence

CANADIAN MUSEUM OF CIVILIZATION
Juliette Gaultier Collection, library, ethnology, III-L-64M.
Marius Barbeau Collection, Correspondence to Juliette Gaultier de la Vérendrye, library, Canadian Centre for Folk Culture Studies.
J. Gaultier de la Vérendrye Collection, 1977, library, Canadian Centre for Folk Culture Studies, Files B218 F1 to F6.

Juliette Gaultier de la Vérendrye, 1975, library, Canadian Centre for Folk Culture Studies, Files 75-31 to 75-98 and 75-2054.

B) Works cited

BECHMANN-KHERA, 1961 : *Report of Field Work, 1961, Among the Algonkin at Rapid Lake, P.Q., Maniwaki, P.Q. and the Ojibway on Bear Island Ont. (Timagami Band).* Canadian Museum of Civilization, library, ethnology, III-L-2M. Manuscript.

– , 1962 : *Lac Barrière Band (Rapid Lake, P.Q.). Family Histories; Report of Field Work, 1962.* Canadian Museum of Civilization, library, ethnology, III-L-3M. Manuscript.

– , 1964 : *Study of Lac Barrière Indians; Field Report. 1964.* Canadian Museum of Civilization, library, ethnology, III-L-4M. Manuscript.

BECK, Horace P., 1947 : "Algonquin Folklore from Maniwaki". *Journal of American Folklore* 60 (237) : 259-264.

BLACK, Meredith Jean, 1980 : *Algonquin Ethnobotany : An Interpretation of Aboriginal Adaptation in Southwestern Quebec.* Ottawa, National Museums of Canada, National Museum of Man, Canadian Ethnology Service, Mercury No. 65.

CHÂTEAU FRONTENAC, May 20-22 1927 : *Canadian Folk Song and Handicraft Festival. Annotated Program.* Under the patronage of the National Museum of Man.

DARRELL, R.D., 1930 : "Folk Song and Phonograph. Gaultier de la Verendrye reveals the treasure store of Canadian folk music." *The Phonograph Monthly Review*, August : 365-366.

DAVIDSON, D. S., 1928 : "Folk Tales from Grand Lake Victoria, Québec". *Journal of American Folk-Lore* 41 : 275-282.

DAY, Gordon M., and Bruce G. TRIGGER, 1978 : "Algonquin", in William C. Sturtevant (ed.), *Handbook of North American Indians,* Vol. 15, *Northeast.* Washington, Smithsonian Institution, pp. 792-797.

KALLMANN, Helmut, Gilles POTVIN, and Kenneth WINTERS (eds.), 1981 : *Encyclopedia of Music in Canada.* Toronto, University of Toronto Press.

JOHNSON, Frederick, 1930 : "An Algonquin Band at Lac Barrière, Province of Québec". *Indian Notes* VII : 27-39.

LEE RUE III, Leonard, 1961 : "Barriere Indians". *Beaver* 292 : 27-32.

MARIE-VICTORIN, Frère, 1964 : *Flore laurentienne.* Montréal, Les Presses de l'Université de Montréal.

McGREGOR, Ernest, n.d. : *Algonquin Lexicon*. Maniwaki, River Desert Education Authority.

MERVEILLE, Jean, 1987 : *La perspective anthropologique de la santé : le cas des patients amérindiens de Lac Rapide au Québec*. PhD dissertation, Department of Anthropology, Université Laval.

ROBERT, Paul, 1984 : *Le Petit Robert 1. Dictionnaire alphabétique et analogique de la langue française*. Paris, Le Robert.

SAVARD, Rémi, 1979 : *Contes indiens de la Basse Côte Nord du Saint Laurent*. Ottawa, National Museums of Canada, National Museum of Man, Canadian Ethnology Service, Mercury No. 51.

SPECK, Frank G., 1915 : *Myths and Folk-Lore of the Timiskaming Algonquin and Timagami Ojibwa*. Ottawa, Department of Mines, Geological Survey Memoir No. 71, Anthropological Series 9.

– , 1929 : "Boundaries and Hunting Groups of the River Desert Algonquin." *Indian Notes* VI (2) : 97-120.

– , 1941 : "Art Processes in Birchbark of the River Desert Algonquin, a Circumboreal Trait." *Bureau of American Ethnology, Bulletin No. 128, Anthropological Papers* 17 : 231-274.

TURBIDE, Nadia, 1986 : *Biographical Study of Eva Gauthier (1885-1958) First French-Canadian Singer of the Avant-garde*. PhD dissertation, University of Montréal.

WOODING, Frederick H., 1982 : *Wild Mammals of Canada*. Toronto, McGraw-Hill Ryerson Limited.

A WEDDING IN THE BUSH :
CONTINUITY AND CHANGE IN ALGONQUIN MARRIAGE

Sue N. Roark-Calnek
State University of New York at Geneseo

On August 20, 1988, Joseph Jr. Wawatie of the Barriere Lake Algonquin Band married Marie Angele Papatie of Lac-Simon, in a "wedding in the bush" (*nîbâwîwin nopimik*). Like all weddings, this event had personal significance for the spouses, their families and friends. Its organizers also conceived the wedding as an occasion for social mobilization and cultural instruction, with lessons for a wider audience of Algonquin people. In this essay I describe the *nîbâwîwin nopimik* and consider its lessons in historical and cultural context. I argue that, both in the forms of its ritual and in the social order it constructs, Algonquin marriage is an evolving adaptive mechanism, developing in parallel with the historical transformation of Algonquin communities in relation to their environment.[1]

Marriage can be examined in two ways : as a social institution or arrangment and as a symbolic performance. From the point of view of social analysis, marriage is an institution through which kinship groups and communities reproduce their structure. In the literature on Algonquin and other Northern societies, the "structure" in question has been taken to be the organization of economic production, primarily hunting and trapping. Marriage is seen as an instrument of the sexual division of labor (Davidson 1929 : 76), or as (in the affinal relationships it creates) an alternative access to hunting and

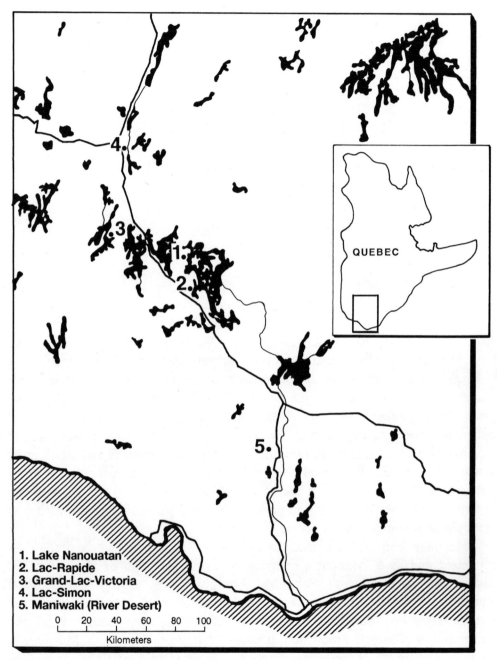

Map. 1
General area of study.

trapping territories (Davidson *idem*; Speck 1915, 1929), or more generally as principle or product of task group formation (Hirbour 1969; Turner and Wertman 1977; Rushforth 1984).

Algonquins recognize two concepts of marital union : *nîbâwîwin*, which has been ceremonially enacted and is today recognized by the laws of the church and state; and *wîdigemâdowin*,[2] consensual companionship, which is recognized by the community as "being with" or "living with" someone. *Wîdigemâdowin* is not initiated by a ritual event; thus, there is no single, unambiguous marker of change in status. Unlike *nîbâwîwin*, it is regarded as a developmental and reversible process of commitment, varying in its obligations among couples and their kin. *Wîdigemâdowin* now frequently precedes *nîbâwîwin* and in the event of separation it frequently also follows it, since Algonquins rarely resort to annulment or civil divorce. Both forms of union are considered in the discussion of marriage as a social and economic arrangement; only *nîbâwîwin* and its ritual antecedents are considered as a symbolic performance.

From the point of view of cultural analysis, marriage rituals are enacted symbolic performances, having as their primary function the communication of meaningful messages about the self in the world. The meanings of the messages are decoded from the intentions and responses of the actors themselves, and not simply (as some authors too often do) from inspection of the symbols alone. The cultural analysis is thus grounded in the historical and interactional context in which the forms are produced. The approach taken here derives from the work of Geertz (1973), Rappaport (1979) and Turner (1969, 1982).

A symbolic performance may have several different relationships to its context. It can simply reflect, and thus validate, the way things are in the world. It can, as Geertz (1973) has suggested, provide an interpretive "metasocial commentary" on the way things are. It can, through symbolic inversion and transformation, ritually deny and compensate for the way things are. It can condense and transmit information about critical states in nature and society (Rappaport 1979). And, since ritual symbols can be employed for persuasion, symbolic performances can actively seek to motivate and instruct their audiences in changing the way things are. I will argue that each of these relationships between performance and context can be discerned in the wedding I describe below.

Barriere Lake Algonquins (*mitcikanâpikokanicinâbek*, "people of the stone fence") occupy a small reserve at Lac-Rapide (hereafter called "Rapid Lake", in accordance with community usage) in the Parc de la Verendrye, and a large, traditional land use area in the Upper Ottawa watershed around Cabonga Reservoir. The band takes its name from its earlier rendezvous place at Barriere Lake. Its members are descended mainly from families trading at the Hudson's Bay Posts at Trout Lake (Des Augustines Lake) and Cawasseicamica (probably Poulter Lake) by 1827. After 1851, they traded at Cabonga and Nichcotea, after 1875 at Barriere, and from 1948 to 1954 at Rapid Lake (HBCA B/221, B/31, B/144. B/96).[3] Oblate mission records of marriages and baptisms begin with a mission to Barriere in 1843 (RMIM : 24-29). Thereafter missionaries came almost every year to Barriere or Cabonga, providing, with the Hudson's Bay Company documents, a nearly continuous record of the demographic and social evolution of this band from the mid-19th to mid-20th century.

Close relations between Barriere Lake and the neighboring bands at Grand-Lac-Victoria and Lac-Simon (which separated from Grand-Lac-Victoria in the 1920s, see Map 1) were noticed by Speck and Davidson. Speck (1929 : 101) regarded Barriere Lake and Grand-Lac-Victoria, in distinction from the River Desert Algonquin, as "part of the primitive population – unmigrated natives of the soil." Davidson described Barriere Lake and Grand-Lac-Victoria as :

> ... fundamentally one and the same people. The two groups live on the most intimate terms of friendship as is demonstrated by their many reciprocal visits as well as by a considerable number of inter- marriages in the past. In considering the close relationship between these two bands, culturally, linguistically, socially, as well as geographically, one cannot easily avoid inclining to the opinion that at some time in the past the two were politically allied and formed one and the same unit (Davidson 1929 : 69-70).

Frederick Johnson visited Barriere Lake at Speck's behest, publishing a brief and uninformative research report (Johnson 1930). The first substantial ethnography of Barriere Lake was produced by Sigrid Bechmann-Khera in three unpublished research reports, 1961-1964. Bechmann-Khera observed a wedding, inventoried patterns of spouse selection, and described trapline successions. Hirbour (1969) followed up Davidson's earlier work on Grand-Lac-Victoria hunting territories with a study of residential and task group composition which reported marriages between Grand-Lac-Victoria and Barriere Lake.

Bechmann-Khera and Hirbour were observing communities in transition. The Cabonga and Dozois Reservoirs flooded much of their traditional land use areas after 1929. By 1961, most members of the Barriere Lake were settling at Rapid Lake. From its beginning as an intermittent service center and summer rendezvous place, Rapid Lake has become a densely occupied year-round community, connected by road to other reserves[4] and towns. It serves as a permanent base camp for hunting, fishing, trapping, and other extractive activities. These activities were supplemented in Bechmann-Khera's time with seasonal work in guiding, at logging camps and on American fur farms. Some seasonal work continues, but government transfer payments and employment contracts with the Band Council now provide more cash income.

In spite of these changes, the bush continues to have a profound economic, social, and spiritual significance for Barriere Lake people. Substantial and quite diverse food and material resources (in particular, distributions of moose meat) flow into the reserve from the bush. All physically able men, and many women, hunt. Not all men have registered traplines, but most families in the community have access to trapping through partnership and other arrangements and have done at least some trapping in recent years. Most families have (or have access to) cabins in the bush, and some people (including members of the family here described) live in the bush for most of the year, with occasional stays in Rapid Lake where they maintain houses.

As is general throughout the Canadian North (Honigmann 1983; Brody 1981), the bush remains the locus of sacred knowledge and power, and a retreat for spiritual renewal. It is also identified with a ideal of autonomy and voluntary cooperation in human affairs that, in Algonquin thinking, contrasts sharply with the dependency and coercion they perceive to be impinging upon them from the outside. In recent years, Barriere Lake people have contended with competing land uses of the Parc – unguided sport hunting and high-technology clear cut logging operations – which both diminish their resource base and deny them cash income. Shortly before the wedding, the community (which has its own electricity generator on the reserve) had successfully mobilized to protest a proposal to extend HydroQuebec power to the reserve. The power line, another umbilical cord to the outside world, became a metaphor for dependency and the erosion of cultural and linguistic identity. Yet in most reserve homes, the generator provides power for television sets and videocassette players which convey images of outside popular culture to the community.

THE SOCIAL ORGANIZATION OF ALGONQUIN MARRIAGE

T o place the "wedding in the bush" in its social context, I first consider Algonquin marriage in relation to four social principles – sex or gender, generational complementarity, sibling solidarity and affinal alliance. These principles are recognized by Algonquin people (today, with varying consistency and effect) as proper to kinship relations. They organize the development of social identity through the life cycle as an unfolding passage from early dependency to autonomous interdependence. I show how these principles also organize spouse selection within a regional marriage network. Finally, I consider domestic and task groups resulting from post-marital residence choices.

RELATIONS BETWEEN THE SEXES

A lgonquins traditionally saw marriage as a natural consequence of gender complementarity : "Long time ago, a man and a woman couldn't live without each other. They were halves only. If one of them died, they couldn't be a whole until they found the other half [remarried] to make the family complete again" (JW). The division of labor is flexible, even reversible in practice : men should be able to cook and women should be able to hunt. Nonetheless, older people conceptualize gender opposition as between facing out into the bush and facing in to the camp : "A man is the boss outside; a woman is the boss inside" (ET).

Men and women are expected to have particular expertise in working with different resources (plant or animal, large or small game), production activities (trapping at a distance versus snaring close to the camp, setting a net versus fishing with a line), stages of processing, and technologies. Their work together draws on this complementarity : "I carve the wood [for a cradleboard]; my wife sews the cover" (JJ); "A woman paddles in the rear, the man in the bow [of the canoe], ready to shoot. A married woman must learn this kind of hunting" (JW).

This phrasing of gender opposition and complementarity is consistent with an organization of domestic and land use relations that is patricentric but not patrilineal, emphasizing cooperation between men in public, out-facing affairs. An ideal but not a requirement is that these men stand to each other as father to son or brother to brother. Conversely, women store up and transmit to each other the genealogical knowledge that maintains the connections between domestic units and communities. Older Algonquin women identify this knowledge with women's reproductive role, and formerly employed it in arranging marriages.

Complementarity between the genders led to the expectation of cooperation and even interchangeability among persons of the same gender. Young people should be trained to work with or replace if necessary other persons of the same sex – parents, parents-in-law, or siblings – before *or* after their marriage "in case something happens" (JW, LN). Traditional Algonquin marriage and post-marital residential practices facilitated this cooperation and interchangeability. They attached people as spouses to domestic groups while young and reattach them through remarriage if widowed (Davidson 1929 : 78).

Contemporary informants say that "long time ago" girls became young women at the menarche, which formerly happened at about 14 or 15 and was marked until early in this century by ritual seclusion. They would marry shortly after thereafter, or occasionally before menstruation if circumstances (orphanhood or domestic abuse) warranted. As a preparation for marriage, girls after the age of seven were given responsibility for household chores and mentoring in the technical skills required for women's roles. Unmarried young women were often taken into observe childbirths, both normal and difficult, as a precautionary instruction in what to do and what to avoid.

Men at first marriage should have undergone puberty ("when their voices changed"), but might be older than their wives, in their late teens or 20s. Visionary experience was formerly sought, but was not a prerequisite for adult status. Like their sisters, boys took on more responsibilities and intensified skills practice after the age of seven. By marriage they were expected to demonstrate some reasonable competence in adult skills, including but not confined to hunting and trapping, and to have "learned their [father's] territory".

As young people approached marriagable age, they were given their own plate and bowl for use at the table : "Now you can start a family, you can fill your own plate with food" (JW). Both sexes were formerly rigidly chaperoned. Sexual experimentation was not approved, and young people who were caught out were promptly married off, often to much older people.

An inspection of ages at first marriage for persons known to be alive in 1871, when the people trading at Cabonga and Grand-Lac-Victoria were censused (PAC C-0025 D92 P2)[5], shows a range from 11 to 30 (clustering between 13 and 16) for women, and a range from 14 to 34 (clustering between 14 and 22) for men. The preferred minimum age at first marriage for women was indeed 14 by 1939, as a dispute case at Barriere shows (HBCA B/96/a/7 : 15), and remained quite stable so long as marriages were arranged by the families. At present, courtship may begin as early as 12 or 13 (for young women), although the onset of living together as a recognized couple (*wîdigemâdowin* or *nîbâwîwin*) happens later, in the middle to late teens or even later.

The later age at first marriage for men reflected competition with older, previously married men for young marriageable women. Until recently men might expect to marry more often than women. 67 of 163 males and 44 of 167 females alive in 1871 who are known to have married were married more than once (and 9 men married four or more times).

Two factors accounted for this : maternal mortality in or after childbirth and, at an earlier period, polygyny. Polygyny was not recognized by the church, but can be sometimes identified from the baptisms of children and also appears in Hudson's Bay Company records. As late as 1871, two households at Grand-Lac-Victoria and one at Cabonga contained elderly men with two or more wives (PAC C-10025 D92 O2). Davidson (1929 : 74) and McPherson (n.d : 100) collected traditions of former polygyny at Grand-Lac-Victoria and Abitibi, where sororal polygyny was the preferred form. It is now only barely recalled at Rapid Lake.

Polygyny would certainly have increased the productive as well as the reproductive output of domestic groups, as McPherson (*idem*) was told at Abitibi. It can perhaps also be understood as an patricentric intensification of gender cooperation and interchangeability.

RELATIONS BETWEEN THE GENERATIONS

Marriage has further been organized by generational complementarity. Elderly Algonquins and some younger traditionalists describe marriage as embedded in a structure of reciprocal obligations between the generations. Seniors (in particular *kôkomik* and *comicik*, "grandmothers and grandfathers" but also parents), are entitled to respect and material support; in return, they admonish and instruct. Relative age is the most distinct and persistent feature of Barriere Lake kinship terminology. It overrides gender when older siblings "look down" to undifferentiated younger siblings, grandparents to grandchildren, and parents' siblings to siblings' children. These latter terms are also alternatives used by some people to distinguish by relative age the collateral relatives of their own generation (more often known collectively as *nitcînuwedâganak*, "my cousins", without distinction as cross or parallel)

Generational authority was expressed until recently in the arrangement of marriages. First marriages were arranged by parents or grandparents. As the repositories of genealogical knowledge, women took an active role in this process, approaching each other informally before their husbands met more formally (LN). Widows and widowers were free to make their own remarriages, although a widow should consider her children's well-being "so he [the step-father] won't abuse them" (LN). A widower who wished to marry a young unmarried woman dealt with her mother.

Hirbour was told by an elderly informant that formerly "elders met and decided if x could be a spouse for y" (1969 : 38), but his suggestion that this may indicate a collective role taken by the community in marriage exchange with other communities – Lac-Simon and Barriere – is not persuasive on his evidence. His "matrimonial exchange group" is more accurately an unbounded marriage network or social field of marrying persons, extending beyond the communities in question and constructed by genealogical knowledge and social interaction.

Minimum estimates and geographic spans for the sector of this network centered on Barriere Lake and Grand-Lac-Victoria can be reconstructed for the past from the known population within which marriages were actually contracted. In 1871 it included families from River Desert, Kipawa, Abitibi, and Quinze Lake (Long Point), Obedjiwan (Attikamek), and Waswanipi (Cree). Its minimum size of 430 persons was consistent with simulation projections of self-sufficient (i.e., self-reproducing) mating networks (475, Wobst 1976) and empirical studies of hunger-gatherer demography (200-800, mean 500, Hassan 1973). The mating network today for the Indian population of the Upper Ottawa is still wider in geographic span, and much larger in size.

Algonquins have organized the marriage field by genealogical knowledge that is laterally extensive but lineally truncated (Rogers and Rogers 1980; Turner and Wertman 1977). Elders look "across" and "down" in reckoning kinship. They have extensive knowledge of marriages, birth order and descent from siblings sets in their own and first ascending generations, in their own and other communities. They acquire and transmit this knowledge through "visiting around", mainly women with women, much as earlier families "traded around".

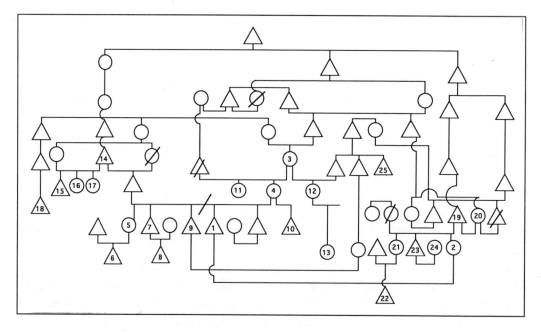

Fig. 1 Genealogical Relations and Performance Roles.

1. Bridegroom 2. Bride 3. Daughter of Tcibanam, the singer 4. Master of ceremonies, kâkîkwewin speaker, drummer 5. Gift presenter, the daughter of Madjikôkom, dancer 6. "Cheetah" (with "Tarzan") 7. Groom's witness, gift announcer, Tcibanam, deer dancer, canoe racer, dancer 8. Deer dancer 9. Drummer, interviewer of Tcibanam, canoe racer, guitarist, singer (country-and-western) 10. "Tarzan", the brother of Madjikôkom, canoe racer 11. Madjikôkom, gift acknowledger, singer, dancer 12. Tcibanam's feet 13. "Jane" (with "Tarzan") 14. Fiddle player 15. Photographer 16. Person in charge of gift wrappings and ribbons 17. Dancer 18. Singer (country-and-western), guitarist 19. Kâkîkwewin speaker, dancer 20. Dancer 21. Bride's witness, gift presenter, dancer 22. Dancer 23. Dancer 24. Dancer 25. Accordionist

However, they are rarely able to trace connecting links in second or higher ascending generations.

Elders sometimes say that "relatives should not marry relatives... A long time ago, that's why we had to go a long way to find someone to marry. Then the priests came and told us it was all right to marry our cousins" (LN). Yet a preliminary analysis of spouse selection in the marriage network since 1871 shows a very high frequency of marriages between people who are second to fourth cousins – patrilateral and matrilateral, cross and parallel.[6] At Grand-Lac-Victoria and Lac-Simon, a common patronym does not exclude marriage; Papaties marry Papaties. Barriere Lake people who have the same patronym do not marry each other. But descendents of brothers often bear different patronyms. Their common ancestry has been forgotten within two or three generations. They therefore can (and do) marry.

Figure 1 presents the genealogical relations between key participants in the Wawatie-Papatie marriage. The connecting links between siblings in the earliest generation shown have been forgotten. The descendents of the two brothers bear different patronyms, and their sister (at the top left of the diagram) is not remembered at all.

Marriages have thus been arranged at the limits of genealogical knowledge, either with people who are regarded as consanguineally unrelated because the connecting links have been forgotten, or with people who are recognized as consanguinally related as the children or grandchildren of first coursins, but who within two generations will not be remembered as having a common ancestor.

SIBLING SOLIDARITY AND AFFINAL ALLIANCE

Sibling solidarity and its extension in solidarity between cousins derive in part from "looking up" together to the same caregiving and instructing senior relatives, parents and grandparents (Turner and Wertman 1977). It is not undifferentiated; gender complementarity and interchangeability in task groups make for different expressions of solidarity between same sex and different sex siblings. Relative age terminology within a sibling set also anticipates parenting, since older siblings are trained intensively to be responsible for younger siblings.

Sibling solidarity and affinal alliance have operated together in spouse selection. The state of relationships among the families was considered in arranging marriages. Prior marriages between two domestic groups established opportunities for friendly visiting and access to resources : "If one man, his daughter, marries another man, his son, you can go there if you're related by marriage" (LN). Through friendly visiting and resource sharing, further marriages were sometimes arranged : sororal polygyny (McPherson n.d : 101) and the sororate and levirate.

In more complex exchanges, closely related consanguineal kin (siblings or first cousins) married people who were themselves related as siblings or first cousins. Some but not all of these exchanges were arranged at a single time by seniors; others followed later as married seniors made marriages for their junior relatives (Bechmann-Khera 1964 : 11 *et seq.*). When this happened, the marriage field was knit into one- or two-generation clusters of marital connection which drew on and reinforced sibling solidarity as well as affinal alliance. Young people continue this process today as they "visit around" with married relatives in other communities and find spouses for themselves; in the 12 recent cases of marriage between Long Point (Winneway) and Rapid Lake people, all the Long Point spouses are related as siblings (in two sets of three siblings each) or first cousins to each other.

POST-MARITAL RESIDENCE, DOMESTIC GROUP AND TASK GROUP COMPOSITION

Post-marital residence structured the setting within which couples continued to move toward autonomy and responsibility. Although young people should be minimally competent by marriage, they were not expected to have perfected all adult skills and would not yet have "learned other territories" : "It was our way to learn, before the marriage and after the marriage, to know all this Indian stuff" (ET) Senior relatives were their principal teachers. Algonquin couples could expect to spend much of their married life with senior relatives, at first as juniors residing and working at least intermittently with seniors (usually parents or parents-in-law), and later as caregivers for elderly parents or grandparents.

This stands in contrast with Davidson's characterization of Grand-Lac-Victoria in the mid-1920s. He reported that hunting territories were allocated to sons or sons-in-law at or shortly after their marriage, and that young married couples usually formed independent nuclear families (1929 : 76-95). But Hirbour counted 21 households at the Grand-Lac-Victoria summer village in 1967; eleven of these were "bilateral extended families" and nine of the remainder were nuclear families living immediately adjacent to the parents of one of the spouses. Couples began living with the husband's or wife's parents, then pitched a tent for themselves by the side of the house, and finally, with help of the father or father-in-law, built their own house (1969 : 35).

Hirbour inventoried the composition of 72 "task groups" between November 1967 and May 1968. 43 of these included among their members married men with one or both parents or parents-in-law. Of the dyadic relations composing these task groups, 138 were close consanguines (father/son or brother), 84 were close affines (father-in-law/son-in-law or brother-in-law), 20 were distant consanguines and 14 were distant affines (Hirbour 1969 : 53-54).

Hirbour's data on post-marital residence and task group formation describe an organization of inter-generational cooperation which, while undoubtedly patricentric, also drew on affinal alliance with the wife's kinsmen. This might take the form of temporary uxorilocal residence : "The new spouse must reside with his father-in-law the first year of marriage. He will later return to his father's residence with his wife" (1969 : 44). Bechmann-Khera (1961 : 23) adds that the couple might remain with the wife's family until the birth of the first child and then join the husband's family.

Contemporary Barriere Lake elders say that it is useful for a young couple to "visit back and forth" between the two families allied by their marriage. "That way you learn both families' ways, both families' territories" (ET, LR). I have earlier noted that this friendly visiting also reinforces relations, with the possibility of subsequent marriages, between the two families themselves. Affinal relations have thus been pathways to alternate resources, diversified sets of knowledge and skills, and future extensions of kinship connection. Today, they serve also as pathways to housing, income and consumption goods.

Affinal alliance may result in permanent attachment to the wife's family or territory. Hirbour reported that of 16 marriages endogamous to the band, 11 resulted in virilocal and 5 in uxorilocal residence; of 21 exogamous marriages, 11 were virilocal and 10 uxorilocal. Forty years earlier, Davidson's trapline succession histories showed that of 42 transfers, six were from father-in-law to son-in-law or the reverse (1929 : 90-95; Cooper 1942 : 10). Coresidence or cooperation with primary affines has been a recognized alternative to the patricentric ideal of father-son succession.

Bechmann-Khera did not conduct a systematic census of households at Rapid Lake, and her data on task group formation is organized by (and largely confined to) trapline use. But much the same pattern can be seen in her anecdotal data. Most married children lived in the summer village with or near senior parents or parents-in-law. 19 separate trapping arrangements during 1963-1964 can be recognized in her trapline histories. In 5 cases, men trapped alone or with unmarried children. In 2 cases, men trapped with non-kin partners. In 5 cases, men trapped with one or more married sons. In 2 cases, brothers trapped together. In 1 case, a man trapped with his brother and his married son. In 1 other case, a step-grandfather trapped with his step-grandsons, married and unmarried. In 2 cases, men trapped with their mothers. Only 1 man was trapping with his son-in-law, but 4 of the 29 traplines registered in the community had gone through affinal transmission in their recent histories (Bechmann-Khera 1964: 84-90). Men might change their trapping arrangements from season to season, or (as Hirbour reported for Grand-Lac-Victoria) join seasonal task and residential groups at fur farms in the United States.

Comprehensive data on contemporary Barriere Lake land use is not yet available, but household composition shows both change and continuity from the past. Of 68 households for which I had information in 1992, 39 were formed around a single marital union, *nîbâwîwin* or *wîdigemâdowin*, (although three included the children of unmarried children or stepchildren). 19 households were formed around two or more unions : a senior couple with children or grandchildren at least one of whom had a recognized and at least intermittently coresident companion. In 11 of all the households formed around marital unions, the companion or spouse came from another community. In 3 cases of the 68 households, widows or widowers lived at least intermittently with unmarried grandchildren. In 2 other cases, widows lived at least intermittently with a married grandchild. In 3 other cases again (two widowers and one young man), men lived alone. In 1 other case, two unmarried siblings shared intermittently the house of a father who lived elsewhere. In 1 last case, two married siblings shared a house intermittently. Of the 25 young couples living with relatives, 10 were living with kin of the men and 15 with kin of the women.

The construction of new housing in the community has not preserved the pattern of grouping by kin, and it has not kept pace with demand. Housing is now the scarcest resource on the reserve. In adaptation to this, kin ties are employed in the succession of occupants; parents have given houses to children and moved elsewhere, to the bush or in with other relatives. Occupancy is fluid; people (particularly young people) move about a good deal – to the bush, to other households or other communities where they have kin or affines, even to Maniwaki where some families now maintain apartments. But most couples now with their own homes have spent time, in the bush or on the reserve, living with parents or parents-in-law, and a young couple now living with older relatives hopes, if they stay together (and *wîdigemâdowin* is often unstable), to have their own house some day.

This is clearly the contemporary expression of the developmental cycle of residence observed at Grand-Lac-Victoria in 1967-1968 by Hirbour. In two other respects, Hirbour's observations apply, with but with some modification, today. First, achieving a separate residence in the village does not mean the end of economic cooperation : juniors and seniors go into the bush together and resources from the bush (in particular, moosemeat and fish) are regularly distributed among closely related households. In these distributions, feeding the "old people" still has the force of moral obligation. Secondly, sharing a common residence does not signal complete incorporation. Hirbour found an etiquette of non-commensality at Grand-Lac-Victoria :

> ... the commensal unit is not the bilateral extended family, but the nuclear family. Each unit indeed has its own provisions and utensils. [Members] need not necessarily eat at the same time or eat the same food ... [but] ... there is however a common cookhouse.
>
> (Hirbour 1969 : 35)

Bechmann-Khera's informants (1962 : 7) recalled a similar separation of household goods and meals when couples shared a common stove and cabin. This is now more variable, but is still common practice, both in Rapid Lake and in the bush. Commensal separation signifies the movement toward economic autonomy within a cooperating group of kin. It will be recalled that previous to marriage young people were formerly given their own dishes and told : "Now you can start a family, you can fill your own plate with food." Marriage thus develops within an unfolding process of movement from dependency toward competent autonomy, in which seniors and juniors adjust their relationships to each other but, ideally, never fully sever them.

This adjustment has not always been easy. Bechmann-Khera's principal informants recalled that after their marriage in 1925 they lived with the husband's parents, but quarreled when the older man kept most of the proceeds from their joint fur sales and refused them access to the canoe. The young couple broke away, spending the next winter with another family while the seniors found another partner "so we knew they were not alone and we could go our own way". They acquired their own canoe At the Christmas rendezvous, the older man took the canoe : "He was [that] mad." In the spring, the younger couple returned to Barriere and "moved back with [his] parents as if nothing happened.

The old man did not say anything either... [but] from then on [the younger man] sold his furs himself." Thereafter they spent some but not all winters with the older couple, each couple finding other partners as needed (Bechmann-Khera 1962 : 8-9).

On the reserve today, income sources from transfer payments and the access to outside technologies and consumer goods they allow have begun to erode the interdependence of genders and generations. Young people now freely contract unions, both *wîdigemâdowin* and *nîbâwîwin*, on their own, and they separate freely. This new autonomy has been achieved, however, at the expense of increasing dependency upon the outside economy. Elderly people regard this state of affairs with somewhat ambivalent alarm :

> I was forced to marry a man I didn't know. I didn't love him for about two years... then we began to know each other. He used to go hunting, bring food back, it took him a whole day. After he came home I'd wash his dirty clothes, I'd hang them up, and his dirty moccasins. We lived with my mother and stepfather for six years before we went on our own... Nowadays if you live just on the reserve it doesn't take a man to go out into the bush to hunt; you just go down to Maniwaki to buy some food [so] Women don't do nothing... You don't need a man. (ET)

ALGONQUIN WEDDING RITUAL

The "wedding in the bush" took place at "Kôkomville" ("Grandma's town") at Lake Nanouatan, 25 miles by car from Rapid Lake. "Kôkomville" is today a group of nine cabins built by descendents of Helene (Lena) Nottaway (age 79). In 1988, its cabins were laid out in two directions from *Kôkom* Lena's cabin, with Jerome and Wawatie children and grandchildren of her first marriage on one side and Nottaway children from her second marriage on another side.

Kôkom Lena and her oldest daughter, Irene Jerome, are accomplished producers of traditional Algonquin crafts. Irene and her children are also vigorous exponents of Algonquin cultural renewal. When her younger son Joseph Jr. Wawatie came together with Marie Angele Papatie from Lac-Simon, their wedding was an opportunity to encourage the revival of craftwork and the return of their people to the bush.

Toward that end, the family devised a wedding ceremony that combined Algonquin customs with the Catholic nuptial mass. They also mounted an elaborate visual display of traditional material culture and wedding regalia inside a bark lodge, and planned events for the day that would both instruct and entertain their guests. Kôkomville was a stage for a form of cultural theater, constructed of dramatic and often playful oppositions between *anicinâbe* (Indian) and *wâbickîwe* (white), "bush" and "reserve", autonomy and dependency, competence and clumsiness, past and present.

The family drew on a tradition of early wedding ritual preserved by Barriere Lake elders. Some features may show post-Oblate borrowing or reinterpretation, but elders regard the essential form as very old. The Catholic mass was grafted onto it, rather than replacing it immediately or completely.

TRADITIONAL WEDDINGS

Weddings were conducted when the band came together at its summer rendezvous. A bride from another band was brought to her husband's band's rendezvous. The arrangers of the marriage selected two mature witnesses, a married man (*opigonickâgewînînî*) and woman (*opigonickâgekwe*). "This means 'they follow behind them, they help them'" (ET/LR). The witnesses accompanied the couple to an island, where they camped for the night. The bride and groom had to obtain their own food and shelter : "When they leave, they don't have anything [except an axe]. He must make shelter, get food for the night, to show he can do this for life" (LN). Each temoin also delivered a moral homily (*kâkîkwewin*) on marital responsibility, the man to the groom and the woman to the bride.

The community had assembled to see the couple and witnesses depart for the island. They assembled again to greet them on their return the next day.

> When they came back, the people asked the witness : "Did you tell him this or that?" If he didn't, he was told that it was his responsibility to preach that advice... The chief (*ogîma*) preached to the married couple, then he preached [to] the witnesses; he told them what they should have preached and taught to the couple. Then the community preached [to] them anything else they thought had been forgotten. (LN, JW)

Some *kâkîkwewin* advice is remembered. Its concern is with domestic harmony through mutual responsibility. A bridgroom was told, for example : "You must treat your wife equally... if your wife gets pregnant, you have to help her, you must carry the heavy burdens during her time." A bride was told : "Now your place is with your husband, you have to help him. You must listen to his mother [because] she is your teacher now." Both were told : "You have to get along together now."

One version of this tradition has "the people drumming and singing Indian songs" while the chief preached to the people. "After the priest came, the people would still sing while the priest was marrying them. They had their own way of singing – Indian worship songs" (ET). Leather thongs were tied at the wrist, connecting the couple to their witnesses; later they were released or the bride and groom alone were connected to each other, as McPherson (n.d. : 100) was told at Abitibi.

The entire community provided food for the feast (*magocewin*) which followed the preaching "so the couple would have a good life and their children would be healthy" (ET). "The feast is like a blessing. [By providing meat from the bush] you bring in the animal [spirit] who blesses the marriage" (JW); a wide range of animals represented in the feast food signified a wide and auspicious blessing. Men were served before women. Birchbark baskets were set aside for offerings of tobacco and food from each person's plate to spiritual patrons – the benevolent "grandfather" (*micomic*) and the dangerous *madjîoc*.

After the feast, the immediate families gave useful presents (*abâdikwe-wanan*) to the new couple – a rabbitskin blanket, a canoe, pots and pans, a gun. This recognized their competence in contributing to household and community production. The people then danced, often all night long. The old social dances, now only dimly recalled, were replaced in the later fur trade period by reels, square- and step (clog)-dances learned at Hudson's Bay posts and logging camps.

CHANGES IN WEDDING RITUAL

Over time, other new forms were incorporated. Originally, new leather clothing was made for the bride and groom by their respective families (ET). By early in this century, grooms wore store clothes while brides made their own ribbon-trimmed cloth dress. Brides wore shawls as a sign of their change in status : "The shawl is the veil" (LN). By 1961, veils were improvised from curtains or other light materials.

Bechmann-Khera (1962 : 102; 1964 : 15-17) observed further elaborations of wedding finery, the introduction of wedding rings, and a procession of cars after the wedding. The night on the island had long since been abandoned. The chief and other senior people still delivered moral homilies, but they might now say : "Don't let relatives meddle in your affairs." A reception line formed after the ceremony, and guests gave gifts of money as they shook hands with the bride and groom. In place of a feast given by the community, the two families hosted a "tea party" for their guests. If the couple came from two different bands, the wedding was now most often held in the bride's community.

Wedding dress and attendants now often copy "white" weddings, and gift-giving is elaborate. At some pre-wedding fetes, the bride and groom may be playfully assaulted with rotten eggs or sour milk. The evolving ensemble of present customs and remembered traditions on which Joseph, Marie Angele, and their families could draw for their wedding was thus eclectic in origin and diverse in meaning. We will see below that they may also have drawn on a still older Algonquin tradition : the theater of the shaking tent.

THE "WEDDING IN THE BUSH"

As an occasion for instructive cultural display, the wedding in the bush was intended for a wide audience. Announcements were circulated in the River Desert (Maniwaki), Grand-Lac-Victoria, and Lac-Simon communities, through kinship and friendship networks and even posting in public places. People from other communities were invited to camp. By the morning of the wedding, a tent village was strung out along the length of Kôkomville. At least 300 people were present at one time or another on the day of the wedding.

THE SETTING

At the foot of this tent and cabin village, a large tipiform lodge (*pikogân*) was erected, about 15' high and 10' in diameter and covered with overlapped sections of birchbark. It was painted by the groom's brother, Jacob Wawatie, with animal symbols : bear, sturgeon, eagle (chiefs of their respective domains of animate life) and beaver. Below was a panel representing the environment : green mountains with yellow sunrise over blue water stripes. Below this again were animal and bird tracks, intended as an exercise in

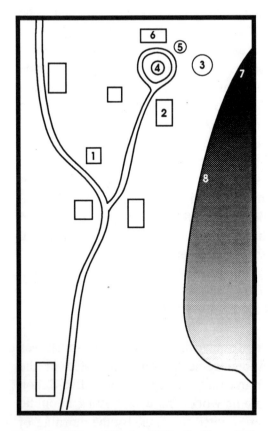

Map 2. Kôkomville in 1988. Outline of the wedding site.
1. Lena Nottaway's cabin 2. Irene Jerome's cabin 3. Bark lodge 4. Cookhouse 5. Sweatlodge 6. Scene 7. Far canoe landing 8. Near (main) canoe landing

identification A painted bear's skull, flanked with eagle feathers, hung over the door.

Objects for use in the wedding were on view : a small birchbark canoe, strung eagle feathers for the altar, two loonskin cushions, two bark baskets for feast offerings, a bow and bark arrow quiver, a moose pericardeum rattle, and a doubleheaded drum with bear's knuckle snares. The lodge was filled also with traditional domestic furnishings, clothing, materials and equipment : "... everything a family would need to survive, long time ago" (IJ). Materials and tools for construction were displayed with finished objects : snowshoes with frames, babiche, netting needles and spacers. Trapping equipment – a crookedstick for exploring a beaver "wash", stakes and stretchers – hung near pelts. There were birchbark moose calls and baskets in all shapes. A rack by the lodge door held common medicine plants and "Indian tea".

These things are made or used regularly by Barriere Lake people. Some other objects displayed, such as rabbitskin blankets, are now rarely made. Still others – an "old time sewing kit" with loon's beak awl, marten's penis needle and "muscle line" thread, a moose legbone scraper, porcupine tail comb, sturgeon gut glue, a treeburl and fungus fire carrier - were reconstructed from oral traditions and early memories as instructive exemplars : "So people will see what we used to use before the white people came" (IJ).

The lodge's contents also represented contemporary cultural interchanges among Native peoples. A Mohawk ash splint basket (gotten in trade at Trois-

Rivières) held the rings for the wedding, and a cradleboard was draped with an embroidered shawl, a gift from Tarahumara visitors from Mexico.

In front of the bark lodge was a circular, boulder-lined fire pit, used for cooking and heating rocks for a small nearby sweatlodge. Joseph and his brothers used the sweatlodge the night before the wedding as a spiritual cleansing. Algonquins traditionally burned dried and powdered pike's liver in a sweatlodge to bring about visions, but not on this occasion.

A dancing platform with a tarpaulin roof was erected near the sweatlodge. From it, a trail led down to the far canoe landing. Another, main landing near the cabins was used for canoe races after the wedding (Map 2).

PREPARATIONS

As campers arrived, they were drawn into preparations for the wedding, under Irene's direction. In every camp with a cookstove, food was prepared and brought to her cabin in the morning. Moose ribs were smoked at the fire and great pots of beans were set to bake in hot sand. Visiting women joined family members for last-minute work, wrapping eagle feathers with ribbon for decorative display and sewing final touches to the wedding clothing. Children were given tasks and errands to run between the camps.

The couple spent the night before the wedding inside the bark lodge. As elders do, *Kôkom* Lena went in early to wake them up : "W*anickan*!" They came out dressed in work clothes and joined in the preparations.

As the time for the ceremony approached, Joseph and Marie Angele and their witnesses dressed with great care and rebraided their hair. Joseph's temoin was his oldest married brother, Jacob Wawatie; Marie Angele's was her older married sister, Mani Papatisse, the wife of the then chief at Grand-Lac-Victoria. The women put on mocassins and two-piece printed calico dresses with ribbon and eyelet trim, everyday dress for some elderly and middle-aged women, but now worn only (if at all) for festive occasions by others. The men put on mocassins and scarlet pow-wow style ribbon shirts over store trousers. For the bride and groom, this was the first of two clothing changes they would make for the ceremony. All their clothing, and new moccasins for the priest, had been made by Irene.

THE CEREMONY

Marie Angele was taken unobtrusively out of the camp, to a place where a bridge crosses the lake. Joseph and Jacob went to the bark lodge, counseled briefly and shook hands. Joseph strung the bow and bark quiver over his shoulder and hefted the bark canoe over his head. A small crowd of children and close family members followed him to the far canoe landing, as his temoin beat the drum. He paddled off, the small canoe riding very low in the water.

Joseph soon returned with Marie Angele, who was wrapped in a green blanket over her ribbon dress and seated in the bow facing him. As they landed, she disembarked first, taking his bow and paddle until he had beached the canoe. More people had come down to meet them, and followed them back up the path to the lodge, where Jacob was beating the drum in slow double-beats. The couple entered the lodge but soon went off to the cabin area, the bride with her witness, to dress for the nuptial mass. Jacob drummed again and briefly addressed the crowd, explaining what was to happen. He then went toward the cabins to escort the groom.

An altar had been erected between the bark lodge and the sudatory. It was covered with a tanned hide and hung with ribbon-wrapped eagle feathers. On it were the chalice, missal, and a small, undecorated bark basket containing communion wafers baked by the groom's mother from "Indian flour – what the Indians used to use a long time ago." A line of mats led to the altar, with the two loonskin cushions on beaver pelts at the front. The officiating Oblate priest, Father Edmond Brouillard, waited by the altar, wearing moccasins and an embroidered moosehide chasuble. The groom's second brother Solomon Wawatie drummed slow single beats as the wedding procession came slowly down from the cabins, followed by a great crowd of guests. The couple were now dressed in fringed deerhide garments, elegantly trimmed with floral beading and fur. They walked with their temoins, joined to them at the wrist by leather thongs. At the line of mats, the witnesses untied the thongs and released the couple. They advanced toward the altar, stepping to slow drumbeats, and sat down cross-legged on the loonskin cushions. Irene, dressed in a feather-trimmed tunic and leggings, now had the drum. She gave the ring basket to the witnesses who stood to the rear.

Kôkom Lena and a woman from Lac-Simon led the responsive singing of the Algonquin liturgy, standing to the right rear of the priest. They were joined from time to time by two of Joseph's aunts. Some visiting women standing by the bark lodge also had hymnals and sang during the communion.

The order of service itself departed only slightly from the canonical nuptial mass. The priest read in Algonquin from a prepared text, abbreviating the Liturgy of the Word. The couple sat throughout the opening prayer and responsive singing, standing only for the exchange of vows. For this rite the witnesses advanced, holding the ring basket upright between them, and presented the rings for blessing. Two sets of rings – one turquoise-and-silver and one beaded – were exchanged.

Fig. 2
Wedding Ceremony at Lake Nanouatan, August 20 1988.
(Photograph by Michael Greenlar)

Following the exchange of rings and general intercessions, the priest performed the Liturgy of the Eucharist, consecrating the wine and the "Indian" communion wafers, leading the Our Father, and conferring the nuptial blessing. The bride and groom were first given communion at their seats. The witnesses then took communion, followed by the siblings and parents of the bride and groom. Only twelve other people joined them.

After communion, the couple stood to receive the final blessing. They sat again for the signing of the mission's register and the marriage certificate. "A long time ago, Indians signed their names with an X" (IJ). After the signing, they kissed each other and playfully rubbed noses.

During the mass, the audience was scattered around the perimeter, from the lodge to the fire. Most people stood, but some visiting women had set up folding chairs to the side. Joseph's aunt arranged seating for elders by the woodpile, and at one point, after the mass had begun, escorted an old couple to a good seat. Small children moved freely, but not noisily, about without admonishment from adults. Marie Angele's father and stepmother stood well to the side, across from Irene but, unlike her and like the rest of the audience, without a visible part in the ritual until its conclusion.

With the signing of the register, the boundary between audience and actors dissolved. People pushed forward to take photographs of the nose-rubbing. Marie Angele's father, the late Jerome Papatie, then went up to the couple and, his back to the crowd, delivered a brief *kâkîkwewin* on their duties to one another. He said to his daughter : "This is your husband; this is where you live now, where you belong." They stood for the homily, eyes respectfully cast down, and shook hands at its end.

A reception line formed and the crowd began to file past. Irene addressed them in her own *kâkîkwewin*, advising them of the family's purpose and its rules for the day :

I'm happy all you people came. Come up and shake hands with the bride and groom, but don't give them money in the handshake, we don't want you to do that. We didn't have money long time ago. The priest didn't have money to preach to us. Why do we have to put money down now? The people who got married don't need any money. And no drinking around here. I know that there was drinking the other day, but we don't want drinking here now. It's our fault, not the white people's fault, that we went over to the white people's way. What we have to do is to go back to the Indian way, stick to the Indian way. That's what we always talk about, we can never forget it [the Indian way].

This public *kâkîkwewin* was met with applause by the crowd. In the reception line, confetti was thrown and people shook hands; women kissed each other on the cheek in customary fashion. Some infirm elders remained at their seats, and other guests went over to shake hands with them in deference to their age.

THE FEAST AND GIFTS

A feast (*magocewin*) followed. The groom's women relatives set moose ribs and bean pots from the fire pit were set beside fried moose meat, bear's meat pie, bannock bread, and other foods contributed from the camps, with wedding cakes at the end. Most people served themselves on paper plates, but infirm elders had food brought to them. Guests sat in small groups on the ground. A long row of women from Lac-Simon and Grand-Lac-Victoria ate facing out to the lake with their backs to the crowd. The bride and groom ate on their cushions near the altar.

Two bark baskets were placed on the altar. Guests came up to put food offerings in the baskets for *micomic* and *madjîoc*. The baskets, with tobacco, were later hung in the bush or left by the lakeshore.

After the feast, the gifts were opened. A wooden canoe, a gift from the bride's brother and his wife, was set on the dance platform. Gifts were brought out in large sacks and loaded into the canoe. Joseph and Marie Angele sat on beaver pelts in front of the canoe. Behind them, their sisters passed gifts from the canoe to Jacob, who read out the cards, translating between Algonquin, French, and English, and handed the gifts to the couple for unwrapping. Wrappings and ribbons were collected by Joseph's father's sister, who tied the decorative bows together. The couple was flanked by Irene, beating the drum as givers were announced, and her sister Mary Whiteduck, who thanked the givers and joked with her nephew.

Gifts from 34 families or individuals were announced, mainly from close consanguines and affines of the couple. Some were substantial : the canoe from the bride's brother and his wife, and a gun, guncase and footlocker from the groom's brother and his wife. Many (but not all) were intended for camping in the bush. Other guests would have made small gifts of money had they not been asked to refrain from this recent custom.

Announcements and unwrapping were conducted with improvised joking, playing upon themes anticipated in Irene's *kâkîkwewin* and elaborated further in the entertainments to follow. Mary joked repeatedly with her sister's son. When an envelope was found to contain a gift of money from a River Desert family, she stuffed it in her dress : "Sorry, it's mine [you don't need it]... hey, take it easy!" (as he made a grab for it).

The bride and groom were reminded by washboards and galvanized tubs that there is no electricity or running water in the bush. Unwrapping fancy gifts, Joseph said : "Indians don't use those things", and he pretended not to recognize or know how to use parts of some complex appliances. Just as the bark lodge display presented a reconstruction of a "traditional" household inventory, joking with the wedding gifts juxtaposed a more recent contrast in material possessions : things of the "bush" and things of the "reserve" (or "town"). But it also playfully recognized the technological dependency that now follows Indian people into the bush. A gift of bullets elicited : "I can't make my own, eh?" And modern cross-bow arrows stuffed into the gun case : "I can use these if the gun doesn't work!"

At the end, the spouses got into the canoe (still on the stage), with the gifts loaded between them, and took up paddles. "You see, you're going on a honeymoon, a honeymoon in the bush", said Mary. The groom called for help in "pushing off". The canoe and gifts were then taken down from the stage.

ENTERTAINMENTS

The first of several entertainments followed, this one a burlesque on the commercialization of sexual displays in the white world. With his mother assisting and prompting ("See what Indian longjohns look like"), Joseph took off his outer garments in turn and paraded about the stag in an artful parody of both a "stripper's" routine and pow-wow dance, while his brother shook a rattle. At the end, he announced : "The show's over. Ten bucks – anybody want to pay ten bucks?" Someone called out that it was the bride's turn, but Joseph retorted : "I don't want anybody to see *my* wife."

A sound system with microphone was now installed on the stage. Dancing followed, led off by the spouses in cloth dress and ribbon shirt, their witnesses, other siblings and close kin. Joseph's grandfather, the late Pierre Wawatie (then living in Lac-Simon with his daughter), played his fiddle for the dance, accompanied from time to time by accordion and guitar.

In Algonquin square dancing, six to eight couples form a square. They dance together three times with intermissions to complete a set. No one "calls" the dance, but older, experienced dancers often stand at the side directing and correcting dancers; this confusion and correction of steps is regarded as part of the entertainment. "Step dance" is a much admired embellishment to the basic progression in which couples, together or changing partners, advance around the square.

Between dances, *kôkom* Lena sang an old Algonquin song about traveling : "Somebody's going with us, somebody's going to get hungry". This was the first of several impromptu performances with the microphone. Others sang American country-and-western songs in Algonquin and English. One singer had his nose pinched to parody the nasal sound of "Willy (Nelson) and Waylon (Jennings)".

The second round of dancing was followed by the appearance of "Tarzan", a primordial "wild man" in white popular culture. Joseph's youngest brother Edward Wawatie ran out from the forest in a leopardskin-print suit, carrying his nephew dressed as an ape ("Cheetah") and followed by his young cousin, also in leopardskin, as "Jane". This "Tarzan" was unable to speak, and more ape than man in behavior. He climbed a tree and swung by his knees, carried his mother off over his shoulder, and jumped into the arms of a guest, to great applause and laughter from the crowd.

Next, canoe races for men and women were announced. They followed a course out and back from the main landing around a small island. In the men's race, five two-man canoes with paddlers from the host and visiting communities competed. It was won by the groom's second and youngest brothers. Joseph and Jacob, both skilled canoers, paddled the small bark canoe used to fetch the bride. This canoe was far too small for two men and sank in the water to its gunwales. As they floundered, far behind the others, the watchers laughed. Four canoes competed in the women's race, which ended in a dead heat. Again, interest and teasing laughter were focused on one floundering canoe.

A Rabbit Dance (*wâbôsnîmî*) was then organized on the stage. *Wâbôsnîmî* is a reel dance, in which men and women face each other in two files. Each couple in turn passes down through the files, separates around them, and each partner comes back behind its own file to "hunt the rabbit", first the man chasing the woman, and then (on the second progression through the reel), the woman chasing the man. As each couple finishes its "hunt", it forms an arch through which the others pass, and then takes its place at the end. The dancers were young people, not very familiar with the dance. Irene and Jacob modeled it for them as Lena called out commands and corrections.

After more impromptu singing, another entertainment was presented. *Madjikôkom* (a bad or cross old woman) was played by Mary Whiteduck. She hobbled onto the stage with her small granddaughter. *Madjikôkom*'s face was blackened with soot and her clothing was torn. Jacob engaged her in dialogue : "What have you got in your packsack?" "Everything!" She pulled out skunkskin and foxskin caps, handing the skunkskin cap to her "son" Edward Wawatie : "This is my son's hat; the other is my husband's." She called loudly for her "daughter" to come out. Joseph's sister, Louise Pien, approached sulkily, complaining : "You've got a big mouth!" *Madjikôkom* demurred : "That little child [her granddaughter] has been making the noise."

She assumed a characteristic "old lady" posture, one leg straight out and the other bent in, and pulled out a pipe from her packsack. Her "son" handed her a lighter, but she said : "I don't know [how to use] that [white] thing." Her "daughter" then handed her matches and explained what they were. *Madjikôkom* tried and failed to strike them. The "daughter" told the "son" to "make a light for her". He did, but the "old lady" grabbed again at the matches : "Let me try!", at last lighting her pipe. "See, you've got it now!"

Madjikôkom then sang about a poor old lady, abandoned and mistreated by her family : "My son is a soldier... my daughter wants to get married and leave me [reaching for her "daughter", who shook her off]... there's no food for me, my clothes are all torn [lifting her torn skirt]. That's all right; I don't care (*mânotc*). I'm going up to heaven early [pointing up to the sky], if someone doesn't feel sorry for me". She finished with : "That's enough; I've got to go back to where I came from", and hobbled offstage.

In the evening, *Tcibinam* appeared on the stage. *Tcibinam* is a far-traveling but shy little man who lives in the bush. His impersonation requires two actors. One actor presents his upper body from behind a curtain; another stands behind the curtain and "dances the feet" with hands in shoes. Like the "cross old woman", *Tcibinam* blackens his face with soot and wears old clothes. On this occasion, Joseph's brother Jacob played *Tcibinam*, while his mother's younger half-sister danced his feet.

A blanket was hung across the back of the stage. Irene, Mary Whiteduck, and Irene's second son Solomon stood to the side with the microphone. The audience was cautioned : "Don't make any noise; you'll scare him... he won't come this way if he's scared." *Tcibinam* emerged, wearing a large brimmed hat over long, unbraided hair which hung in his face. "See what he looks like with his long hair! He wants to dance." *Tcibinam* danced to the fiddle, turning his head from side to side, elbows askew. He could not control his feet, grabbed at them to stop dancing, and went behind the curtain.

When *Tcibinam* reappeared, Solomon asked him questions : "Where do you come from?" "I come over here from far, far away. I did this [dancing] a long time ago." He answered once in English – "yeah, yeah, yeah" – an amusing dissonance for one listener who complained : "*Tcibinam*'s not supposed to say *that*!" But when Marie Angele's sister 's camera flashed, he became frightened; the camera was an unfamiliar object from the white world.

The dialogue continued : "Did you bring somebody?" "Yes, my daughter is coming out". *Kôkom* Lena appeared, wrapped in a rabbitskin blanket. *Tcibinam* asked his "daughter" if she wanted to dance. She step-danced to the fiddle, first alone and then with her "son", and then stomped off stage. Again, *Tcibinam* could not stop his own dancing feet : "I've got to check on this out in the back." He returned with the wedding drum, and was asked : "Do you want someone to play the fiddle?" "No, I don't want anything to play from the white people, I've got my own [music]. [White people's music] would be confusing." He called his "daughter" out again, and drummed and sang for her as she danced energetically. *Tcibinam* cried "*pekâtc* ["slow down!"]... do you like this dance better?" "*Eheh*!" ["yes!"]. They talked about turning back to "the Indian way" : "This is the way I'm going to travel, where my language is". *Tcibinam* said : "I'm going to finish dancing, and go back to where I came from". People were then invited to ask him questions – "How do you do that [with his feet]?" "I don't know" and again "Where do you come from?" "Far away" – to much laughter.

After this entertainment, dancing resumed until midnight. Jacob and his son danced a Deer Dance which mimes a father instructing his son how to track, stalk and shoot. This dance had been last seen some 25 years earlier : "We haven't seen [how to revive] all of our old dances yet."

AFTER THE WEDDING

By the evening of the next day the tent village had been dismantled and most people had gone back to their reserves. The couple stayed on for some time in the bush; they have since built a cabin just outside the reserve at

Rapid Lake, where they now live.

Friendly contacts have continued between their families, mainly at Nanouatan, and mainly between women. Marie Angele returned frequently to visit with her (late) father and her brother at Lac-Simon. The following summer, her sister witness Mani spent a week with Irene to learn hide tanning and other skills; her mother's sister likewise came to visit *kôkom* Lena, and went moose hunting with Lena and Irene that fall.

THE WEDDING IN THE BUSH AS A SYMBOLIC PERFORMANCE

The "wedding in the bush" was a complex symbolic performance which was meaningful at more than one level for its actors and audience. As a rite of passage (Van Gennep 1960; Turner 1969), its overt and obvious intention was to mark a change in status identity for the bride and groom. Other lessons were intended as well, and other effects were achieved. Their explication requires that we consider the full range of performance events – interludes and ludic divertissements as well as the wedding ritual itself – in relation to each other and in relation to the larger contexts of Algonquin society and history.

Rites of passage have three phases. In the first phase, participants are separated from their old social identity. In the liminal or transitional phase, they are "betwixt and between" (Turner 1969 : 95), no longer occupying their former position in society but not yet asuming their new social identity. In the aggregation or reincorporation phase, participants rejoin society in their new social identity.

Of these stages, liminality is the most analytically interesting. Turner has noted that liminal ritual contains ambiguous imagery in which symbolic inversions or reversals appear. It also presents in condensed form reenactments of the instruction that prepared its subjects for their new status. Public rites of passage involve the entire community in this "pedagogics of liminality".

Traditional Algonquin wedding ritual symbolized : the separation and reincorporation of the couple in relation to consanguines and affines; their evolution toward competent autonomy; the complementarity of genders and generations; the integration and reproduction of the seasonally dispersed community as a whole.

The ritual recognized the primary interest of domestic groups in reproducing themselves through the marriages they arranged, and their primary responsibility for training and equipping their children for adult life. It also separated couples from their families and community, and required them to demonstrate social and technical competence. This demonstration was witnessed and confirmed by the witnesses, who delivered the first of the instructional homilies, man to man and woman to woman. The witnesses represented the differentiation of gender roles and the accrued knowledge of community seniors in relation to juniors. The homilies were reiterated by the chief, in his role as spiritually powerful moral exemplar, and by other community members. Their right to "preach" other advice derived both from their own autonomous experience and their common interest in the competence of persons with whom they might want or need to cooperate. Community interest was also expressed in the "reincorporation" ritual of the commensal feast and the dance.

In the "wedding in the bush" at Lake Nanouatan we can see elements of these customs, selected and reinterpreted. The canoe journey to fetch the bride was intended to reprise both the old patricentric ideal of domestic group composition and the return of the couple from the island. The burden of demonstrating competence was now carried by an elaborate and stylized display of traditional skills – the lodge and its contents – in which Joseph's entire family participated. They collectively stood as hosts and instructors for their guests.

On the other hand, the witnesses' symmetrical ritual roles and parallel relationships with the couple implicated both families equally in the union. The witnesses' representation of gender difference is self-evident. Their relative age, as older married siblings of the same sex, also mediated between sibling solidarity and generational authority. They were thus ideal exemplars for their younger siblings.

In former times, the chief's *kâkîkwewin* was addressed to the community as well as the couple. At this wedding, the public "preaching" was divided between the bride's father and the groom's mother, but in different ways. He "faced in" to the couple, counseling them on their duties to each other. She "faced out" to the audience, counseling them on appropriate behavior – again as host and instructor for her guests.

This "facing out" role is consistent with changes in the community itself. Weddings and other festive events at the rendezvous place once provided ritual integration for a dispersed community of domestic and land use groups coming in from the bush. In the settled life of the reserve, these events (in which women play increasingly visible organizing roles) punctuate everyday life and intensify, but do not create, community solidarity for the people who attend them.

The "wedding in the bush" was a temporary and partial reversal of settling down, but it was also different in its organization from the earlier band rendezvoux. The transient tent-and-cabin village that formed in the bush was recruited from several reserve communities. Its residents were invited guests who chose to attend. The feast and dance had once been the community's responsibility and seal of acceptance; they were now hospitalities organized by the hosts for their guests.

It will be recalled that the host family wished to use this occasion to champion the cause of Algonquin cultural renewal. As they and other traditionalists understand it, this means turning again to the bush as the source of the sacred, and turning away from economic and political dependency toward autonomy and self-sufficiency.

The events and material displays of the performance can be understood as ritualized transformations from "the way things are" (in outside society and its impacts on Native people) to "the way things once were", and in some measure also "the way things can be again", from linear to reversible or cyclical time. These transformations represent successive approximations to an ideally authentic Algonquin identity : "*anicinâbe* (Indian)" is opposed with "*wâbickîwe* (white)", then reduced into an opposition of "how we live in the bush" (hunting and trapping) and "how we live on the reserve" (dependency on cash income, electricity, VCRs). "How we live in the bush" in turn is reduced into an opposition of "how we live now in the bush" (the cabins and their contents, contemporary canoes, cookstoves), and "how we (Indian people) lived in the bush a long time ago, when we made things for ourselves" (the bark lodge and its contents, birchbark canoe, open hearth). This progressive distillation of Algonquin culture and history was on view as guests came to Kôkomville and in the progressive visual transformations of the bride and groom themselves, from sweat pants through ribbon shirt and dress to buckskin for the nuptial mass.

The nuptial mass represents, to be sure, the historical penetration of Algonquin communities by Roman Catholicism, to which many but not all Barriere Lake Algonquins now adhere. It is even possible, as I suggested earlier, that the shape of the remembered "traditional" wedding – its witnesses and moral homilies – reflects Oblate influence. But cultural penetrations can run in more than one direction, as we saw in the priest's vestments, the consecrated host, and the feast baskets on the altar. Algonquin Catholicism coexists with continuities in traditional ritual practice. Cultural syncretisms, ambiguities, dissonance and compromise are "the way things are".

Recognition of this truth sheds some light on the last events to be considered – the entertainments which followed the ceremony and the feast. These games and theatrical displays amused the crowd greatly, but they also instructed it, through an ironic "metasocial commentary" (Geertz 1973) on the ritual text. I mean by this, paraphrasing Geertz, that the performances are stories that Algonquins tell themselves about being Algonquin :

> Performances are reflective in the sense of showing ourselves to ourselves. They are also capable of being reflexive, arousing consciousness of ourselves as we see ourselves... At once actor and audience, we may then come into the fullness of our human capability – and perhaps human desire to watch ourselves and enjoy knowing that we know. (Meyerhoff, in Turner 1982 : 75)

The enjoyment, and the knowing, is in the humor. Honigmann (1983) observes that in Northern cultures humor resides in absurdity and paradox. People laugh at incongruities of behavior : incompetence where competence is expected, or behavior that crosses the line between social, natural, or spiritual categories. "Joking define(s) the ambiguous and disable(s) the threatening" (1983: 735). This may explain the ribald clowning and joking dialogues between spirits and audience that startled early observers of shaking tent ceremonialism among the Ojibwa and Cree (*idem*; Vecsey 1983 : 105)

The ultimate source of the wedding entertainments is an early Algonquin version of this theater of the sacred absurd. It was secularized and performed at festive occasions in the past, and revived for the wedding. Since then, elaborate games and skits have been produced for the community's Feast of the Three Kings (Epiphany). Characters from Algonquin folklore are impersonated and, like the shaking tent spirits, engage in amusing dialogue.

The entertainments often reverse gender and generation roles : men and women stalk each other in *wâbôsnîmî* or even dress as each other, women assert expressive authority over men, old people pose as the "children" of young people (e.g., *Tcibinam* and his "daughter"), or complain that they are neglected. Such reversals enact and perhaps exorcise the social tensions that arise as the bonds of interdependence are loosened. Thus it is funny (because it is incongruous) but also sad when *Madjikôkom* sings that "there's no food for me, my clothes are all torn... I don't care."

A persistent theme in this theater is a play upon cultural contrast, sometimes linked with gender or generation reversals. The funniest female impersonations are when men are "made up" at the "beauty parlor", or play "waitress walk" in high heels with trays. At the wedding, Joseph's "strip tease" artfully inverted and satirized the sexual displays of the "white" world.

It is also amusing when Indians and whites cross the line into each other's domains. The inarticulate and apelike "Tarzan" burlesques "white" images of the forest, and, perhaps Indian images of "white" incompetence and regression in the bush. *Madjikôkom* does not know how to use a lighter or matches to light her pipe; *Tcibinam* is "confused" by the fiddle, and prefers the drum. On the surface, the joke turns on the incongruity of crossing the cultural line.

There is a deeper irony here, since the audience knows that Indian people use fiddles and matches (and other borrowed objects) with perfect ease. The canoe race offered an inverse and equally ironic counterpoint when two skillful canoeists were (because of their size) unable to paddle the small birchbark canoe, the very emblem of traditional competence and self-sufficiency.

Irony was apparent again in the wedding gifts. It will be recalled that the development of adult autonomy – being separate and together, able to feed yourself – has been symbolized by acquiring one's own household utensils. This is now elaborated into conspicuous displays of purchased gifts. The accompanying joking repeated but also subverted the message of the bark lodge and *kâkîkwewin* : "Indians don't use those things", "Indians don't need money."

CONCLUSION

Taken together as a single complex performance, the wedding ritual and its entertainments can be understood as a commentary on dependency and autonomy. They present themselves two forms, one cyclical and reversible, the other linear and perhaps irreversible. In the relationship between genders and generations developing through the life cycle and represented in marriage, childhood dependence transforms into adult autonomy and interdependence as competence in production is acquired. In the evolving relationship between Indians and the non-Indian economy which began with the fur trade, Algonquins have become consumers as well as (or instead of) producers. Competence in the new technologies has resulted in an increasing dependency which they recognize, deplore and resist.

Marriage was described earlier as a rite of passage in which participants pass through a liminal or transitional phase. Liminal ritual time is ambiguous and instructive. Native communities today are at the liminal edge of history, "betwixt and between" (Turner 1969 : 95) two cultural worlds. In this "wedding in the bush", Algonquin people reflected on their past and their present predicament. As in the old "shaking tent", they also looked to traditional knowledge as power, to divine and direct the course of their future.

NOTES

[1] This article is based on ethnographic work with Barriere Lake Algonquins supported in part by the BOCES Geneseo (N.Y) Migrant Center (with funding by the New York State Council for the Arts), and by the Canadian Ethnology Service of the Canadian Museum of Civilization. The Barriere Lake Band Council granted permission for my work in the community.

[2] Interviews on which this article are based in part were conducted in English or in Algonquin with English-fluent interpreters to aid the author's as yet limited competence in Algonquin. Algonquin terms and their translations represent contemporary community usages, as provided by Algonquin speakers at or after events described; extended passages quoted are verbatim transcriptions of relatively free translations. Lemoine (1909) gives *witikendiwin* as "union par contrat naturel". McGregor's lexicon of River Desert Algonquin (n.d. : 435) gives this term as "marriage before the advent of the missionaries... mated for life"; the verb *wîdabindiwag* means "staying together; cohabiting".

[3] Hudson's Bay Company post documents are archived by unique numbers for each trading post. When the Cabonga post was moved to Barriere, its records kept the same number (B/96). Only partial records survive for Cabonga/Barriere. They include yearly journals (B/96/a/) and account books (B/96/d/).

[4] The term "reserve" is used throughout this article in the sense of a settled community rather than as a legally constituted entity. The lands on which Algonquins are settled at Grand-Lac-Victoria, Lac-Simon, and Rapid Lake have varying legal status.

[5] First ages at marriages and the "minimum marriage field" for 1871 has been reconstructed from the marriage choices known to have been. Sources include : the 1871 Census for North Pontiac District (Unorganized Territories) D/92, Schedule 1 (PAC C - 10025); Hudson's Bay Company Post Records for Grand-Lac-Victoria (HBCA B/82) and Cabonga (B/96); Oblate mission records of births, marriages, and deaths preserved at Rapid Lake, Maniwaki, Weymontachie, Lac-Simon, and Amos; and oral traditions.

[6] A detailed quantitative analysis of spouse selection is in process. It is looking at the marriage field at critical points in time – 1843, when the first Oblate mission came to Barriere, 1871 (just before the Cabonga post removed to Barriere), 1900, 1929 (when the effects of the flooding of the Cabonga Reservoir were felt at Barriere), 1962 (when the community settled on the reserve), and the present.

ACKNOWLEDGEMENTS

I am deeply indebted to the friendship and hospitality of Helene (Lena) Nottaway, Irene Jerome, Jacob Wawatie, Joseph Jr. Wawatie, Marie Angele Papatie, and their families, and to other community elders – in particular, Louise Ratt, Emilie Thomas, and Jim Jerome, from whom I have learned much. The "wedding in the bush" was videotaped by Jean Baptiste Wawatie, the groom's father's brother. I am grateful to Mr. Wawatie and to Irene Jerome for access to this videotape, which has greatly facilitated the reconstruction of the performance. I also thank Mr. Daniel Clément from the Canadian Ethnology Service at the Canadian Museum of Civilization for his comments on earlier versions of this article and for his generous help during my research. Michael Greenlar, professional photographer from Syracuse, New York, who is a friend of the Jerome-Wawatie family, has allowed me graciously to use one of his picture to illustrate this article.

BIBLIOGRAPHY

A) Archival sources

HBCA : *Hudson's Bay Company Archives, Manitoba Provincial Archives, Winnipeg. Post Journals and Account Books, Trout Lake (Temiskaming), Grand-Lac-Victoria, Cabonga/Barriere, Nescutia.*

PAC : *Public Archives of Canada, Ottawa. Microfilmed Census Records 1871 North Pontiac (Unorganized Territories) C-10025 D92 02.*

RMIM : *Registre du Missionnaire Itinérant de la Région de Maniwaki, 1843 -1864.* Église de l'Assomption, Maniwaki.

B) Works cited

BECHMANN-KHERA, Sigrid, 1961-1964 : *Field Reports, Lac Barrière Indians.* Canadian Ethnology Service, Canadian Museum of Civilization, Hull.

BRODY, Hugh, 1981 : *Maps and Dreams.* Douglas and McIntyre, Vancouver.

COOPER, Arch, 1942 : *Ecological Aspects of the Family Hunting Territory System of the Northeastern Algonkians*. Master's thesis, Department of Anthropology, University of Chicago.

DAVIDSON, D. S., 1929 : "The family hunting territories of the Grand Lake Victoria Indians", in *Atti del XXII Congresso Internazionale degli Americanisti, Rome*, pp. 69-95.

GEERTZ, Clifford, 1973 : *The Interpretation of Cultures*. Basic Books, New York.

HASSAN, F., 1973 : "Determination of the size, density and growth rate of hunting-gathering populations", in S. Polgar (ed.), *Population, Ecology and Social Evolution,* pp. 27-52. Mouton Publishers, The Hague and London.

HIRBOUR, René, 1969 : *Étude de trois niveaux d'intégration sociale d'une société de chasseurs-cueilleurs. Kitchezagik Anichenabe.* Master's thesis, Department of Anthropology, University of Montréal .

HONIGMANN, John J., 1983 : "Expressive Aspects of Subarctic Indian Culture", in June Helm (ed.), *Handbook of North American Indians,* Vol. 6. pp. 718-738. Smithsonian Institution, Washington.

JOHNSON, Frederick, 1930 : "An Algonkian Band at Lac Barrière, Province of Québec". *Indian Notes* 7 (1) : 27-39.

LEMOINE, Geo., 1909 : *Dictionnaire français-algonquin*. G. Delisle, Chicoutimi.

McGREGOR, Ernest, n.d. : *Algonquin Lexicon*. River Desert Education Authority, Maniwaki.

McPHERSON, John T., n.d. : *An Ethnological Study of the Abitibi Indians*. Canadian Ethnology Service, Canadian Museum of Civilization, Hull.

RAPPAPORT, Roy A., 1979 : *Ecology, Meaning, and Religion*. North Atlantic Books, Richmond.

ROGERS, Mary, and Edward S. ROGERS, 1980 : "Adoption of patrilineal surname system by bilateral Northern Ojibwa : mapping the learning of an alien system", in *Proceedings of the 11th Algonquian Conference,* pp. 198-230. Carleton University, Ottawa.

RUSHFORTH, Scott, 1984 : *Bear Lake Athapaskan Kinship and Task Group Formation*. Canadian Ethnology Service, Mercury Series No. 96, National Museum of Man, Ottawa.

SPECK, F. G., 1915 : *Family hunting territories and social life of various Algonkian bands of the Ottawa Valley*. Anthropological Series 9, Memoirs of the Canadian Geological Survey, Ottawa.

– , 1929 : "Boundaries and hunting groups of the River Desert Algonquin". *Indian Notes* 6 (2): 97-120.

TURNER, David H., and Paul WERTMAN, 1977 : *Shamatawwa : The Structure of Social Relations in a Northern Algonkian Band.* Canadian Ethnology Service, Mercury Series No. 36, National Museum of Man, Ottawa.

TURNER, Victor, 1969 : *The Ritual Process.* Aldine, Chicago.

– , 1982 : *From Ritual to Theater: The Human Seriousness of Play.* Performing Arts Journal Publications, New York.

VAN GENNEP, Arnold, 1960 : *The Rites of Passage.* Routledge and Kegan Paul, London.

VECSEY, Christopher, 1983 : *Traditional Ojibwa Religion and Its Historical Changes.* American Philosophical Society, Philadelphia.

WOBST, H., 1976 : "Boundary conditions for paleolithic social systems : a simulation approach". *American Anthropologist* 39: 147-179.

"MAKWA NIBAWAANAA" : ANALYSIS OF AN ALGONQUIN BEAR-DREAM ACCOUNT

Roger Spielmann
University of Sudbury

T his paper examines one Algonquin account and two related teachings about bear-dreams with an interest in discovering and describing some of the performative features of Algonquin narrative and expository discourse. Careful attention to the features of spoken discourse sheds light on what at first appears to be common knowledge about Algonquin discourse but in the final analysis reveals something previously unexplored about the nature of Algonquin ethnography of speaking[1] (Chief and Spielmann 1986; Spielmann 1987). In examining natural discourse we make the claim that Algonquin narrative discourse, in general, and this dream account, specifically, are characterized by a distinct form-content parallelism which turns on two different aspects of the account itself; the structure of the account and the significance of the account, the latter embedded within the former. Algonquin expository discourse is characterized by a generic-specific (deductive) structure at the beginning of the discourse, a related specific-generic (inductive) structure at the end of the discourse, an appeal to personal experience and/or the defusing of contrary opinions with an appeal to authority within the discourse itself, and the inclusion of a final challenge or related piece of advice along with the appeal to authority. When these discourse features are explored in the context of teachings about bear-dreams and compared with teachings about warning animals and dream visitors in a related dialect (Odawa), these observations enable us to better understand the relationships between performative features of Algonquian discourse, culture-specific techniques of transmitting cultural knowledge and Algonquin cosmology.

The data for this paper come primarily from the Algonquin community of Pikogan, Quebec, and the Ojibwa community of Wikwemikong, Ontario. The Algonquin texts examined in this paper were obtained by the author in the spring of 1985. They were recorded on cassette tape during an evening of visiting and storytelling. The Wikwemikong interviews were conducted in the spring of 1992.

Pikogan is one of nine Algonquin communities in northwestern Quebec. Most of the community originates from the Abitibi region of Quebec, with a few members from the Témiscamingue area. In the village of Pikogan (which means "tent" or "teepee"), the Algonquin language is still in vigorous use among the 550 people living there, although there is a considerable amount of functional bilingualism and in many cases trilingualism among the population. The majority of families live in their reserve homes, making frequent trips to their trapping grounds throughout the year. Although Algonquin is linguistically considered to be a northern dialect of Ojibwa, Algonquins generally distinguish their language and culture from Ojibwa. The major matrix language spoken throughout Algonquin territory is French. English is also used to a lesser degree. The community of Wikwemikong is situated on the eastern peninsula of Manitoulin Island. It is the largest of the five Ojibwa/Odawa reserves on the Island. The population of Wikwemikong stands at around 5,000 (2,400 living on the reserve itself with 2,600 living off-reserve). While the majority of the people at Wikwemikong over the age of 35 speak Ojibwa fluently (as well as English), most of those under the age of 35 speak English exclusively.

DREAMING ABOUT A BEAR IN ALGONQUIN COSMOLOGY

Everybody dreams, no matter what culture they belong to or what they believe, but how people *view* their dreams and *interpret* their dreams depends greatly on what they believe. At Pikogan, for example, there's a very strong belief that the Creator uses dreams to *communicate* with people; to warn them about possible misfortune, to help people make important decisions, to know where to go to find game when hunting, and so on (Albert Mowatt, pers. comm.). People would tell us their dreams regularly and matter-of-factly, as if to say, "Of course it's the Creator communicating with us. What's so strange about that?" Having lived in the community for eleven years, we discovered that one very strong tradition at Pikogan is dreaming about a bear. Many of the Elders believe that the bear is sent as a dream *visitor* to warn people about possible misfortune.[2] The Elders at Pikogan would teach us about the importance of dreaming about a bear by regularly calling to tell us about their dream about a bear from the night before. Sometimes we would be warned not to drive on the highway for the next three days because the Elder had dreamt about a bear on the side of the road. One time an Elder told us about a dream where a mother bear was playing with her cubs and the mother bear fell down and was hurt. The Elder said : "Watch. Within three days something bad is going to happen." The next day, her daughter, who is a teacher at the community school, was out at recess with her Grade 4 students. The daughter slipped and broke her ankle while playing outside with her students. When we saw the Elder the next day she said : "Kinisidotan na? [Do you understand?]. My daughter, the teacher, is like a mother bear to her students, who are like cubs." It made sense and eventually we began to believe that these Elders were tuned into something that we weren't.[3]

From the perspective of the Elders at Pikogan, there exists a very fuzzy boundary between what is commonly called in non-Native thinking the "natural" and the "supernatural". In the minds of most people I know at Pikogan, everything that happens, including dreams, visions, dream visitors and warnings, are all part of the *natural*. Animals who are sent to visit people in dreams or visions are not seen as somehow "beneath" human beings but are considered to be other-than-human *persons* and messengers from *Kitcie Manitou*, the Creator. Most people at Pikogan seem to experience a powerful transformation of self in their contact with animals, either in the bush or in dreams and visions. For them, the prime means of access to personal knowledge and spiritual awareness seems to be through dreams and visions. Most, if not all, people at Pikogan are motivated and directed by their dreams as a part of their everyday experience. There's nothing strange or unusual about it. That's just the way it is and the way it has been for thousands of years.

What we are dealing with in the following instances, however, are not specifically dream recountings, but a story and two separate-but-related aphorisms about bear-dream accounts and lucky dreams. In the community of Pikogan, a commonplace conversational activity is telling stories and listening to stories. Sometimes those interactional situations which include storytelling result in the telling of a story followed by non-narrative teachings relating to the story that has been told. In our Algonquin materials referred to in this paper, what we have is a series comprised of a story and related teachings told contiguously. The storyteller, Mrs. Anna Mowatt, is recognized as an Elder in the community and is one who understands her dreams to be an avenue of communication between humans and the spirit world. Her story and related teachings are presented immediately below and the reader is encouraged to examine them carefully before proceeding to the analysis.[4]

TEXT NO. 24 : DREAMING ABOUT A BEAR LONG AGO

24 : 1   Makwa e-aadisookanaaganiwij.
          [The story is told of the bear.]

24 : 2   Gichi-weshkaj-gookom gii-wiidamaage egaa e-minwaashig makwa bawaanaj.
          [A long time ago a really old woman told about how it's not good to dream of a bear.]

24 : 3   Noopimig dazhiikewaagoban weshkaj-gookom ashij idash naabe ashij owiidigemaaganan
          awe naabe.
          [A long time ago an old woman and her man were staying in the bush.]

24 : 4   Gegapiich nigodin e-gizhebaawagag ikido awe naabe, oo, gichi-minwendam e-
          gizhbaawaganinig.
          [After awhile one morning the man said, "Oh, I'm really happy this morning."]

24 : 5   "Makwa nibawaanaa," ikido awe naabe.
          ["I dreamed about a bear," said the man.]

24 : 6   "Oo," ikido dash gookom.
          ["Oh," says the old woman.]

24 : 7   "Giga-wii-wiisin ihi gaa-inaabadaman. Gaawin minwaashisinoon gaabawaanaj makwa,"
          ikido awe gichi-gookom.
          *["You will be hungry because of that dream. It's not good to dream about a bear," that
          old woman says.]*

24 : 8   "Aan dash wiin ihi?" ikido dash ahawe naabe.
          ["Why's that?" the man then says.]

24 : 9   Miinawaj idash ikido ahawe gichi-gookom, "Gigikendaan na?
          [Again then that woman says, "Don't you know?]

24 : 10   Makwa gaawin wiisinisii gabe-biboon.
          [The bear doesn't eat all winter.]

24 : 11   Mii eta nibaa.
          [He/she only sleeps.]

24 : 12   Mii dash ihi gaa-oji-egaa-minwaashig makwa bawaanaj."
          [So then that's why it's not good to dream about a bear."]

24 : 13   Naabe dash wiin ahawe ikido, "E-bawaanag makwa, nigichibabeweyaabadaan,
          nidinendaanaaban," ikido ahawe naabe.
          *[So then that man says, "I thought when I dreamed about a bear that it
          was a lucky dream", that man says.]*

24 : 14   Gookom dash gii-wiidamaage, "Gaawin minwaashisinoon e-bawaanaaganiwij makwa.
          [So the old woman tells him, "It's not good to dream about a bear.]

24 : 15   Gimasagwaabadaan ihi gaa-inaabadaman.
          [It was unlucky that you dreamed it.]

24 : 16   Giga-bakade naage, giga-gichi-wii-wiisin naage," gii-ikido awe gookom.
          *[You will be starving later. You will really be hungry later." That's what that old woman
          said.]*

TEXT NO. 25 : DREAMING ABOUT A BEAR TODAY

25 : 1   Ogaazhigag idash.
[So then today.]

25 : 2   Mii giiyaabaj ezhiseg bawaanaj makwa.
[This is what happens when someone dreams about a bear.]

25 : 3   Giishpin makwa inaabadaman gigichi-masagwaabadaan ihi gaa-inaabadaman.
[If you dream about a bear it will really be unlucky that you dreamed it.]

25 : 4   Gegoon giga-izhi-majise.
[Something bad will happen to you.]

25 : 5   Gonimaa ogaazhigag, gonimaa waabag, gonimaa bezhigo dawateyaan.
[Maybe today, maybe tomorrow, maybe in one week.]

25 : 6   Giga-gichi-majise gaa-inaabadaman makwa bawaanaj.
[Something will go wrong for you if you dream about a bear.]

25 : 7   Mii giiyaabaj noogom ezhi-miikimoomagak ihi inaabadaman.
[That's the way it still works (today) when you dream about him/her.]

25 : 8   Gigichi-masagwaabadaan makwa bawaanaj.
[It's really unlucky when you dream about him/her.]

25 : 9   Gonimaa gaawin giga-mikasiin miikimowin.
[Maybe you won't be able to find a job.]

25 : 10   Gonimaa giga-wanitoon hiwe gimiikimowin.
[Maybe it will go bad for you on the road in your car.]

25 : 11   Gonimaa giga-aakozinan.
[Maybe you will get sick.]

25 : 12   Gonimaa miikanaakaag gada-majise odaabaan bimibizowan.
[Maybe something bad will happen to you on the road when you're driving around.]

25 : 13   Gegoon sa igoj giga-majise giishpin bawaanaj makwa.
[Something bad will happen to you if you dream about a bear.]

25 : 14   Gonimaa gaawin gada-dagwasinoon debwe ge-miijiyan, anooj igoj gegoon gada-izhi-majise bawaanaj makwa.
[Maybe you won't have anything to eat, something will go wrong when you dream about a bear.]

25 : 15   Mii giiyaabaj noogom ezhi-miikimoomagak ihiwedi makwa bawaanaj.
[That's how it still works when you dream about a bear.]

25 : 16   Debwe igoj gekwaan gaawin anishaa ikidonaaniwasinoon gaa-inweyaan, mayaa igoj debwe igoj ihi ikidonaaniwan ihi inaaniwag.
[It's true, I'm not just saying this for fun, this has been said (known) for a long time.]

25 : 17   Giishpin naagajitoowan ihiwedi giga-waabadaan, giga-debwetaan dash naage apiich gikendaman wegonen ihi weji-inaabadaman.
[If you look carefully you will see it, you will believe it and then later you will know why you dreamed it.]

TEXT NO. 26 : LUCKY DREAMS

26 : 1   Ohowedi dash, miinawaj godag, giishpin inaabadaman e-nibaayan.
[This one then is another, if I dream while I am sleeping.]

26 : 2   Nimikaan gegoon, gichi-weshaj gegoon, gonimaa igoj azhishkiikaag nimikaan gegoon, inaabadaman, gigichi-minwaabadaan ihi gaa-inaabadaman.
[If I find something, something old, maybe in the dirt I find it while I'm dreaming, that's a really good dream.]

26 : 3   Mii bezhigwan, gichi-weshkaj miigiwaam nimikaan noopimig gaa-dazhiikaaniwag inaabadaman, gichi-minwaashin ihi gaa-inaabadaman.
[The same way, I found a really old house to stay in the bush once when I was dreaming, that was a really good dream.]

26 : 4   Mii bezhigwan nimikaan gichi-weshkaj onaaganan gonimaa gichi-weshkaj akikwag nimikawaag inaabadaman, gichi-minwaashin ihi gaa-inaabadaman.
[Then I found some really old dishes or old buckets I found, it was good that I dreamed it.]

26 : 5   Giga-minose naage, gonimaa giga-mikaan miikimowin, gonimaa gigad-ayaawaa zhooniyaa, gada-minose gegoon gimiigiwaamikaag giishpin ihi inaabadaman.
[It will be good for later, maybe you will find work, maybe you will have money, it will be something good for your house(hold) if you dream it.]

26 : 6   Naanigodin gidinaabadaan weshkaj gaa-dazhiikeyan ihi e-abinoojiizhiwiyan.
[Sometimes you dream of where you used to live as a child.]

26 : 7   Gakina giwaabadaan ihi, gakina gegoon gimikaan ihimaa gaa-dazhiikeyaban, noogom dash aazha gaawin dagwasinoon ihi gegoon ihimaa.
[Everything you see, everything you will find it in that place you were living, though now those things are not there.]

26 : 8   Giiyaabaj idash giwaabadaan e-bawaadaman e-nibaayan.
[Again you will see (those things) when you are dreaming.]

26 : 9   Ihiwe dash inaabadaman, gichi-minwaashin hi gaa-inaabadaman.
[That kind of dream is really good when you dream it.]

26 : 10   Gigad-ayaan gegoon naage, gonimaa gigad-ayaawaa zhooniyaa naage, gonimaa miijim maane gigad-ayaan.
[You will have something for later, maybe you will have money later, maybe you will have lots of food.]

26 : 11   Mii ezhiseg giishpin weskaj gegoon bawaadaman.
[That's what happens when you dream of something from long ago.]

26 : 12   Mayaa igoj debemagan ihi gaa-inweyaan.
[It is really true what I'm saying.]

26 : 13   Gaawin anishaa nidikidosii ihi gaa-inweyaan.
[I'm not just saying these things for fun.]

SOME DISCOURSE FEATURES OF ALGONQUIN NARRATIVES

In the storytelling portion of this series, Mrs. Mowatt recounts the significance of dreaming about a bear *gichi-weshkaj* or "long ago". She uses the narrative format as a heuristic device to teach the listener about the importance of bear-dreams and some of the reasoning behind their significance. It should be noted, as well, that the relations between the story and the two teachings are not capricious, but are instead the products of Mrs. Mowatt's attention and careful management. As a forum for teaching about matters of tradition and culture, appreciation of the kind of attention such a series provides may be obtained by the following observation. Mrs. Mowatt's narrative which opens the series, which we have glossed as "Dreaming About a Bear Long Ago", is structured in such a fashion that the underlying theme of the story (that it is not good to dream about a bear) is made clear in the following utterances :

Fig. 1
Drying beaver skins and roasting beaver, the natural context for story-telling and transmitting knowledge. (Photo : Roger Spielmann)

24 : 2   Gichi-weshkaj-gookom gii-wiidamaage egaa e-minwaashig makwa bawaanaj.
[A long time ago a really old woman told about how it's not good to dream of a bear.]
24 : 7   "Giga-wii-wiisin ihi gaa-inaabadaman. Gaawin minwaashisinoon gaa-bawaanaj makwa,"
ikido awe gichi-gookom.
["You will be hungry because of that dream. It's not good to dream about a bear," that old woman says.]
24 : 12   Mii dash ihi gaa-oji-egaa-minwaashig makwa bawaanaj."
[So then that's why it's not good to dream about a bear."]
24 : 14   Gookom dash gii-wiidamaage, "Gaawin minwaashisinoon e-bawaanaaganiwij makwa.
[So the old woman tells him, "It's not good to dream about a bear.]

What we are pointing to here are not a random cluster of utterances which are merely thrown into the story in haphazard fashion, but instead we have a sequence of utterances which are progressively organized and realized so as to highlight the important theme of the story. The technique of bringing the hearer's attention back to the important theme of the story via repetition is found throughout this text and, according to Lisa Valentine (1992), appears to be typical of Algonquian discourse in general. She writes : "Narrative texts from many Algonquian languages display a pervasive use of doublet constructions, which are repetitions of phrases or lines, occurring at crucial points in the narratives" (1992 : 3). Valentine claims that this feature is considered "old-fashioned" by some younger speakers, one of whom complained that "the old people are always repeating themselves." In my analysis, it seems clear that this rhetorical device is quite important for storytellers in general and one which Mrs. Mowatt uses in this story to great advantage as a local structuring device and as a means of adding force to the teaching she is giving though the repetition. Redundancy appears to be an extremely important means of highlighting the important theme of the discourse and lightening the information load for the hearer(s).

There is another type of parallelism at work in this opening story in the story/teaching series which other stories told in Algonquin seem to exhibit. While telling this particular story, Mrs. Mowatt not only takes on the task of structuring her narration, but she also gives the listeners some subtle and not-so-subtle clues as to what the story is about. In storytelling situations at Pikogan, it is frequently the case that the significance of individual stories is made available to listeners within the context of the story itself. In Mrs. Mowatt's opening story in this series, for example, both aspects of story organization and their functions are represented. There is a recounting of a particular *aadisokaan* or legend which is prefaced by an introductory statement which informs the listener about what the story is about :

24 : 2   Gichi-weshkaj-gookom gii-wiidamaage egaa e-minwaashig makwa bawaanaj.
          [A long time ago a really old woman told about how it's not good to dream of a bear.]

    This introductory statement, which precedes the actual telling of the story, provides the listener with the appropriateness and relevance of the story which follows. Then the story about the "long time ago woman" and the "man" (*weshkadj-gookom* and *naabe*, respectively), serves as a source of evidence which supports the two related teachings which follow ("Dreaming About a Bear Today" and, "Lucky Dreams"). The two teachings are, in a sense, informed by the opening story, and this reflexive relationship operating between the story and the teachings testifies to the competency of the speaker and provides the observer with a window into the mind of the speaker. It's not as if Mrs. Mowatt was merely stringing together a story and some teachings, but the teachings are occasioned by the opening story which provides the listeners with a context for understanding the teachings. That is to say, Mrs. Mowatt's opening story can be viewed as providing a source of testimony occasioning the significance and coherence of the teachings which follow. The means by which Mrs. Mowatt introduces what she is going to provide teaching about in the form of an opening story seems to follow a pattern that we see as quite common in Algonquin ways of transmitting tradition and culture.

SOME FEATURES OF ALGONQUIN EXPOSITORY DISCOURSE

In the first teaching following the narrative, Mrs. Mowatt uses a standard format found in most Algonquian expository texts (Valentine 1992). In our Algonquin materials, expository texts invariably begin with the speaker telling the hearers what is going to be talked about. Note the following from Texts No. 25 and No. 26 (above) :

25 : 1   Ogaazhigag idash.
          [So then today.]
25 : 2   Mii giiyaabaj ezhiseg bawaanaj makwa.
          [This is what happens when someone dreams about a bear.]

---

26 : 1   Ohowedi dash, miinawaj godag, giishpin inaabadaman e-nibaayan.
          [This one then is another, if I dream while I am sleeping.]

Fig. 2
Mrs. Anna Mowatt, an Elder from Pikogan.
(Photo : Roger Spielmann)

Another feature frequently found in Algonquian expository discourse is a generic-specific structure at the beginning of a discourse and a related specific-generic structure at the end of the discourse. By generic-specific I am referring to a contextual use of deductive reasoning in transmitting cultural knowledge. By specific-generic I am referring to a contextual use of inductive reasoning. The same features can also be found in another Algonquian language, Attikamek (Boo Stime, linguist working among the Attikamek, pers. comm.). One can see these features in operation in the two expository texts following the opening story. First, the generic-specific feature in first half of Text 25 and the beginning of Text 26.

25 : 7   Mii giiyaabaj noogom ezhi-miikimoomagak ihi inaabadaman.
          [That's the way it still works (today) when you dream about him/her.]
25 : 8   Gigichi-masagwaabadaan makwa bawaanaj.
          [It's really unlucky when you dream about him/her.]
25 : 9   Gonimaa gaawin giga-mikasiin miikimowin.
          [Maybe you won't be able to find a job.]

---

26 : 1   Ohowedi dash, miinawaj godag, giishpin inaabadaman e-nibaayan.
          [This one then is another, if I dream while I am sleeping.]
26 : 2   Nimikaan gegoon, gichi-weshaj gegoon, gonimaa igoj azhishkiikaag nimikaan gegoon,
          inaabadaman, gigichi-minwaabadaan ihi gaa-inaabadaman.
          *[If I find something, something old, maybe in the dirt I find it while I'm dreaming, that's
          a really good dream.]*
26 : 3   Mii bezhigwan, gichi-weshkaj miigiwaam nimikaan noopimig gaa-dazhiikaaniwag
          inaabadaman, gichi-minwaashin ihi gaa-inaabadaman.
          *[The same way, I found a really old house to stay in the bush once when I was dreaming,
          that was a really good dream.]*

Then the specific-generic structure near the end of the discourse :

25 : 14 Gonimaa gaawin gada-dagwasinoon debwe ge-miijiyan, anooj igoj gegoon gada-izhi-
         majise bawaanaj makwa.
         *[Maybe you won't have anything to eat, something will go wrong when you dream about
         a bear.]*
25 : 15 Mii giiyaabaj noogom ezhi-miikimoomagak ihiwedi makwa bawaanaj.
         [That's how it still works when you dream about a bear.]

---

26 : 10 Gigad-ayaan gegoon naage, gonimaa gigad-ayaawaa zhooniyaa naage, gonimaa miijim
         maane gigad-ayaan.
         *[You will have something for later, maybe you will have money later, maybe you will
         have lots of food.]*
26 : 11 Mii ezhiseg giishpin weskaj gegoon bawaadaman.
         [That's what happens when you dream of something from long ago.]

Another feature of expository discourse in our Algonquin materials is the appeal to personal experience and/or the defusing of contrary opinions with an appeal to authority, as in the following :

25 : 16 Debwe igoj gekwaan gaawin anishaa ikidonaaniwasinoon gaa-inweyaan, mayaa igoj
         debwe igoj ihi ikidonaaniwan ihi inaaniwag.
         [It's true, I'm not just saying this for fun, this has been said (known) for a long time.]
26 : 12 Mayaa igoj debemagan ihi gaa-inweyaan.
         [It is really true what I'm saying.]
26 : 13 Gaawin anishaa nidikidosii ihi gaa-inweyaan.
         [I'm not just saying these things for fun.]

In tandem with this consideration is that expository texts frequently include a final challenge or advice along with the appeal to authority, as we see occurring in 25 : 16 and 26 : 13. Another salient discourse feature in these expository texts is that the strength of the challenge at the end of the text is directly proportional to (a) the relative positions of the speaker and hearer (i.e. mother-daughter, old person-young person), and (b) the consideration of importance in what is being said. In Text 25, for example, the speaker uses the 2nd person construction almost exclusively throughout the text, indicating the importance of what is being said, particularly highlighted in the final exhortation :

Fig. 3
Mrs. Mowatt in the bush. (Photo : Roger Spielmann)

25 : 17   Giishpin naagajitoowan ihiwedi giga-waabadaan, giga-debwetaan dash naage apiich
         gikendaman wegonen ihi weji-inaabadaman.
         *[If you look carefully you will see it, you will believe it and then later you will know why
         you dreamed it.]*

    By examining some of the salient features of Algonquin discourse we can see
that there are certain interactional benefits for one transmitting traditional knowledge
and teachings in the *structural positioning* of the story and teachings themselves.
That is to say, the meaning and relevance of a particular teaching, as exhibited in the
story/exposition series we have been examining, is not something that can be
determined merely by inspecting the details of the story and following teachings.
What one can see happening in this instance is a *social occasion*; a traditional
teaching which emerges in the context of the particulars of a culture-specific
situation. The analysis thus far is best perceived as relating to how traditional
teachings from one Algonquian tradition are structured and transmitted in a

contemporary setting. I have made the claim that Algonquin narrative discourse is characterized by a form-content parallelism which turns on two different aspects of the account itself; the structure of the account and the significance of the account, the latter embedded within the former. When these features are explored in the context of teachings about "animals who warn people of possible misfortune" and compared with findings in a related dialect (Odawa), these observations enable us to better understand the relationships between performative features of Algonquian discourse and culture-specific ways of retaining and transmitting cultural knowledge.

WARNINGS AND DREAM VISITORS IN THE ODAWA TRADITION

In comparing this bear-dream account found in Algonquin with other accounts collected in a related dialect, Odawa, I discovered that, while our Algonquin data suggest that the significance of bear-dreams and bear visitors seem to be Algonquin-specific, there are some thematic similarities when examined in the context of "animals who warn people of future misfortune".[5] In order to explore the comparative element between two related traditions, I asked my colleague, Mary Ann Corbiere, a member of the community of Wikwemikong, to interview some Odawa Elders from her community in order to find out what similar themes are at play involving dream visitors and animals who bring warnings in both conscious and dream states to Anishinabe (Ojibwa) people. While we were, unfortunately, unable to elicit tape-recorded responses, we were able to ask four Elders, all in their seventies, for their responses to the bear-dream tradition among the Algonquins and for their thoughts on animal warnings in their own tradition. Another colleague, Barry Ace, interviewed one Elder in the same tradition from the community of Sagamok.

The strongest tradition of a warning animal for these Elders revolves around the fox figure. All of the Elders agreed that the fox is one who warns of imminent misfortune, usually related to death. More specifically, the sound of the fox barking, rather than one seeing a fox, is what provides the warning. One of the Elders questioned stated that the bark of the fox is, in her words, "our relatives screaming" as a warning to prepare oneself for the death of a relative or family member. Speaking with some of the younger community members, there seems to be a strong sense of the reliability of the fox's warning. As one respondent in her early thirties noted : "When I was growing up, the thing I heard most about was the fox and if you heard a fox bark at you or hang around your house, that was a warning or a sign that something bad was going to happen." Responding to this comment, one of the Elders acknowledged : "Yes, the fox is generally the big one, the one commonly associated with a bad sign." In relation to the fox as a dream visitor, as per the Algonquin bear-dream teaching, one younger respondent answered: "I've never heard of anyone dreaming about a fox. Hearing it [in a conscious state] is the important thing."

During our visits with the Elders, we related the Algonquin tradition of dreaming about a bear (Texts 24-26, above). Responding to those teachings, the Elders we spoke with from Wikwemikong were unanimous in their answers. One responded : "We don't have those kind of stories." Interestingly, the Elder we talked to from Sagamok, upon hearing of the Algonquin bear-dream tradition, agreed that "it's a bad sign to dream about a bear." When questioned further, she noted that the "bad sign" had more to do with the color black than with the bear figure. This exchange did trigger a response from this particular Elder, however, about dreaming about a horse. She told us that dreaming about a horse is a warning that someone (usually a relative) is going to become very sick.

Another animal who warns people of possible misfortune is the woodpecker. Particularly strong in the mind of the Elder from Sagamok, a woodpecker pounding on one's house is another warning of the imminent death of a relative. One Elder also mentioned the dog as an animal who warns of death. She recounted one story of how one man's dog began howling for three successive nights prior to the accidental death of the dog's master. In fact, almost every response by these five Elders was accompanied by real-life stories relating the particular warning animal with recent and not-so-recent experiences related to validate the power and efficacy of the animal's warning.

In relation to the "dream visitor" theme in the two traditions, there does seem to be a sense that dream visitors, both human and other-than-human, are still active. One story about a dream visitor told to us was about how one family member who had recently died came to visit a relative in her dream.[6] This family member's accidental death caught the family by surprise. One of his cousins was particularly shocked and, according to the recounting, one night soon after his death she heard someone come around the house and into the back. Then she remembers hearing the person come up the stairs and into her room. It was her cousin who had recently died. He said to her : "I know you're really depressed about me dying, but don't feel bad. I'm very happy where I am, other family members are here, so put your mind at ease and don't be so sad about me anymore." This kind of recounting seems to be common in the Algonquin tradition as well, with stories of the recently deceased visiting people in dreams in order to set the minds of family members at ease and encourage them to stop mourning and to go on with their lives.

CONCLUSION

Our Algonquin materials on this bear-dream account and the teachings related to that tradition, while decidedly preliminary, provide us with a variety of insights into some of the discourse structures and interactional techniques available to Algonquin speakers for retaining and transmitting cultural knowledge and traditional teachings as well as providng us with a window into Algonquin cosmology. The field of discourse analysis among Algonquian languages is still relatively young and much remains to be done before one can begin to make rigorous connections between linguistic traditions. Recent work by J. Randolph Valentine and Lisa P. Valentine (Valentine 1990, 1992; Valentine and Spielmann 1990) looks promising, although these studies have yet to be published. In this paper I have discovered and described some of the similarities and differences between Algonquin and Odawa traditions as a way of highlighting culture-specific teachings and structural and interactional transmission techniques in order to better understand the relationships between performative features of Algonquian discourse, culture-specific techniques of transmitting cultural knowledge and Algonquin cosmology.

NOTES

[1] By ethnography of speaking I am referring to the study of linguistic genres and their culture-specific use and distribution. According to Lisa Valentine (1990 : 3), "the ethnography of speaking is not a field or a discipline, rather it is a perspective, an orientation toward the relationship between language, culture and society". This paper follows the general ethnography of speaking tradition by systematically studying a community's language use within its cultural context.

[2] This perspective receives support from the existing literature relating to the Algonquian evaluation of the bear as the most intelligent other-than-human person. The bear as spiritually powerful is well-known and has been discussed by Hallowell (1926), Speck (1935), and Skinner (1912), among others. In *Legends of My People The Great Ojibway* (1965), Norval Morriseau writes about some of the beliefs of his people concerning the bear. He writes, for example, that his people "... held this animal to be very sacred" (p. 39). He continues : "Legend states that the bear was at one time in the early history of the Ojibway a human, or had human form. Then it turned into an animal [...]

If Indians meet a bear, they address it as 'Our Grandfather to all of us, the great Ojibway', and start to talk to it".

Morriseau gives us a clue as to the significance of bear-dreams when he writes : "My grandfather on my father's side at the time of his fasting year had a great medicine dream of a bear. The bear said to him in his dream : 'My son, I will be a guardian to you and give you some special power [...]. You will have power to do good. I will also give you good luck, but you must respect me in my present form and never kill me.'" (p.45)

[3] Jennifer Brown and Robert Brightman (1988), citing Densmore (1928) and Landes (1968), write, "Among some Southwestern Ojibwa... [the] bear was identified as [one of the] spirit guardians of shamans" (p. 175). As for the connection between dreaming about a bear and its association with "warnings", Brown and Brightman (1988) quote from one of George Nelson's unpublished journals (1825) : "The Bear is a rough beast and makes a devil of a racket", implying a cultural outsider's view of what may constitute a cultural member's understanding of one feature of a "warning". While Mrs. Mowatt characterizes bear visitors in dream states as *Gimasagwaabadaan* ("It was an unlucky dream"), certainly dreaming about a bear is beneficial in the sense that, as Mrs. Mowatt emphasizes, if one pays attention to the details of a bear-dream, one may be able to avoid the possible misfortune of which the bear visitor warns. But here I am on shaky ground.

[4] The orthography used in this paper generally follows the Fiero tradition, an alphabet designed by linguist Chuck Fiero for transcribing Ojibwa. This tradition is loosely based on the phonetic principle of one letter representing one sound. The salient features of this orthography include a distinction between long and short vowels (one vowel representing the short vowel sound and double vowels representing the long vowel sound) and connecting preverbs, person and tense markers with the dash sign (-).

[5] While I refer to bear-dream accounts in this paper as Algonquin-specific, I recognize that bear-dream accounts as warnings do appear in other Algonquian traditions. In speaking with a member of another Algonquian tradition, I was informed that bear-dreams and bears as dream visitors are common and also signify, as in Algonquin, warnings about future misfortune (Schuyler Webster, Mennominee Nation – pers. comm.). I use the term Algonquin-specific only in the comparative sense between Algonquin and Odawa. There is, however, one feature of bear-dreams which does seem to be specific to the Algonquin tradition; that is, one may pay attention to the details of one's dream about a bear in order to avoid the potential misfortune. I have not, as yet, heard of techniques for avoiding the misfortune of which the bear forewarns in other Algonquian traditions.

[6] The way the story was told, I wasn't sure if the visitor appeared in a dream or while the one giving the account was in a conscious state. The details of the story itself lead me to believe that it was a dream experience.

ACKNOWLEDGEMENTS

I wish to express my deepest gratitude to Mary Ann Corbiere of the Department of Native Studies, University of Sudbury, for her contribution to this paper. Ms. Corbiere graciously took the time to speak with some of the Elders from the community of Wikwemikong. While she declined an invitation of co-authorship, the comparative elements of this paper would not have been possible without her assistance. I would also like to thank Anna and Albert Mowatt of Pikogan for their patience and generosity in sharing their insights and dreams with me over the past 13 years. Further, great thanks are due the Elders from Wikwemikong; Kate Assinewai, Madeline Enosse, Violet Naokwegijig and Mary Corbiere, and the Elder from Sagamok, Annie Owl McGregor, for taking the time to share their valuable insights. I would also like to thank Barry Ace of the Department of Native Studies at the University of Sudbury for interviewing Mrs. McGregor on my behalf.

WORKS CITED

BROWN, Jennifer S., and Robert BRIGHTMAN, 1988 : *The Orders of the Dreamed : George Nelson on Cree and Northern Ojibwa Religion and Myth, 1823*. Winnipeg, The University of Manitoba Press.

CHIEF, Bertha, and Roger SPIELMANN, 1986 : "Requesting and Rejecting in Algonquin : Notes on a Conversation", in William Cowan (ed.), *Actes du dix-septième congrès des algonquinistes*. Ottawa, Carleton University Press, pp. 313-325.

DENSMORE, Frances, 1928 : "The Use of Plants by the Chippewa Indians". *Annual Report of the Bureau of American Ethnology* 44 : 275-397.

HALLOWELL, Irving A., 1926 : "Bear Ceremonialism in the Northern Hemisphere". *American Anthropologist* 28 : 1-175.

LANDES, Ruth, 1968 : *Ojibway Religion*. Madison, University of Wisconsin Press.

MORRISSEAU, Norval, 1965 : *Legends of My People the Great Ojibway*. Toronto, McGraw-Hill Ryerson.

NELSON, George, 1825 : *Unpublished Reminiscences*. George Nelson Papers, Metropolitan Toronto Library.

SKINNER, Alanson, 1912 : "Notes on the Eastern Cree and Northern Saulteaux". *Anthropological Papers of the American Museum of Natural History* 9 (1) : 1-177.

SPECK, Frank G., 1935 : "Montagnais and Naskapi Tales". *Journal of American Folklore* 38 : 1-32.

SPIELMANN, Roger, 1987 : "Preference and Sequential Organization in Algonquin", in William Cowan (ed.), *Papers of the Eighteenth Algonquian Conference*. Ottawa, Carleton University Press, pp. 321-334.

VALENTINE, Lisa P., 1990 : *"Work to Create the Future You Want" : Contemporary Discourse in a Severn Ojibwe Community*. PhD dissertation, University of Texas at Austin.

– , 1992 : "Wemihshoohsh and the Vurned Shoes". Manuscript.

VALENTINE, Randall J., and Ruth SPIELMANN, 1990 : "Amik Anishinaabewigoban : Rhetorical Structures in an Algonquin Traditional Tale". Manuscript.

THE ABORIGINAL PEOPLE OF ALGONQUIN ORIGIN IN VAL-D'OR : MIGRANTS OR CITY DWELLERS?

Christiane Montpetit
Department of Anthropology
University of Montreal

One particularly crude caricature of the Native person in an urban environment still persists : a drunkard engaging in his favourite activity with others in downtown bars or streets; culturally disoriented; fond of nature, game hunting and freedom; someone who cannot be at ease on concrete. This picture is not an accurate reflection of reality. From the tropical forests of Brazil to the northern deserts of Arctic ice, the aboriginal world of the Americas, whether nomadic or sedentary, forms a cultural mosaic. Closer to home, this cultural and social diversity is similarly reflected in the responses of aboriginal people to the demands of urbanization.

THE URBANIZATION OF ABORIGINAL PEOPLE

In both Canada and the United States, the past 20 years have seen a steady increase of the aboriginal[1] population in urban areas.[2] This phenomenon is quite well documented, although the anthropological and sociological literature on aboriginal urbanization chiefly concerns the major cities of the United States and English-speaking Canada.[3] Little is known about the situation in Quebec cities, as well as in smaller American or Canadian cities, usually located close to reserves.

While the "Indian problem" of the "megacities" has drawn a great deal of attention, it would be worthwhile to investigate the variety of ways in which aboriginal people have adapted to urban environments, as illuminated by a less "culturalistic" approach, as well as the specific situation of the urbanization of aboriginal people in a city that is near their reserve.[4]

Our object here is to describe one such situation, in which two aboriginal populations, in the same familiar urban context, have different experiences of integration. In a study conducted in fall 1988[5] of the urbanization of aboriginal people of Algonquin origin in Val-d'Or, Abitibi, I was interested in the various factors explaining their presence in the town and the possibility of their integration there. I was struck by certain dissimilarities between Algonquins originally from reserves and Métis of Algonquin origin who were born in the towns or villages of Abitibi-Témiscamingue. At first glance, the Métis do not seem very different from the reserve Indians : in the town, they work with the Algonquins and Crees in aboriginal organizations, and many share the same ideological orientation and nationalist politics as the Amerindians. And they frequently encounter the same socio-economic problems. In the course of my stay, however, I noted certain distinct behaviour patterns – in their degree of participation in social and recreational activities addressed to the aboriginal population, their perception of urban life, their plans, and their movements back to their communities of origin.

The aboriginal population of Algonquin origin is in fact characterized by two types of urban experience. Unlike the Algonquins, who perceive city life as a temporary necessity – for educational purposes or to take on a job that is unavailable on the reserve – the Métis are much more inclined to put down roots in the town. This different relation with the town is largely explained by their life and employment history in white society, as well as by the relationship they have established with their communities of birth.

Aboriginal adaptation to the urban environment is not a uniform process, contrary to the image conveyed by adherents of the acculturation view (Hawthorn 1966-1967; Nagler 1970; Graves 1970; Roy 1962; Chadwick and Stauss 1975; Paredes 1973; Holden 1969). Researchers have long regarded the cultural traits and rural and traditional origin of aboriginal peoples as insurmountable obstacles to urban adaptation.

From this point of view, abandonment of such rural and traditional behaviour is the only way this kind of adaptation can be successful. Urbanization, perceived as a force directing societies to so-called higher levels of organization, is seen as destroying these less complex forms. Hence it is not surprising that, in the recent past, researchers have been mainly concerned with the various socio-economic problems of Native peoples, which are seen as irrefutable proof of the disruptive effect of the urban environment on these communities and their members.

However, there is reason for caution here. How is it possible to see the process of urban adaptation as solely responsible for all of the socio-economic problems encountered by aboriginal people? Those problems exist on the reserves themselves, that is, long before any migration, and so have deep roots (Honigmann 1965, 1968; Balikci 1968; Dunning 1964). Furthermore, the whole issue of tradition and rurality as alleged obstacles to successful urbanization needs to be re-evaluated. On many reserves, the old traditions are dying out and life has taken on an urban, "modern" dimension. Even on reserves located in rural or isolated areas, such as the Algonquin reserves of Abitibi-Témiscamingue, there are few Indians who have not had some kind of contact with the urban environment. Sooner or later, they come there to study, work, take in supplies, or simply have a good time. Moreover, part of the urban aboriginal population, such as the Métis or non-status Indians, does not come from the reserves but from towns or villages where they have lived for a long time. In light of these facts, one cannot claim that tradition and rurality are significant factors for all aboriginal migrants.

A few researchers have taken an interest in the diversification of aboriginal urban experience. Many Native city dwellers in fact manage to preserve the foundations of their aboriginal identity. They organize a community life for themselves around their own neighbourhoods, schools, or political or cultural agencies, and present none of the classic symptoms associated with "the Indian problem". The urban aboriginal population is socio-economically diverse, and can be distinguished according to cultural history, place of origin, type of occupation and political orientation (Tax 1978; Stanley and Thomas 1978; Dosman 1972; Guillemin 1975; Einhorn 1973; Garbarino 1971; Mucha 1983 and 1984). Nor does the urban environment automatically lead to the disappearance of all so-called "traditional" modes : ancestral medicine (Waldram 1990) and spiritual and ceremonial practices (Einhorn 1973; Krutz 1973) still persist.

While aboriginal populations generally have been faced with these kinds of events, it therefore appears that each ethnic group has its own history of contacts with the dominant population. In urban settings, these contacts are manifested in differences in lifestyle and in the particular problems with which aboriginal migrants may be confronted. To fully understand this diversity, it is helpful to adopt a perspective that takes account of the historical and cultural antecedents of the population studied and the lives of the migrants (frequency and duration of moves to cities, education in urban areas, work experience, etc), for these are factors which influence integration. From this new perspective, I have tried to get a better grasp of the urban experience of the aboriginal population of Algonquin origin which is transient or resident in Val-d'Or.

This article will identify certain aspects of the urbanization of aboriginal people, with particular emphasis on the differing experiences of the Algonquins born on reserves and the Métis born in Belleterre, Témiscamingue, who took part in my survey. For a better idea of these differences observed in urban areas, we must first of all sketch an overview of the recent history of the Algonquins and Métis of Abitibi-Témiscamingue.

THE ALGONQUIN RESERVES

As early as end of the 19th century, the Amerindian populations of southern Quebec were playing a role in the industrial economy, whereas those of central Quebec, such as the Montagnais, Algonquin and Cree, were not affected by urban and industrial development until much later. Progressively, and in particular since the 1950s, with the deforestation of their hunting and trapping grounds by the lumber and mining industries and the drop in fur prices, many Amerindians were obliged to take on salaried work in order to obtain sufficient or extra income. However, they usually have to be content with only casual or seasonal work in mining exploration, logging or commercial fishing, or as hunting and fishing guides (Laplante 1979a; Lambert 1979).

Until just recently, the Algonquin had been able to maintain many of their cultural and social activities within the context of a trapping economy. Today, settlement on the reserves is practically completed, and these reserves unfortunately seem to be no exception to the sad lot of poverty and social problems typical of reserves generally. That at least is the picture that emerges from certain documents (Kistabish 1982, 1987; Statistics Canada 1988; Couture 1983) and from the testimony of the Algonquins who took part in my survey.

In the regions of Abitibi-Témiscamingue and the Quebec side of the Ottawa valley, over 4,000 Algonquins now make up nine communities, seven of which have the status of Indian reserves : these are, for the northern Algonquins, Grand-Lac-Victoria, Lac-Simon, Winneway, Pikogan and Timiskaming, and for the southern Algonquins, Kipawa, Wolf Lake, Lac-Rapide and Maniwaki (Quebec 1987). Most of the northern Algonquin reserves were established recently, in the late fifties and early sixties. Logging and mining, hydro-electric development, government hunting regulations in Algonquin territory, and the introduction of a law prescribing the compulsory education of Amerindian children forced many families to abandon their camps to settle on these sites which became reserves. The exception in the northern Algonquin communities is the Timiskaming reserve, which was founded in 1853. And indeed, the Algonquins of Timiskaming were affected much earlier than those of Abitibi by colonization and logging activities (Laplante 1979a; Quebec 1987).

On the whole, the economy of these reserves is today underdeveloped : the Algonquins now sell just a few furs and crafts. According to the 1986 census data (Statistics Canada 1988), they are very dependent on federal government programs. The unemployment rate is high, particularly among young people aged 15 to 24, for whom it reaches 50 to 75% at Lac-Simon and Pikogan. There are in fact hardly any jobs on the reserves. On average, each reserve offers only about 30 full-time jobs connected with the band council or through government programs. To work, people must leave the reserve to seek employment in logging or construction. Like most Amerindian communities, the Algonquin population is not well educated : the majority of those over 15 years of age have not completed Grade 9. Many dwellings are overcrowded and unsanitary, resulting in numerous health problems (Kistabish 1982, 1987; Statistics Canada 1988).

These difficult socio-economic conditions lead some Algonquins to leave the reserve and settle in urban areas. It would appear, however, that this migration to urban environments, whether temporary or definitive, is not yet widespread. First, it concerns only those generations which have been sedentary since birth, a phenomenon which, as we have seen, occurred in the fairly recent past. The elders, who have spent most of their lives in the woods and have little knowledge of English or French, have few contacts with urban communities, except as visitors or leaders working with the Amerindian movements. Hence those involved in this migration are relatively young – under 40 years of age.

Yet even among this age group, one cannot say there are numerous migrations to seek work.[6] Many of the Algonquins interviewed say they have few relatives or friends who have left the reserves to settle in urban areas, whether Val-d'Or or elsewhere. Although some may be racked by a desire to leave the reserve, the young people seem to fear the non-aboriginal world. They have bad memories of their schooling, which was poorly adapted to their lives, and their relations with white people have been marked by discrimination. Their limited education and lack of work experience do not prepare them for the labour market. The employment structure in Val-d'Or and in the region chiefly requires a specialized work force that is qualified in mining and the service sector. The Algonquins who leave the reserves thus form a small minority, often more educated or engaged in political affairs, and hence with the advantage of good contacts for landing a job in an aboriginal agency or an organization with aboriginal clientele, which as we shall see are the main employers. Even in a context of prevailing unemployment and poverty, therefore, not all Algonquins can act upon their plans to migrate.

Then again, others want to live on the reserve. For example, a document produced by young Algonquins from various reserves expresses their attachment to their communities, despite the difficulties and social tensions that are so acute on the reserves : very high unemployment, welfare, juvenile delinquency, drug and alcohol abuse, violence against women, to name just a few. Rather than leave, they far prefer to develop jobs within the community (Rankin, McKenzie and McDougall 1985). Of those Algonquins who justified their departure on the grounds that it was impossible to live under such conditions, some returned to the reserve without hesitation after losing their jobs. By choice, obligation or for lack of anything better, the reserves still seem to be the Algonquins' principal mooring post.

If there is no change on the reserves, over the years the migration destinations and networks will probably expand. In the meantime, it is the young people who are bearing the brunt : excluded from the infrequent jobs that come up which are set aside for those older, and lacking education, training and work experience, they do not see what type of employment might be open to them on the outside.

THE MÉTIS VILLAGES

While it is difficult to count the Métis and non-status Indian population of Abitibi-Témiscamingue, a survey by Employment and Immigration Canada estimated it to be 1119 individuals in 1976 (Gauvreau et al. 1982). The Métis and non-status Indians share many socio-economic characteristics, together with their related problems, with the rest of the aboriginal population. Unlike registered Indians, however, they do not have the benefit of government assistance, although in the last few years some of them have regained this status with Bill C-31. Studies done by the Laurentian Alliance of Métis and Non-Status Indians in 1975 have shown that health, income and housing conditions for the great majority of Métis and non-status Indians are deplorable. These Native people are located mainly in villages or towns near reserves (Chalifoux 1975). In rural communities, their socio-economic situation is similar to that of reserve Indians. Many are on welfare and have to deal with the problems that often accompany insufficient income : crime, juvenile delinquency, dropping out of school, and job loss (Gendron 1983). However, the Métis and non-status Indians in urban areas enjoy better conditions than registered Indians as regards education, employment, income and housing (Statistics Canada 1984). Often the former have more experience of life and salaried work in non-aboriginal society than registered Indians.

As we have seen, the Algonquin population in Témiscamingue was the earliest to suffer the effects of logging activities and agricultural colonization. The region was officially opened up in 1894 when the Canadian Pacific railway arrived in southern Témiscamingue. From that moment, outside loggers, farmers and trappers began to settle there. In the Kipawa region of Témiscamingue there were numerous marital unions between Eurocanadian men and Indian women. According to Moore (1982), their descendants were the first aboriginal people in the region to combine life in the woods with life in the villages and to approach the labour market in a more open manner. Their expertise in the forest and their knowledge of the dominant language made them in demand as employees. The men's jobs included lumbering, prospecting, dam building and preventing forest fires. At the time, their families lived in small villages, settlements which indeed were often created by Métis families : for example, Hunter's Point, Wolf Lake and Brennan Lake. To help meet their own needs and the demand created by the lumber camps, the Métis families engaged in some farming. But these agricultural occupations and temporary salaried work were not enough to support them. Trapping always remained the main source of stable income, and game the staple of their diet.

In the thirties and forties, on account of the scarce chances of employment and hard living conditions after the Depression years, the Métis families that lived in these villages moved to other communities, in or outside the Kipawa region. The extremely low price of furs had forced trappers to increase their catches, causing a decline in the number of animal species (Moore 1982). Government legislation in 1947 also jeopardized the trapping activities of the Métis and non-status Indians :

> The 1947 statute carved up the traditional territories into registered traplines, allowing others the right to hunt on Indian land. It dealt a fatal blow to what remained of aboriginal economic activity : the white trappers came to snatch up the territories. Status Indians were entitled to hunt on the reserves, but the non-status, that is to say much of the aboriginal population of the Northwest, were progressively dispossessed. It was simply done : a father could no longer bequeath his land; he had to cede it back to the Department, which allocated it to the trapper at the top of the waiting list. In less than 20 years, the very great majority of non-status Indians lost their trapping grounds in this way. (Laplante 1979b : 229)

Most of the Native people born in Hunter's Point, Brennan Lake and Wolf Lake thus had to move to the village of Kipawa, where they could find work while remaining on their traditional land. Some migrated to the towns of Timiskaming or to North Bay, while others moved farther north to Belleterre, Rouyn-Noranda and Val-d'Or (Moore 1982).

Many of the Métis established in Val-d'Or are originally from Belleterre. In that village they used to work in the gold mine, at the sawmill, in the outfitters' lodges and in the forestry sector. The Métis are generally acknowledged to share many cultural behaviours and practices characteristic of Amerindians. Trapping, hunting, fishing and aboriginal crafts used to be common activities among the Métis and non-status Indians (Gendron 1983). These practices did not hold much importance for the Métis interviewed in Val-d'Or, especially the women and persons who left Belleterre at a very young age, but the men frequently engaged in them as recreational activities. In the village of Belleterre, the Métis mainly kept their own company, and had numerous ties to relatives and friends in Winneway, an adjacent Amerindian community. But relations with non-Natives were also good, and their life and work experience with the latter was much more substantial and positive than that of the Algonquins living on the reserves.

When the gold mine was operating, the village numbered several thousand inhabitants. Since the closure of the mine in 1969, shortly followed by a prolonged strike at the sawmill, the village population declined considerably. Today it stands at only about 500 (Statistics Canada 1988). After 1969 the Métis families, like the non-aboriginal families, left the village one after the other.

The first Métis migrants chose Val-d'Or for the employment prospects it offered, notably in mining, a field in which a number of men had acquired some experience. In the beginning, then, the migration was not connected with the presence of aboriginal organizations, as is the case today. Métis with experience in the gold mine or sawmill generally had no trouble finding work. In addition, the Alliance of Métis and Non-Status Indians, founded in 1972, had an office in Val-d'Or and sponsored several projects which generated employment for the Métis. And then the presence of relatives and friends was a deciding factor, for it guaranteed the socialization and mutual assistance networks necessary for their integration. In fact, it appears that Métis families related by marriage always grouped together and followed each other's moves (Moore 1982). The Métis who left the village in the late 1970s say that Belleterre at that time had become a ghost town where there was hardly any work. Only a few elderly people remained there.

The successive migrations that followed the plant closures thus almost completely emptied the village of its Métis families. The migration affected entire families, unlike the reserve Algonquins where the emigrants were mainly childless young adults. Almost all the Métis ended up in Val-d'Or, where they comprise most of the resident aboriginal population. As we shall see, this situation lends certain distinctive features to their urban experience.

THE URBAN CONTEXT

The Native people of Abitibi-Témiscamingue who went to Val-d'Or found themselves in a familiar context. In the 1970s, this town effectively became the "capital" of the aboriginal people in the Abitibi-Témiscamingue/James Bay region. The aboriginal population of Val-d'Or is highly visible because of the influx of Amerindian visitors who use the many government services and health services oriented toward the region's Indian communities. Certain Cree organizations created by the James Bay Agreement have their headquarters there. Val-d'Or was also the seat of the Algonquin Council of Western Quebec until very recently, and of the provincial office of the Laurentian Alliance of Métis and Non-Status Indians, which was very active in the late seventies and early eighties. Finally, it also features a Friendship Center, whose specific purpose is to serve the transient and resident aboriginal populations of Val-d'Or.

The transient aboriginal population, that is, people who are there to use the various services or are "in transit" (looking for work and accommodation, or doing temporary work before moving on to something else), is much larger than the resident aboriginal population. The 1986 Census reported the number of residents as being about 260 (Statistics Canada 1988). In a recent study on the aboriginal people in Val-d'Or, Monique Laplante (1991) and her research team enumerated 250 and questioned 191, the latter consisting of 120 Algonquins, 50 Crees, 9 Métis, 4 Inuit and 8 from various nations. Algonquins would thus seem

Third Avenue in Val-d'Or, a place where aboriginal people meet and talk.
(Photo : Paul Brind'Amour)

to make up almost two thirds of the total aboriginal population of Val-d'Or. However, many of these Algonquins are in fact apparently Métis of Algonquin origin. This survey shows that most of the Native people residing in Val-d'Or were born in a town, and that almost a third of them have been living in Val-d'Or for over 10 years. These are probably Métis or non-status Indians who have obtained their status. The study goes on to note that very few of these aboriginal people are fluent in an Amerindian language : they prefer to use English. Yet most of the reserve Algonquins whom I met with, even the youngest, always use their mother tongue, with French as their second language. This would mean that very few Algonquins born on reserves have settled in Val-d'Or. As for the Cree, this survey estimates that they account for a little over one quarter of the aboriginal population of Val-d'Or. However, some 60 Crees refused to take part in the survey, while most of the Cree respondents were high school students boarding with families in Val-d'Or. Consequently it is difficult to assess their exact proportion in terms of the total aboriginal population of Val-d'Or.

Although Amerindians originally from reserves make up few of the permanent residents of Val-d'Or, many Algonquins and Crees, even from remote communities, visit this town on a regular basis. For example, Algonquins come from Grand-Lac-Victoria, one of the most isolated and traditional Algonquin communities, located 66 km south of Val-d'Or. Some go there several times a week to make purchases, take their children to the arena or meet acquaintances. A great many Crees also make a brief visit to Val-d'Or on weekends, mainly during the holiday season, to the delight of the merchants for whom they are said to provide a most lucrative clientele, bringing in two or three million dollars during the annual Cree hockey tournament in December (Vastel 1992). In addition, many children from the Algonquin and Cree reserves attend high school in Val-d'Or. Finally, certain sociocultural events organized by the aboriginal peoples, such as bingo, an aboriginal film festival, a ball tournament and a "Jam Session" music festival over several summers, have progressively become very popular, attracting Amerindians from the surrounding communities.

The town's familiarity tends to prevent certain problems for the aboriginal people settling there. They know the places in Val-d'Or that can be of assistance to them in the event of difficulties, and rarely do they feel isolated. Since the aboriginal population is small, everyone knows everyone else, or almost. And the smallness of the town makes it possible to meet many people on the one main street, in the bars with an almost exclusively aboriginal clientele, or in the restaurants. Also, one does not see the homeless Indians typical of big urban centres, who make up much of the clientele of support agencies such as the Salvation Army (Dosman 1972). For example, there are at present few homeless Amerindians at the Friendship Center : most of those housed there are Cree patients visiting the town for health care.

That being said, certain problems do exist, the main one being housing. Aboriginal people do not complain as much about discrimination as about the high cost of rent, which is based on mine wages. Peer accommodation is a common practice to address this problem. Another solution is a low-rent housing co-operative for aboriginal people called "the Wawaté Residences". This was set up through the efforts of the Val-d'Or Friendship Center and the Waskahegen housing corporation, an aboriginal company which has carried out projects in most areas of Quebec. Inaugurated in 1986, the Wawaté Residences were a response to the precarious housing conditions of many aboriginal families in Val-d'Or. Rent is based on income, and cannot exceed 25 percent of gross salary. In 1989 there were 27 family units, with plans to build new ones, since some 30 Val-d'Or families were on the waiting list, not counting applications from outside the town.

This aboriginal initiative has both its positive and negative aspects. Many Natives, especially Algonquins who have lived on the reserves, have told me that, for them, the Wawaté Residences are "the reserve in the city" because of certain similar features : identical houses lining unpaved, treeless streets swarming with children who are often left to themselves. In addition, everyone knows about everyone else's affairs, and the drinking problems of certain individuals increase the incidence of family violence or juvenile delinquency. On the other hand, there are certain advantages : affordable rent, families assisting each other with child care, transportation, repairs and financial emergencies. Friendly visits, particularly among the Métis who make up many of the residents, help to maintain bonds among the people.

Employment is another source of problems. The situation seems more difficult for the younger Native people, Algonquins and Métis, who are excluded from both the private sector and the aboriginal community if they are not involved in training or community work reserved for welfare recipients. However, these employment problems are not peculiar to aboriginal people, since the entire urban and rural population of Abitibi-Témiscamingue is suffering the repercussions of the recession and the difficulties in the mining sector (Vastel 1992).

WORK IN ABORIGINAL COMMUNITIES

Monique Laplante's survey (1991) and a poll done by a Labour Quebec officer whom I interviewed in Val-d'Or show that a little over 70 percent of employed aboriginal people are hired by aboriginal agencies or recruited by various organizations that have an aboriginal clientele. There are various reasons for this : lack of education or experience, discrimination, decision to work in one's own community.

The reserve Algonquins whom I questioned had had next to no experience of the non-aboriginal working world. They said they had encountered no discrimination when applying for employment since very often they had never even made such an application. On this subject, they speak of their desire to work with and for their peers, and to avoid the excessively compartmentalized and stressful work structure characteristic of white people. Some young Métis also told me they like work in tree planting, provided they can form teams with other aboriginal people. Instead of doing an exhaustive job search, many Algonquins return to the reserves and wait for a new opening when there is no longer any chance of work in aboriginal organizations. The older Métis men and Métis women in general have greater work experience in the private sector in Val-d'Or, the former in companies linked to mining, forestry or construction, and the latter in the services or restaurant sector.

Consequently the aboriginal organizations play a crucial role, because they enable Native people to acquire training and work experience that they have difficulty finding elsewhere, or which they are not inclined to look for elsewhere. What is more, they provide a meeting place for the aboriginal peoples, for Algonquins from the reserves and Métis, whose relations outside the working context are limited. Indeed, there seems to be a wall between them, a division that is evident in the comments of the Native people interviewed. Some Algonquins refer to the Métis as "acculturated Indians".

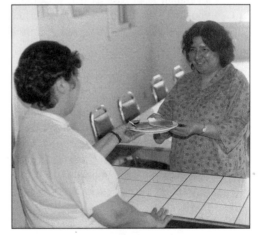

Various services are available at the Val-d'Or Friendship Center, including inexpensive meals. (Photo: Paul Brind'Amour)

Some Métis say they are ignored in the street by Amerindians or regarded as intruders during certain public assemblies :

> When I am with Indians I feel different, apart. When I eat at the Center, for example, I sometimes feel the Indian patients watching me as if I had no business there. Last summer I was at the last annual meeting of the Algonquin Council. I had been asked to act as secretary. There was a traditionalist atmosphere at this meeting. They had the tent of purification there. During the meeting, one Algonquin pointed at me along with a few white people who were there and asked what we were doing there, saying we had no business there. I felt very bad. I must say I have trouble understanding the traditionalists, this return to the traditions. That's why I feel better with the Métis, with people whose lives are the same as mine. (Danielle, 26 years old, Belleterre)[7]

However, there is a similar division between Amerindians – between the traditionalists and those who know nothing of the traditional culture, between city dwellers and those who cherish the ideal of life on the ancestral lands. Here is the testimony of two Amerindian women who have spent many years of their lives in an urban environment :

> There is racism between Indians, not just between Indians and whites. For example, the expression "apple", which means someone is red outside and white inside. Someone called me that once, because I have lived a long time in the city. I was shocked. When an Indian is in Montreal it is perfectly natural that he will not be hunting or fishing : you don't need an ethnologist to understand that. It doesn't mean you're no longer Indian. (Marie, 35 years old, Témiscamingue)

> When I was in an Inuit community, the people knew I was Indian but they didn't consider me to be an Indian. The more traditions people have, the more they see people differently. Myself, I do not engage in traditional activities, I have never learned tradition. I like the bush, but I don't like hunting and I hardly eat any meat. Since I was a child I have known that I belong to the Indian nation. I try to understand what is around me, those who are aboriginal people, and to have a relationship with them. I like to explore the aboriginal spiritual world. I don't feel obligated to do so, I do it out of interest, out of curiosity. I seek knowledge about the aboriginal people, rather than tradition.

> I feel closer to aboriginal people who, like me, have not been raised in the tradition. In the city, I feel comfortable with those who have lived with non-aboriginal people, like me. (Pauline, 37 years old, Odanak)

Staff members at the Val-d'Or Friendship Center.
(Photo : Paul Brind'Amour)

Natives usually form groups with relatives or friends from the same place of origin or with people who share the same life or work experiences in urban areas. There is little exchange between the different groups, although the aboriginal workplace provides a common ground. While Métis and Algonquins do not associate much outside working hours, I have observed very friendly relations in the office. Certain Métis and Amerindians who had learned nothing about tradition say that work in an aboriginal environment has given them better knowledge of the Amerindian reality and allowed them to renew ties, which have at times been interrupted, with their culture of origin. In addition, some individuals are making efforts to break down this division and reunite the aboriginal peoples by organizing a range of sociocultural and recreational activities.

PARTICIPATION IN ABORIGINAL ACTIVITIES

These efforts are being made chiefly by persons working at the Friendship Center. In the 1970s, the Center was oriented mainly toward assistance, referral and accommodation services, since it served a transient clientele and had reduced funding. With the 1980s, programs and activities designed to facilitate meeting and discussion among the aboriginal population of Val-d'Or were increased and diversified. Certain activities of the Center, which collaborates with the Algonquin Council and the band councils of the closest reserves, such as Lac-Simon and Pikogan, are obviously intended to maintain relations between urban and rural Native people and to encourage them to preserve their cultural identity. For example, in 1985 the Center organized a meeting of Algonquin Elders on a traditional assembly ground on Siscoe Island.[8] At this meeting, the Elders joined with the participants in discussing a number of subjects, such as the spiritual life and cultural survival. A voyage for young aboriginal people on traditional Algonquin canoe routes was also greatly appreciated. The Cree are little involved in the Center's various events, although these are open to all aboriginal peoples. Since the founding of the Center, few Crees have been members of its board of directors or staff. There are fewer Crees than Algonquins who are permanent residents of Val-d'Or, and certain Cree communities are fairly far away, but the main impression is that they maintain few relations with Natives of Algonquin origin, and another division is evident between these two groups. Nonetheless, the Center is constantly in touch with the Cree communities to plan the travel, reception and accommodation of Cree patients staying in Val-d'Or for health care.

Despite the success of a few projects, numerous attempts at organization frequently run up against the indifference of the aboriginal people, something that is not unrelated to the low number of aboriginal residents and the proximity of the reserves. On the other hand, a number of studies on the urbanization of aboriginal people in general note their efforts to build themselves a community life in an urban environment, or at least to associate so as to participate in activities which are reserved for them. Such efforts are proving successful in many large American cities. Native people concentrate in the same neighbourhoods and gravitate, for example, toward very active Amerindian political organizations and Amerindian social clubs, schools and colleges (Stanley and Thomas 1978; Mucha 1983 and 1984; Garbarino 1971). One fact deserving of attention is that these cities are located far from the reserves and contain a large Indian population. In Los Angeles, San Francisco, Chicago and Detroit, for instance, there are thousands of aboriginal people from various nations who have developed a distinct social life and a collective urban identity. In many other cities, the true hub of aboriginal social life simply consists of networks of relatives and friends, or local bars (Stanley and Thomas 1978; Guillemin 1975; Brody 1971). These data are consistent with my observations at Val-d'Or. In this town located close by the reserves, it is difficult to completely dissociate the urban context from the communities of origin. Relations between the urban aboriginal population and members of the community of origin are constant, especially among the Algonquins. While such relations may exist in cities far removed from the reserves, they are apparently more frequent in urban centres situated closer by, and it is probably for this reason that Amerindians in those centres do not develop any distinct, organized social life (Stanley and Thomas 1978).

LINKS MAINTAINED WITH THE COMMUNITIES OF ORIGIN

In Val-d'Or, it is always the same families, principally Métis, that take part in the activities for aboriginal people. The Métis indeed seem much more interested in creating an aboriginal community life in Val-d'Or than the Algonquins from the reserves. On the whole, the latter have little desire to make a commitment to the urban environment and are far from considering themselves city dwellers. They maintain close relations with their kin living on the reserves, and continue to participate in political assemblies and various events in their communities. I have noticed that many Algonquins move back to the reserve in periods of unemployment or when there is a chance of employment there. Others spend these slack periods trapping on their hunting grounds.

It seems, then, that the existence of the reserves lends a distinctive quality to the urban experience of the Amerindians. Studies have shown that Amerindian migrations follow a particular pattern of frequent movements between reserve and city, and also mention the significance of moves back to the reserve after a certain period of migration (Price and McCaskill 1974; Bernèche 1984; Guillemin 1975). For many migrants, the reserve can be considered a safer place to live out their remaining days. Some adult migrants sometimes even leave their children on the reserve to be brought up there (Guillemin 1975).

Returns to the place of origin can be perceived as signs of failure at urbanization. But some Amerindians apparently return to the reserve after settling in an urban area simply because they never intended to put down roots in the city or to become model city dwellers. Despite its problems, the reserve always remains their home. That being said, movements are also related to the types of jobs to which Amerindians are confined, chiefly temporary situations which offer no employment security.

In other respects, not all Indians cherish the ideal of returning to the community, whether on the reserve or on ancestral lands. In this regard, certain Amerindian women seemed to me to be far less anxious to leave the town to return to the reserve. One question remains : to what extent is the reality of women on the reserve, where they are often victims of incest and violence, responsible for this difference between the plans of men and of women? According to Algonquin women who had married non-Amerindians, mixed marriages are another obstacle to returning to the reserve, since non-aboriginal spouses are in general rarely accepted :

> I married a white man at 17. For my father, the family was very important. He always wanted the family to be united, and he wanted me to stay with the family on the reserve. My husband came to live on the reserve. At that time, an Indian woman who married a white man automatically lost her status. The community never accepted my living with my husband on the reserve. People made us feel that we had no business there. I had ostracized myself in some way. I was shocked, and my contact with the community cooled off for quite a while. (Suzanne, 38 years old, Pikogan)

CONCLUSION

The reserve seems to play an ongoing role in the existence of most Amerindians living in urban environments, for that is where most members of the community reside. The reserve is a centre of political organization, and always a home to return to in case of need. Most Métis do not have such ties, which may explain why they tend more to settle in permanent fashion in urban areas and regard themselves as city dwellers. What is more, as they have greater life and work experience in non-aboriginal society, they probably integrate the urban environment better than the Algonquin, for whom urbanization is a fairly recent reality. As to their future in Val-d'Or, it will be interesting to see whether an aboriginal enclave is eventually formed, around the

Wawaté Residences for example, or at least to examine more specifically their role in the future development of the aboriginal community.

For the Algonquins of the Abitibi-Témiscamingue region, migration to the cities is still a marginal and relatively recent phenomenon, compared with other Amerindian populations living in southern Quebec such as the Mohawks (Einhorn 1973). While the Algonquins feel themselves to be on familiar ground in Val-d'Or, many refuse to be integrated there. They know and appreciate the urban environment, but cannot yet be considered accomplished "city dwellers". They are better described as migrants oscillating between the two environments, not quite sure of what the future holds for them :

> I would like to have children. But I wouldn't raise them in Pikogan, because the people would be a bad influence. People there talk a lot but do nothing, because of Catholic brainwashing. There is no more energy. My life on the outside, my travels, my spiritual experience, these are important. But my brothers on the reserve do not understand. They look at me like a little child. Yet it has been my life on the outside that has renewed my ties with my culture. For my brothers, experience on the outside is work experience : they don't understand that there could be anything else of value [...]. But city life is not ideal for protecting culture, especially not in houses all standing in a straight line like those on Louise Lemay Street [Wawaté Residences] : it's like a reserve. I would like to live in a community close to a town but with houses that are scattered, with some space. Another thing that's missing in the city, but also on the reserves, is cultural and spiritual leaders. In Val-d'Or there are only political leaders. (Marc, 27 years old, Pikogan)

The younger generations are going through a major transition in the history of the Algonquins, who in recent decades have experienced significant upheavals. For the moment, they are involved mainly on the aboriginal side of the equation, possibly because they feel the need to affirm their identity and are afraid of being rejected or assimilated by non-Amerindian society. However, emigration to the urban areas should increase, or at least remain stable, in view of the economic underdevelopment characteristic of most reserves and the growth of the Algonquin population.

NOTES

[1] The term "aboriginal" here refers to all descendants of the first inhabitants of the country, including status and non-status Indians, Métis and Inuit.

[2] According to Statistics Canada (1984), four Native people out of ten have chosen to reside in urban areas.

[3] New York (Einhorn 1973), Chicago (Garbarino 1971; Mucha 1983 and 1984), Denver (Graves 1970), Boston (Guillemin 1975) and Los Angeles (Price 1968); in Canada: Saskatoon (Dosman 1972), Winnipeg (McCaskill 1970), Toronto (Nagler 1970) and Vancouver (Stanbury 1975), to name just a few.

[4] The migration of aboriginal people to towns surrounding reserves is a phenomenon that has received little study. In Canada, it would seem that very few Natives head for the big urban centres, since only 24% of urban aboriginal people live in cities with a population over 100,000 (Statistics Canada 1984). In the United States, Indians relocate as much to small cities near reserves as to the major centres (Neils 1971). By concentrating on the lives of aboriginal people in these big cities, with which they are less familiar and where they may well feel isolated, researchers have in a way contributed to an exaggeration of the difficulties experienced by Native people in urban environments.

[5] The data that provide the framework for this article chiefly derive from documentary research and life histories collected from some 20 aboriginal people living in Val-d'Or, which were used to prepare a master's thesis (Montpetit 1989). During a six-month field survey in Val-d'Or, I did research on the history of the Val-d'Or Friendship Center and took part in activities which brought together aboriginal people from the town and from the surrounding areas.

[6] This emerges from the accounts given by the Algonquins interviewed in Val-d'Or. Another survey done in Val-d'Or by Monique Laplante (1991) shows that very few aboriginal people born on reserves reside in Val-d'Or.

[7] Names are fictitious. Place indicated is the community of birth.

[8] "Askigwash", produced by Radio-Québec.

WORKS CITED

BALIKCI, Asen, 1968 : "Bad Friends". *Human Organization* 27 (3) : 191-199.

BERNÈCHE, Francine, 1984 : "La migration de la population indienne du Québec, 1966-1974", in L. Normandeau and V. Piché (eds.), *Les populations amérindiennes et inuit du Canada. Aperçu démographique*. Les Presses de l'Université de Montréal, Collection "Démographie canadienne" 8 : 224-257.

BRODY, Hugh, 1971 : *Indians On Skid Row*. Ottawa, Information Canada.

CHADWICK, Bruce A., and Joseph STAUSS, 1975 : "The Assimilation of American Indians into Urban Society : The Seattle Case". *Human Organization* 34 : 359-369.

CHALIFOUX, Fernand, 1975 : "Les Métis et Indiens sans statut ou les pires conditions de logement au Québec". *Recherches amérindiennes au Québec* 4 (4) : 70-74.

COUTURE, Yvon H., 1983 : *Les Algonquins*. Val-d'Or, Éditions Hyperborée.

DOSMAN, Edgar J., 1972 : *Indians : The Urban Dilemma*. Toronto, McClelland and Stewart.

DUNNING, R. W., 1964 : "Some Problems of Reserve Indians Communities : A Case Study". *Anthropologica* 6 (1) : 3-38.

EINHORN, Arthur, 1973 : "The Indians of New York City", in J. O. Waddell and O. M. Watson (eds.), *American Indian Urbanization*. Purdue University, Institute Monograph Series 4 : 90-100.

GARBARINO, Merwyn S., 1971 : "Life in the City : Chicago", in J. O. Waddell and O. M. Watson (eds.), *The American Indian in Urban Society*. Boston, Little, Brown and Company, pp. 168-203.

GAUVREAU, Danielle, Francine BERNÈCHE, and Juan A. FERNANDEZ, 1982 : "La population des Métis et des Indiens sans statut : essai d'estimation et de distribution spatiale". *Recherches amérindiennes au Québec* 12 (2) : 95-103.

GENDRON, Gaétan, 1983 : *L'affirmation ethnique chez les Métis et Indiens sans statut du Québec : ambiguité et tensions*. Master's thesis, Department of Anthropology, Université Laval.

GRAVES, Theodore D., 1970 : "The Personal Adjustment of Navajo Indian Migrants to Denver, Colorado". *American Anthropologist* 72 : 35-54.

GUILLEMIN, Jeanne E., 1975 : *Urban Renegades : The Cultural Strategy of American Indians*. New York, Columbia University Press.

HAWTHORN, H. B., 1966-1967 : *A Survey of the Contemporary Indians of Canada*. Ottawa, Indian Affairs Branch.

HOLDEN, D. E., 1969 : "Modernization among Town and Bush Cree in Québec". *Canadian Review of Sociology and Anthropology* 6 (4) : 237-248.

HONIGMANN, John J., 1965 : "Social Disintegration in Five Northern Canadian Communities". *Canadian Review of Sociology and Anthropology* 4 (2) : 199-214.

– , 1968 : "Interpersonal Relations in Atomistic Communities". *Human Organization* 27 (3) : 220-229.

INDIAN AND NORTHERN AFFAIRS CANADA, 1989 : *1986 Census Highlights on Registered Indians : Annotated Tables*. Ottawa, Supply and Services Canada.

KISTABISH, Richard, 1982 : "La santé chez les Algonquins". *Recherches amérindiennes au Québec* 12 (1) : 29-32.

– , 1987 : *Santé algonquine. Document de réflexion*. Algonquin Council of Western Quebec.

KRUTZ, Gordon V., 1973 : "Compartmentalization as a Factor in Urban Adjustment : the Kiowa Case", in J. O. Waddell and O. M. Watson (eds.), *American Indian Urbanization*. Purdue University, Institute Monograph Series 4 : 101-116.

LAMBERT, Carmen, 1979 : "Les Amérindiens du Québec", in *Perspectives anthropologiques. Un collectif d'anthropologues québécois*. Ottawa, Éditions du Renouveau pédagogique, pp. 267-287.

LAPLANTE, Monique, 1991 : *Les autochtones de Val-d'Or : études sur les autochtones vivant en milieu urbain*. Val-d'Or, Université du Québec en Abitibi-Témiscamingue.

LAPLANTE, Robert, 1979a : *L'enfermement des Algonquins*. Manuscript. Société d'histoire de Val-d'Or.

– , 1979b : "Kipawa – Chronique des commencements". *Recherches amérindiennes au Québec* 9 (3) : 219-236.

McCASKILL, Don N., 1970 : *Migration, Adjustment, and Integration of the Indians Into the Urban Environment*. Master's thesis, Carleton University, Ottawa.

MONTPETIT, Christiane, 1989 : *Trajectoires de vie de migrants autochtones à Val-d'Or*. Master's thesis, Department of Anthropology, University of Montréal.

MOORE, Kermot A., 1982 : *Kipawa : Portrait of a People*. Highway Book Shop, Cobalt, Ontario.

MUCHA, Janusz, 1983 : "From Prairie to the City : Transformation of Chicago's American Indian Community". *Urban Anthropology* 12 (3-4) : 337-371.

– , 1984 : "American Indian Success in the Urban Setting". *Urban Anthropology* 13 (4) : 329-354.

NAGLER, Mark, 1970 : *Indians in the City*. Ottawa, Canadian Research Centre for Anthropology, Saint Paul University.

NEILS, Elaine M., 1971 : *Reservation to City : Indian Migration and Federal Relocation*. Chicago, University of Chicago Press.

PAREDES, J. Anthony, 1973 : "Interaction and Adaptation Among Small City Chippewa", in J. O. Waddell and O. M. Watson (eds.), *American Indian Urbanization*. Purdue University, Institute Monograph Series 4 : 51-73.

PRICE, John A., 1968 : "The Migration and Adaptation of American Indians to Los Angeles". *Human Organization* 27 (2) : 168-175.

PRICE, John A., and Don N. McCASKILL, 1974 : "The Urban Integration of Canadian Native People". *Western Canadian Journal of Anthropology* 4 (2) : 29-47.

QUEBEC, 1987 : *The Aboriginal People in Quebec*. Secretariat for Aboriginal Affairs, Les Publications du Québec.

RANKIN, Sandra, Hanson MCKENZIE and Gordon McDOUGALL, 1985 : *En images et en mots*. Document deposited at the Val-d'Or Frienship Center.

ROY, Prodipto, 1962 : "The Measurement of Assimilation : The Spokane Indians". *American Journal of Sociology* 67 : 541-551.

STANBURY, W.T., 1975 : *Success and Failure : Indians in Urban Society*. Vancouver, UBC Press.

STANLEY, Sam, and Robert K. THOMAS, 1978 : "Current Demographic and Social Trends Among North American Indians". *Annals of the American Academy of Political and Social Sciences* 436 : 111.

STATISTICS CANADA, 1984 : *Canada's Native People. 1981 Census of Canada*. Ottawa, Supply and Services Canada.

– , 1988 : *Canada 1986 Census. Profiles*. Ottawa.

TAX, Sol, 1978 : "The Impact of Urbanization on American Indians". *Annals of the American Academy of Political and Social Sciences* 436 : 121-136

VASTEL, Michel, 1992 : "La reconquête de l'Abitibi". *L'Actualité*, August : 52-58.

WALDRAM, James B., 1990 : "The Persistence of Traditional Medecine in Urban Areas : the Case of Canada's Indians". *American and Alaska Native Mental Health Research* 4 (1) : 9-29.

*T*HE ALGONQUINS :
A THEMATIC BIBLIOGRAPHY

Daniel Clément and Jacques Frenette

Translated by Nicole Beaudry

T he main objective of this thematic bibliography on the Algonquins is to provide the general public, as well as specialists, with a research tool useful for developing our understanding and knowledge of the Algonquin people of Eastern Canada. Presently, we believe that there is no bibliography focusing specifically on Algonquins and we hope here to fill this gap.

For the purpose of this bibliography the name "Algonquin" (or "Algonkin") is to be distinguished from the similar name "Algonquian" (or "Algonkian"), a possibly confusing term. The latter term refers to a linguistic and cultural family comprising, among other groups, not only the Algonquins proper – whom this bibliography concerns – but also the Montagnais, Crees, Ojibwas, Micmacs, Atikamekws, etc. Moreover, the name "Algonquin" refers to all the Native people clustered around ten communities in the Ottawa valley and Abitibi-Témiscamingue regions. These are Golden Lake in Ontario, and in Quebec, Pikogan, Lac-Rapide, Grand-Lac-Victoria, Kebaowek, Lac-Simon, Winneway, Maniwaki, Timiskaming and Hunter's Point. In our bibliography, the prehistoric inhabitants of the Ottawa valley and Abitibi-Témiscamingue regions, the Algonquians' presumed ancestors, are also included within this appellation.

The bibliography is thematically organized. General works are followed by documents pertaining to archaeology and prehistory, history, linguistics, toponymy, material culture, traditional social organization, religion, oral tradition, ethnoscience, indigenous rights and present living conditions. The last section includes a partial list of audio-visual documents. With some exceptions, the documents listed are easily accessible either through universities or through other institutions such as museums and Native organizations.

Excluded from this bibliography are the documents referring in their title or in some of their comments to Algonquins or to Algonquians but which do not directly concern the Algonquins as previously defined. In the same manner, manuscripts in the strict sense of the term (hand-written texts) as well as newspaper articles have not been retained.

Several people and institutions have contributed to this bibliography and we wish to thank them warmly. These are Pierre Dumais, Regina Flannery-Herzfeld, Charles Martijn, François Trudel and, more specifically, Sylvie Laflamme, who is responsible for interlibrary loans at the Canadian Museum of Civilization. We also wish to thank those whom we may have inadvertently forgotten.

BIBLIOGRAPHIES

ABLER, Thomas S., and Sally M. WEAVER, 1974 : *A Canadian Indian Bibliography 1960-1970*. Toronto and Buffalo, University of Toronto Press.

CARRIÈRE, Gaston, 1970 : "Catalogue des manuscrits en langues indiennes conservés aux archives oblates, Ottawa". *Anthropologica* XII (2) : 151-179.

DOMINIQUE, Richard, and Jean-Guy DESCHÊNES, 1985 : *Cultures et sociétés autochtones du Québec. Bibliographie critique*. Québec, Institut québécois de recherche sur la culture, Instruments de travail 11.

FREEMAN, John F., 1966 : *A Guide to Manuscripts Relating to the American Indian in the Library of the American Philosophical Society*. Philadelphia, Memoirs of the American Philosophical Society, Vol. 65.

FRIED, Jacob, 1955 : "Bibliography and Survey of the Literature", in Jacob Fried (ed.*), A Survey of the Aboriginal Populations of Quebec and Labrador*. Montréal, McGill University, Eastern Canadian Anthropological Series 1, pp. 1-64.

GOURD, Benoît-Beaudry, 1973 : *Bibliographie de l'Abitibi-Témiscamingue*. Rouyn, Université du Québec, Direction des études universitaires dans l'Ouest québécois.

– , 1975 : *Bibliographie de l'Abitibi-Témiscamingue. Supplément*. Rouyn, Université du Québec, Direction des études universitaires dans l'Ouest québécois.

HELM, June, 1976 : *The Indians of the Subarctic : A Critical Bibliography*. Bloomington and London, Indiana University Press.

LAFORTE, Esther, and Roland VIAU, 1987 : *Bibliographie du patrimoine culturel de l'Outaouais québécois*. Montréal, University of Montréal, Department of Anthropology. Manuscript.

MURDOCK, George Peter, and Timothy J. O'LEARY, 1975 : *Ethnographic Bibliography of North America*. Vol. 2, *Arctic and Subarctic*. 4th ed. New Haven, Human Relations Area Files Press.

NATIONAL CAPITAL COMMISSION, 1978 : *A Bibliography of History and Heritage of the National Capital Region/Une bibliographie de l'histoire et du patrimoine de la région de la capitale nationale*. Ottawa, National Capital Commission.

– , 1982 : *1982 Supplement. History and Heritage Bibliography of the National Capital Region/Supplément 1982. Bibliographie de l'histoire et du patrimoine de la région de la capitale nationale*. Ottawa, National Capital Commission.

PENTLAND, David H., C. Douglas ELLIS, Carol A. SIMPSON, and H. Christoph WOLFART, 1974 : *A Bibliography of Algonquian Linguistics*. Winnipeg, University of Manitoba, Anthropology Papers 11.

PENTLAND, David H., and H. Christoph WOLFART, 1982 : *Bibliography of Algonquian Linguistics*. Winnipeg, The University of Manitoba Press.

PILLING, James Constantine, 1891 : *Bibliography of the Algonquian Languages*. Washington, Government Printing Office, Bureau of American Ethnology Bulletin 13.

PRESTON, R. J., 1970 : *Boreal Forest Algonkian Ethnographic Bibliography*. Canadian Museum of Civilization, Library, Ethnology document III-L-12M. Manuscript.

SAINT-AMOUR, Jean-Pierre, 1978 : *L'Outaouais québécois. Guide de recherche et bibliographie sélective*. Hull, Université du Québec, Centre d'études universitaires dans l'Ouest québécois.

VINCENT, Sylvie, 1984 : *Bilan des recherches ethnohistoriques concernant les groupes autochtones du Québec*. Report submitted by the Centre de recherche et d'analyse en sciences humaines (ssDcc inc.) to the Direction régionale du Nouveau-Québec et service aux autochtones. 5 vols. n.p., Quebec's ministère des Affaires culturelles.

GENERAL WORKS

ASSINIWI, Bernard, 1972a : "La Femme indienne. Interview de Mme Mary Commanda", in *À l'indienne*. Ottawa, Éditions Leméac inc., pp. 15-25.

– , Bernard, 1972b : "La survie en forêt. Interview de William Commanda", in *À l'indienne*. Ottawa, Éditions Leméac inc., pp. 83-94.

BECHMANN-KHERA, Sigrid, 1961 : *Report of Field Work, 1961, Among the Algonkin at Rapid Lake, P.Q., Maniwaki, P.Q. and the Ojibway on Bear Island Ont. (Timagami Band)*. Canadian Museum of Civilization, Library, Ethnology document III-L-2M. Manuscript.

– , 1964 : *Study of Lac Barrière Indians; Field Report, 1964*. Canadian Museum of Civilization, Library, Ethnology document III-L-4M. Manuscript.

CÔTÉ, Marc, and Gaëtan L. LESSARD (eds.), 1993 : *Traces du passé, Images du présent. Anthropologie amérindienne du Moyen-nord québécois*. Rouyn-Noranda, Cégep de l'Abitibi-Témiscamingue.

COUTURE, Yvon H., 1983 : *Les Algonquins*. Val-d'Or, Éditions Hyperborée, Collection Racines amérindiennes.

CUOQ, J. A., 1894 : "Anotc Kekon". *Proceedings and Transactions of the Royal Society of Canada* 11 (1) : 137-179.

DAY, Gordon M., 1979 : "The Indians of the Ottawa Valley". *Oracle* 30, Ottawa, National Museums of Canada, National Museum of Man.

DAY, Gordon M., and Bruce G. TRIGGER, 1978 : "Algonquin", in William C. Sturtevant (ed.), *Handbook of North American Indians*, Vol. 15 *Northeast*. Washington, Smithsonian Institution, pp. 792-797.

DROUIN, Rita (ed.), 1989 : *Femmes algonquines – anecdotes*. Témiscamingue, Multi-Diffusion enr.

ERICKSON, Vincent O., 1974 : "Algonquin", in *Encyclopedia of Indians of the Americas*. Vol. 2. St. Clair Shores, Michigan, Scholarly Press Inc., pp. 102-106.

HESSEL, Peter, 1983 : "The Algonkins of Golden Lake". *Beaver* 314 (3) : 52-57.

– , 1987 : *The Algonkin Tribe. The Algonkins of the Ottawa Valley : An Historical Outline*. Arnprior, Ont., Kichesippi Books.

JENKINS, William H., 1939 : *Notes on the Hunting Economy of the Abitibi Indians*. Washington, The Catholic University of America, Anthropological Series 9.

JOHNSON, Frederick, 1928 : "The Algonquin at Golden Lake, Ontario". *Indian Notes* V (2): 173-178.

JUDGE, Leonard, 1986 : *The Elders Gift – Origins*. Winneway, Amo Osowan School. Manuscript.

LAURIN, Serge, 1989 : "L'occupation amérindienne", in *Histoire des Laurentides*. Québec, Institut québécois de recherche sur la culture, Les Régions du Québec 3, pp. 47-75.

LEE RUE III, Leonard, 1961 : "Barriere Indians". *Beaver* 292 : 27-32.

MacPHERSON, John T., 1930 : *An Ethnological Study of the Abitibi Indians*. Canadian Museum of Civilization, Library, Ethnology document III-G-38M. Manuscript.

MOORE, Kermot A., 1982 : *Kipawa : Portrait of a People*. Cobalt, Highway Book Shop.

POIRIER, Jeanne, (ed.), 1978 *: Survival Through Cultural Understanding : From Conversations with the Elders of the Cree, Algonkian and Metis Nations of North Western Québec and Temiscaming*. Val-d'Or, Laurentian Alliance of Metis and Non-Status Indians Inc.

VINCENT, Sylvie, 1971 : *Les Amérindiens dans les Annales de la Propagation de la Foi. Étude pilote : dépouillement de lettres de missionnaires, classification et annotation des informations concernant les Algonquins, Cris et Tête de Boule dans les Annales de Québec 1877-1930*. n.p., Quebec's ministère des Affaires culturelles. Manuscript.

ARCHAEOLOGY - PREHISTORY

BENMOUYAL, J., 1971 : *Reconnaissance archéologique dans la région du Parc de la Gatineau*. Ottawa, National Museum of Man and National Capital Commission. Manuscript.

BOYLE, David, 1896 : "Rock Paintings or Petrographs. Rock Paintings at Lake Massanog. Other Rock Paintings", in *Archaeological Report 1894-95. Appendix to the Report of the Minister of Education, Ontario*. Toronto, Warwick Bros. & Rutter, pp. 44-51.

CÔTÉ, Marc, 1991 : "Une pipe de plâtre du XVIIe siècle en Abitibi-Témiscamingue". *Wigwas* IV (2) : 2-8.

EMERSON, J. N., 1949 : "Preliminary Report on the Excavations of the Kant Site, Renfrew County, Ontario", in *Annual Report of the National Museum for the Fiscal Year 1947-1948*. Ottawa, National Museum of Canada, Bulletin 113, pp. 17-22.

– , 1955 : "The Kant Site : A Point Peninsula Manifestation in Renfrew County, Ontario". *Transactions of the Royal Canadian Institute* XXXI, Part 1 : 24-66.

ETHNOSCOP, 1980 : *Étude de potentiel archéologique. Axe Maniwaki - Témiscaming, secteur rivière Dumoine et Maniwaki*. Québec, ministère de l'énergie et des Ressources, Secteur de la voirie forestière. Manuscript.

– , 1983 : *Étude synthèse sur l'occupation amérindienne en Abitibi. Rapport final*. n.p., ministère des Affaires culturelles. Manuscript.

– , 1984 : *L'occupation amérindienne en Abitibi-Témiscamingue*. Québec, ministère des Affaires culturelles.

KENNEDY, Clyde C., 1958 : "Ancient Man in the Ottawa Valley", in *Pembroke Centennial Souvenir Book*. Pembroke, pp. 81-88.

– , 1959 : "On the Trail of Champlain". *Ontario History* LI (1) : 50-52.

– , 1960 : "Charmstones in the Ottawa Valley". *Ontario History* LII (1) : 67-70.

– , 1962 : "Archaic Hunters in the Ottawa Valley". *Ontario History* LIV (2) : 122-128.

– , 1967 : "Preliminary Report on the Morrison's Island-6 Site", in *Contributions to Anthropology V : Archaeology and Physical Anthropology*. National Museum of Canada, Bulletin 206, pp. 100-125.

LAIDLAW, G. E., 1919 : "Algonquin Pottery", in R. B. Orr (ed.), *Thirty-First Annual Archaeological Report 1919 being Part of Appendix to the Report of the Minister of Education, Ontario*. Toronto, A. T. Wilgress, pp. 100.

LEE, Thomas E., 1962a : "A Patination Problem at Lake Abitibi, Canada". *New World Antiquity* 9 (11-12) : 167-172.

– , 1962b : "A Small Beach Site on the South Shore of Lake Abitibi, Québec". *New World Antiquity* 9 (11-12) : 152-161.

– , 1962c : "A Small Prehistoric Quarry at Lake Abitibi, Québec". *New World Antiquity* 9 (11-12) : 162-167.

– , 1967 : *Archaeological Investigations at Lake Abitibi 1964*. Québec, Université Laval, Centre d'études nordiques, travaux divers No. 10.

– , 1974 : *The Fort Abitibi Mystery*. Québec, Université Laval, Centre d'études nordiques, Paléo-Québec 4.

MAROIS, Roger J. M., 1974 : *Les schémes d'établissement à la fin de la préhistoire et au début de la période historique : le sud du Québec*. Ottawa, National Museums of Canada, National Museum of Man, Archaelogical Survey of Canada, Mercury Series, Paper No. 17.

– , 1981 : "Modes d'établissements des Amérindiens dans l'Outaouais", in P. L. Lapointe (ed.), *L'Outaouais : Actes du colloque sur l'identité régionale de l'Outaouais, tenu à Hull les 13, 14 et 15 novembre 1981.* Hull, Institut d'histoire et de recherche sur l'Outaouais inc., pp. 8-11.

MAROIS, Roger, and Pierre GAUTHIER, 1989 : *Les Abitibis.* Ottawa, Canadian Museum of Civilization, Archaeological Survey of Canada, Mercury Series, Paper No. 140.

PHILIPS, W. H. C., 1907 : "Rock Paintings at Temagami District", in David Boyle (ed.), *Annual Archaeological Report 1906 being part of Appendix to the Report of the Minister of Education, Ontario.* Toronto, L. K. Cameron, pp. 41-47.

RIBES, René, 1973 : *La collection Bérubé au Musée de La Sarre 1950-1970. Les sites Bérubé dans la partie québécoise du lac Abitibi.* Trois-Rivières, Université du Québec à Trois-Rivières, Groupe de recherche en histoire des religions et en archéologie préhistorique. Manuscript.

RIDLEY, Frank, 1956 : "An Archaeological Reconnaissance of Lake Abitibi, Ontario". *Ontario History* XLVIII (1) : 18-23.

– , 1958 : "Sites on Ghost River, Lake Abitibi". *Pennsylvania Archaeologist* XXVIII (1) : 39-56.

– , 1962 : "The Ancient Sites of Lake Abitibi". *Canadian Geographical Journal* LXIV (3) : 86-93.

– , 1966 : "Archaeology of Lake Abitibi, Ontario-Québec". *Anthropological Journal of Canada* 4 (2) : 2-50.

SOWTER, T. W. Edwin, 1895 : "Notes on the Antiquities of Lake Deschênes". *The Ottawa Naturalist* IX (5) : 114-116.

– , 1900 : "Archaeology of Lake Deschênes". *The Ottawa Naturalist* VIII (10) : 225-238.

– , 1901 : "Prehistoric Camping Grounds Along the Ottawa River". *The Ottawa Naturalist* XV (6) : 141-151.

– , 1909 : "Algonkin and Huron Occupation of the Ottawa Valley". *The Ottawa Naturalist* XXIII (4) : 61-68, XXIII (5) : 92-104.

– , 1915 : "The Highway of the Ottawa". *Ontario Historical Society. Papers and Records* XIII: 42-52.

– , 1917 : "Indian Village Sites. Lake Deschênes", in R. B. Orr (ed.), *Twenty-Ninth Annual Archaeological Report 1917 being Part of Appendix to the Report of the Minister of Education, Ontario*. Toronto, A. T. Wilgress, pp. 78-85.

TASSÉ, Gilles, and Selwyn DEWDNEY, 1977 *: Relevés et travaux récents sur l'art rupestre amérindien*. Montréal, Laboratoire d'archéologie de l'Université du Québec à Montréal, Paléo-Québec 8.

WATSON, G. D., 1972 : "A Woodland Indian Site at Constance Bay, Ontario". *Ontario Archaeology* 18 : 1-24.

WINTEMBERG, W. J., 1924 : "Unusual Stone Artifacts From Ontario", in R. B. Orr (ed.), *Thirty-Fourth Annual Archaeological Report 1923 being Part of Appendix to the Report of the Minister of Education, Ontario*. Toronto, Clarkson W. James, pp. 81.

– , 1929 : "Distinguishing Characteristics of Algonquian and Iroquoian Cultures". *Annual Report for 1929*. Canada, Department of Mines, National Museum of Canada, Bulletin No. 67, pp. 65-125.

HISTORY

ANONYME, 1938 : "La vallée de l'Outaouais avant la Conquête", in *Le Nord de l'Outaouais. Manuel-Répertoire d'histoire et de géographie régionales*. Ottawa, Le Droit, pp. 103-129.

BARBEZIEUX, Alexis de, 1897 : *Histoire de la province ecclésiastique d'Ottawa et de la colonisation dans la vallée de l'Ottawa*. 2 vols. Ottawa, La Cie d'Imprimerie d'Ottawa.

BEAULIEU, Alain, 1987 *: Convertir les fils de Caïn. Jésuites et Amérindiens nomades en Nouvelle-France, 1632-1642*. Québec, Nuit Blanche éditeur.

BLACK, Meredith Jean, 1989 : "Nineteenth-Century Algonquin Culture Change", in W. Cowan (ed.), *Actes du vingtième congrès des Algonquinistes*. Ottawa, Carleton University, pp. 62-69.

BOND, C. C. J., 1966 : "The Hudson's Bay Company in the Ottawa Valley". *Beaver* (Spring) 296 : 4-21.

BOUCHARD, Serge, 1980 : *Mémoires d'un simple missionnaire. Le père Joseph-Étienne Guinard, o.m.i., 1864-1965*. Québec, ministère des Affaires culturelles, Collection Civilisation du Québec.

CANADA, DEPARTMENT OF INDIAN AND NORTHERN AFFAIRS, 1973 : *Historical Notes on the Abitibi Dominion Band*. Ottawa, Claims and Historical Research Centre. Manuscript.

CARON, Ivanhoé, 1913 : "Au Grand lac Victoria". *Bulletin de la Société de géographie de Québec* 7 (2) : 87-95, 7 (3) : 139-150.

– , 1914 : "De Témiscamingue à l'Abitibi en canot". *Bulletin de la Société de géographie de Québec* 8 (2) : 67-72, 8 (3) : 131-145.

CARRIÈRE, Gaston, 1963 *: Missionnaire sans toit. Le P. Jean-Nicolas Laverlochère, O.M.I. 1811-1884*. Montréal, Rayonnement.

CHARRON, Yvon, 1951 : "Monsieur Charles de Bellefeuille missionnaire de l'Outawais (1836-1838)". *Revue d'histoire de l'Amérique française* V (2) : 193-226.

COUTURE, Gilles, 1979 : *L'Écologie d'une invasion. La dépossession progressive des territoires du peuple algonquin en Abitibi-Témiscamingue*. n.p., Bureau de recherche de l'Alliance laurentienne des Métis et Indiens sans-statut du Québec inc. Manuscript.

DUNN, G., 1975 : *Les Forts de l'Outaouais*. Montréal, Les Éditions du Jour.

EINHORN, Arthur, 1974 : "Iroquois – Algonquin Wampum Exchanges and Preservation in the 20th Century. A Case for In Situ Preservation". *Man in the Northeast* 7 : 71-86.

GEORGE, Paul, 1986 *: Étude ethno-historique des sites de sépultures autochtones de l'Outaouais*. n.p., Alliance autochtone du Québec. Manuscript.

GOUGER, Lina, 1987 : *L'acculturation des Algonquins au XVIIe siècle*. Master's thesis, Department of Literature, Québec, Université Laval.

GRASSMANN, Thomas, 1966 : "Oumasasikweie", in George W. Brown (ed.*)*, *Dictionary of Canadian Biography*. Vol. 1. Toronto and Québec, University of Toronto Press and Les Presses de l'Université Laval, pp. 527.

JOLY DE LOTBINIÈRE, Pauline, 1991 : *Western Perspectives and Algonquin Narratives : Divergent Interpretations of the Wampum Tradition*. Master's thesis, Department of Anthropology, University of Montréal.

JURY, Elsie M., 1966a : "Batiscan" in George W. Brown (ed.), *Dictionary of Canadian Biography*. Vol. 1. Toronto and Québec, University of Toronto Press and Les Presses de l'Université Laval, pp. 80.

– , 1966b : "Iroquet", in George W. Brown (ed.), *Dictionary of Canadian Biography*. Vol. 1. Toronto and Québec, University of Toronto Press and Les Presses de l'Université Laval, pp. 381-382.

– , 1966c : "Pieskaret", in George W. Brown (ed.), *Dictionary of Canadian Biography*. Vol. 1. Toronto and Québec, University of Toronto Press and Les Presses de l'Université Laval, pp. 547-548.

– , 1966d : "Pigarouich, Étienne", in George W. Brown (ed*.), Dictionary of Canadian Biography*. Vol. 1. Toronto and Québec, University of Toronto Press and Les Presses de l'Université Laval, pp. 548-549.

– , 1966e : "Tessouat", in George W. Brown (ed.), *Dictionary of Canadian Biography*. Vol. 1. Toronto and Québec, University of Toronto Press and Les Presses de l'Université Laval, pp. 638-639.

– , 1966f : "Tessouat (Le Borgne de l'Île)", in George W. Brown (ed*.), Dictionary of Canadian Biography*. Vol. 1. Toronto and Québec, University of Toronto Press and Les Presses de l'Université Laval, pp. 639.

– , 1966g : "Tessouat, Paul", in George W. Brown (ed*.), Dictionary of Canadian Biography*. Vol. 1. Toronto and Québec, University of Toronto Press and Les Presses de l'Université Laval, pp. 640-641.

KENNEDY, Clyde C., 1961 : "Ancient Man; The Champlain Trail; The Fur Trade", in Carl Price and Clyde C. Kennedy. *Notes on the History of Renfrew County*. Pembroke, Renfrew County Council, pp. 13-33.

– , 1970 : *The Upper Ottawa Valley*. Pembroke, The Renfrew County Council.

KEPLER, Joseph, 1929 : "The Peace Tomahak Algonkian Wampum". *Indian Notes* VI (2) : 130-138.

LATULIPE, E., 1902 : *Visite pastorale de Monseigneur Lorrain, évêque de Pembrooke, chez les Algonquins du Grand lac Victoria et du lac Barrière*. Québec, Imprimerie S.-A. Demers.

MALCHELOSSE, Gérard, 1922 : "Ki8et et la Chaudière-Noire". *La Revue nationale* 4 (II) : 341-345.

MITCHELL, Elaine Allan, 1977 : *Fort Timiskamimg and the Fur Trade*. Toronto and Buffalo, University of Toronto Press.

NICOLAS, Louis, 1974 : *Les raretés des Indes "Codex Canadiensis". Album manuscrit de la fin du XVIIe siècle contenant 180 dessins concernant les indigènes, leurs coutumes, tatouages, la faune et la flore de la Nouvelle France, plus deux cartes. Reproduit intégralement, en* *fac-similé par le procédé d'héliotypie Léon Marotte. Précédé d'un avant-propos par le baron Marc de Villiers.* Montréal, Les Éditions du Bouton d'Or.

ORR, R. B., 1922 : "Algonquin Subtribes and Clans of Ontario", in R. B. Orr (ed.), *Thirty-Third Annual Archaeological Report 1921-22 being Part of Appendix to the Report of the Minister of Education, Ontario.* Toronto, Clarkson W. James, pp. 24-31.

PARISEAU, Claude, 1974 : *Les troubles de 1860-1880 à Oka : choc de deux cultures.* Master's thesis, Department of History, Montréal, McGill University.

POIRE, Charles Ed., 1841 : "Relation d'une mission faite en l'été de 1839, le long de la rivière de l'Ottawa jusqu'au lac de Témiskaming, etc." *Rapport de l'Association de la Propagation de la Foi* 3 : 3-26.

PROULX, Jean-Baptiste, 1882 : *Voyage au lac Abbitibi ou Visite pastorale de Mgr J. Th. Duhamel dans le haut de l'Ottawa.* Montréal, J. Chapleau et Fils.

– , 1886 : *À la baie d'Hudson, ou récit de la première visite pastorale de Mgr N. Z. Lorrain, Évêque de Cythère et Vicaire apostolique de Pontiac, dans ses missions sauvages de Témiscamingue, d'Abbitibi, de New-Port, de Moose et d'Albany.* Montréal, Librairie Saint-Joseph.

St. LOUIS, A. E., n.d. : *Early History of the Algonquin Indians of Golden Lake.* n.p. Manuscript. (Claims and Historical Research Centre, Department of Indian and Northern Affairs Canada).

– , 1951 : *Ancient Hunting Grounds of the Algonquin and Nipissing Indians Comprising the Watersheds of the Ottawa and Madawaska Rivers.* n.p. Manuscript. (Claims and Historical Research Centre, Department of Indian and Northern Affairs Canada)

SULTE, Benjamin, 1898 : "The Valley of the Grand River, 1600-1650". *Proceedings and Transactions of the Royal Society of Canada.* Second Series IV (II) : 107-135.

– , 1915 : "The Valley of the Ottawa in 1613". *Ontario Historical Society, Papers and Records* XIII : 31-35.

LINGUISTICS

AUBIN, George F., 1979. "Golden Lake Algonquin : A Preliminary Report", in W. Cowan (ed.), *Papers of the Tenth Algonquian Conference.* Ottawa, Carleton University, pp. 121-125.

– , 1981 : "Remarks on Golden Lake Algonquin", in W. Cowan (ed.), *Papers of the Twelfth Algonquian Conference.* Ottawa, Carleton University, pp. 39-46.

– , 1984 : "Some Verb Paradigms in Golden Lake Algonquin", in W. Cowan (ed.), *Papers of the Fifteenth Algonquian Conference*. Ottawa, Carleton University, pp. 217-224.

– , 1987 : "Three Texts in Golden Lake Algonquin", in W. Cowan (ed.), *Papers of the Eighteenth Algonquian Conference*. Ottawa, Carleton University, pp. 1-6.

– , 1988 : "'Girls Hunting Groundhogs' : A Text in Golden Lake Algonquin", in W. Cowan (ed.), *Actes du vingtième congrès des Algonquinistes*. Ottawa, Carleton University, pp. 1-5.

– , 1989 : "Some Verb Paradigms in Golden Lake Algonquin : II", in W. Cowan (ed.), *Actes du vingtième congrès des Algonquinistes*. Ottawa, Carleton University. pp. 1-16.

– , 1991 : "Comments on Some Demonstratives in Golden Lake Algonquin", in W. Cowan (ed.), *Papers of the Twenty-Second Algonquian Conference*. Ottawa, Carleton University, pp. 1-10.

BROUILLARD, Edmond, and Marie DUMONT-ANICHINAPÉO, 1987 *: Grammaire algonquine respectant les règles langagières coutumières propres aux communautés du Lac Simon ainsi que du Grand lac Victoria*. Lac-Simon, Centre culturel Amikwan. Manuscript.

CHARENCEY, H. de, 1903 : "Études algiques". *Journal de la Société des américanistes de Paris* 4 : 8-54.

COUTURE, Yvon H., 1982 : *Lexique français-algonquin*. Val-d'Or, Éditions Hyperborée, Collection Racines amérindiennes.

COWAN, William, 1991 : "Philological Spadework in the Jesuit Relations : A Letter in Algonquin", in W. Cowan (ed.), *Papers of the Twenty-Second Algonquian Conference*. Ottawa, Carleton University, pp. 48-57.

CUOQ, J. A., 1864 : *Jugement erroné de M. Ernest Renan sur les langues sauvages*. Montréal, Eusèbe Senécal.

– , 1865 : *Catéchisme algonquin avec syllabaire et cantiques*. Montréal, John Lovell.

– , 1866 : *Études philologiques sur quelques langues sauvages de l'Amérique*. Montréal, Dawson Brothers.

– , 1872 : "Cantique en langue algonquine". *Actes de la société philologique* 1 : 73-76.

– , 1873 : "Fragments de Chrestomathie de la langue algonquine". *Actes de la société philologique* 3 : 39-50.

– , 1874a : "La salutation angélique (Texte algonquin avec glose)". *Actes de la société philologique* 4 : 207-209.

– , 1874b : "L'oraison dominicale (Texte algonquin avec glose)". *Actes de la société philologique* 4 : 199-205.

– , 1876 : "Fragments de Chrestomathie algonkine". *Actes de la société philologique* 5 : 287-305.

– , 1886 : *Lexique de la langue algonquine*. Montréal, J. Chapleau & Fils.

– , 1892-93 : "Grammaire de la langue algonquine". *Proceedings and Transactions of the Royal Society of Canada* IX (1) : 85-114, X (1) : 41-119.

– , 1893 : *Ocki mino masinaigans*. Montréal, J.M. Valois.

DAVIAULT, Diane, 1981 : "Dialectologie algonquine : les démonstratifs". *Recherches linguistiques à Montréal/Montréal Working Papers in Linguistics* 16 : 1-20.

– , 1982 : *Une analyse des particules introduisant les structures enchassées en algonquin*. Master's thesis, Department of Linguistics and Philology, University of Montréal.

– , 1986 : "La structure d'argument en algonquin", in W. Cowan (ed.), *Actes du dix-septième congrès des Algonquinistes*. Ottawa, Carleton University, pp. 81-91.

– , 1987 : "Un aperçu de la morphologie verbale dans la grammaire du Père Nicolas", in W. Cowan (ed.), *Papers of the Eighteenth Algonquian Conference*. Ottawa, Carleton University, pp. 69-94.

DAVIAULT, Diane, M. DUFRESNE, S. GIROUARD, J. D. KAYE, and P. LEGAULT, 1978 : "L'algonquin du Nord", in W. Cowan (ed.), *Papers of the Ninth Algonquian Conference*. Ottawa, Carleton University, pp. 55-60.

DAY, Gordon M., 1972 : "The Name 'Algonquin'". *International Journal of American Linguistics* 38 (4) : 226-228.

DUFRESNE, Monique, 1981 : *Les comparatives en algonquin du Nord*. Master's thesis, Department of Linguistics, Université du Québec à Montréal.

DUMONT, Marie, and Mani DUMONT, 1985 : *Lexique algonquin/français*. Lac-Simon, Lac-Simon Band Council. Manuscript.

FAFARD, F.-X., 1954 : *Niina Aiamie Masinaigan. Recueil de prières et de cantiques en algonquin à l'usage des Indiens de Maniwaki, de l'Abitibi, du Témiscamingue et du Haut St-Maurice*. Trois-Rivières, Les Missionnaires Oblats de Marie Immaculée.

GILSTRAP, Roger, 1978 : *Algonquin Dialect Relationships in Northwestern Québec*. Ottawa, National Museums of Canada, National Museum of Man, Canadian Ethnology Service, Mercury Series, Paper No. 44.

HANZELI, Victor Egon, 1969 : *Missionary Linguistics in New France. A Study of Seventeenth – and Eighteenth – Century Descriptions of Amnerican Indian Languages*. The Hague, Paris, Mouton. (Phd Dissertation 1960, Indiana University, Department of French and Italian).

– , 1970 : "The Algonquin R-Dialect in Historical Records". *Actes du Xe Congrès international des linguistes*, Bucarest, August 28 – September 2 1967 : 85-89.

HENDERSON, T. S. T., 1971 : "Participant-Reference in Algonkin". *Cahiers linguistiques d'Ottawa* 1 : 27-49.

– , 1973 : "Verbal Modes in Algonkin". *Studies in Linguistics* 23 : 57-62.

JONES, David J., 1976a : *An Algonquin Word-List Showing How Maniwaki-Algonquin Words Might Be Written*. Maniwaki, River Desert Band Council. Manuscript.

– , 1976b : *Extracts from A Basic Algonquin Grammar Written under Contract for the River Desert Band Council*. Maniwaki, River Desert Band. Manuscript.

– , 1977 : *A Basic Algonquin Grammar for Teachers of the Language at Maniwaki, Quebec*. Maniwaki. Manuscript.

LEMOINE, George, 1907 : "Le génie de la langue algonquine". *Congrès international des Américanistes*. XVth Session held in Québec in 1906. II : 225-242.

– , 1909 : *Dictionnaire français-algonquin*. Chicoutimi, G. Delisle, Bureaux du journal "Le Travailleur".

– , 1910 : "Les Algonquins du Canada". *Bulletin de la Société de géographie de Québec* 4 (3): 184-196.

MATHEVET, Jean-Claude, 1890 : *Aiamie-tipadjimowin. L'Histoire sainte en algonquin*. First ed. 1860. Montréal, J. M. Valois.

– , 1968 : *Ka titc Jezos Tebeniminang ondaje aking enansinaikatek masinaigan. Vie de Notre-Seigneur Jésus-Christ*. First ed. 1861. Amos, Les Missionnaires Oblats de Marie Immaculée.

McGREGOR, Ernest, n.d. : *Algonquin Lexicon*. Maniwaki, River Desert Education Authority.

PAGOTTO, Louise, 1980 : "On Complementizer Adjuncts in the Rapid Lake Dialect of Algonquin", in W. Cowan (ed.), *Papers of the Eleventh Algonquian Conference.* Ottawa, Carleton University, pp. 231-246.

PIGGOTT, G. L., 1977 : "Ordered Rules? An Innovation in Algonquin". *Recherches linguistiques à Montréal/Montréal Working Papers in Linguistics* 9 : 159-174.

– , 1978 : "Algonquin and Other Ojibwa Dialects : A Preliminary Report", in W. Cowan (ed.), *Papers of the Ninth Algonquian Conference.* Ottawa, Carleton University, pp. 160-187.

SPIELMANN, Roger, 1987 : "Preference and Sequential Organization in Algonquin", in W. Cowan (ed.), *Papers of the Eighteenth Algonquian Conference.* Ottawa, Carleton University, pp. 321-333.

– , 1988 : "What's so Funny? Laughing Together in Algonquin Conversation", in W. Cowan (ed.), *Papers of the Nineteenth Algonquian Conference.* Ottawa, Carleton University, pp. 201-212.

SPIELMANN, Roger, and Bertha CHIEF, 1986 : "Requesting and Rejecting in Algonquin : Notes on a Conversation", in W. Cowan (ed.), *Actes du dix-septième congrès des Algonquinistes.* Ottawa, Carleton University, pp. 313-326.

SZABO, Laszlo, 1977 : "Lemoine's French-Algonquin Dictionary", in W, Cowan (ed.), *Actes du huitième congrès des Algonquinistes.* Ottawa, Carleton University, pp. 168-170.

TAUBE, Edward, 1955 : "Tribal Names Related With Algonkin". *Names. Journal of the American Name Society* III (2) : 65-81.

TOPONYMY

KISTABISH, Norman, 1980 : *Inventaire toponymique en territoire algonquin. Réserve indienne de Pikogan.* Québec, Government of Quebec, Commission de toponymie. Manuscript.

LAROSE, François, 1986 : *Inventaire toponymique. Lac Simon.* Québec, Government of Quebec, Commission de toponymie. Manuscript.

McKENZIE, Agnès, 1981a : *Rapport toponymique. Harricana.* Québec, Government of Quebec, Commission de toponymie. Manuscript.

– , 1981b : *Rapport toponymique. Pikogan 1981.* Québec, Government of Quebec, Commission de toponymie. Manuscript.

MORISSET, Danièle, 1989 : *Projet d'inventaire toponymique du Lac Simon. Rapport de recherche soumis à la Commission de toponymie du Québec.* Lac-Simon Band Council, Centre culturel Amikwan. Manuscript.

WINTEMBERG, W. J., 1938 : "Early Names of the Ottawa River". *Proceedings and Transactions of the Royal Society of Canada, 3rd series* 32 (2) : 97-105.

YOUNG, Norman, 1980 : *Inventaire toponymique en territoire algonquin. Réserve indienne de Kipawa.* Québec, Government of Quebec, Commission de toponymie. Manuscript.

– , 1981 : *Inventaire toponymique. Kipawa.* Québec, Government of Quebec, Commission de toponymie. Manuscript.

MATERIAL CULTURE

ALSFORD, Denis, 1970 : *Background and Acknowledgements on the Building of a Birch Bark Canoe.* Canadian Museum of Civilization, Library, Ethnology document III-L-53M. Manuscript.

EINHORN, Arthur, 1970 : *Interim Report on Contract to Investigate Bark and Leather Craft Industries Practiced in Maniwaki, Quebec.* Canadian Museum of Civilization, Library, Ethnology document III-L-7M. Manuscript.

GIDMARK, David, 1980 : *The Indian Crafts of William and Mary Commanda.* Toronto, McGraw-Hill Ryerson Limited.

– , 1985 : "Algonquin Birchbark Canoe Construction", in W. Cowan (ed.*)*, *Papers of the Sixteenth Algonquian Conference.* Ottawa, Carleton University, pp. 25-46.

– , 1988a : *The Algonquin Birchbark Canoe.* Aylesbury, Shire Publications Ltd.

– , 1988b : "The Birchbark Canoe Makers of Lac Barrière", in W. Cowan (ed.), *Papers of the Nineteenth Algonquian Conference.* Ottawa, Carleton University, pp. 75-79.

– , 1989 : *Birchbark Canoe.* Burnstown, Ont., General Store Publishing House Inc.

GILLIES, D. A., 1958 : "Canot du maître or Montréal Canoe". *Canadian Geographical Journal* LVI (3) : 114-119.

JAY, Roger, 1970 : "A New People, A Prevailing Old Trade". *Tawow* 1 (3) : 26-29.

JOHNSON, Frederick, 1930 : "An Algonquian Band at Lac Barrière, Province of Québec". *Indian Notes* VII : 27-39.

LEE-WHITING, Brenda, 1966 : "Daniel Sarrazin Still Makes Birchbark Canoes". *Canadian Geographical Journal* LXXII (4) : 124-129.

PETRULLO, Vincent M., 1929 : "Decorative Art on Birch-bark Containers from the Algonquin River du Lièvre Band". *Indian Notes* VI : 225-242.

ROULEAU, Serge, 1989 *: Fort Témiscamingue. Répertoire des costumes algonquin et chef de poste 1850.* Québec, Environment Canada, Parks Service, Collection Management. Manuscript.

SAINT-ARNAUD, Marie, 1991 : *Acériculture algonquine à Kitcisakik (Abitibi) et limite nord de répartition de l'érablière à sucre.* Report submitted to Université du Québec à Montréal as partial fulfillment for the degree of Master of Environmental Sciences.

SPECK, Frank G., 1927 : "River Desert Indians of Québec". *Indian Notes* 4 (3) : 240-252.

– , 1941 : "Art Processes in Birchbark of the River Desert Algonquin, a Circumboreal Trait". *Bureau of American Ethnology, Bulletin 128, Anthropological Papers* 17, pp. 231-274.

– , 1947 : "Northwestern Extent of Stamp Decoration. Algonquin, Québec", *in Eastern Algonkian Block-Stamp Decoration. A New World Original or An Acculturated Art.* Trenton, New Jersey, The Archeological Society of New Jersey, pp. 24-29.

SOCIAL, ECONOMIC, TERRITORIAL ORGANIZATION

BECHMANN-KHERA, Sigrid, 1962 : *Lac Barrière Band (Rapid Lake, P.Q.). Family Histories; Report of Field Work, 1962.* Canadian Museum of Civilization, Library, Ethnology document III-L-3M. Manuscript.

COOPER, Arch E., 1942 : *Ecological Aspects of the Family Hunting Territory System of the Northeastern Algonkians.* Master's thesis, Department of Anthropology, The University of Chicago.

DAVIDSON, D. S., 1926 : "The Family Hunting Territories of the Grand Lake Victoria Indians". *International Congress of Americanists, Proceedings* XXII (2) : 69-95.

DESCHÊNES, Jean-Guy, and Jacques FRENETTE, 1987 : *Les Algonquins de la rivière Désert : le territoire de la bande et son occupation depuis 1850.* Report submitted to the River Desert Band Council. Montréal, ssDcc inc. Manuscript.

HALLOWELL, A. Irving, 1949 : "The Size of Algonkian Hunting Territories : A Function of Ecological Adjustment". *American Anthropologist* 51 : 35-45.

HIRBOUR, René, 1969 : *Étude de trois niveaux d'intégration sociale d'une société de chasseurs cueilleurs : Kitchezagik Anichenabe*. Master's thesis, Department of Anthropology, University of Montréal.

McGEE, John T., 1950 : *Notes on Present and Past Systems of Land Tenure in the Kippewa Area of Temiscamingue Québec, Canada*. Master's thesis, Department of Anthropology, Washington, The Catholic University of America.

– , 1951 : "Family Hunting Grounds in the Kippewa Area, Québec". *Primitive Man* 24 (3) : 47-53.

MECHLING, W. H., 1916 : "Review of 'Family Hunting Territories and Social Life of Various Algonkian Bands of the Ottawa Valley' and 'Myths and Folk-lore of the Timiskaming Algonquin and Timagami Ojibwa' by F. G. Speck". *American Anthropologist* 18 (2) : 281-282.

ROARK-CALNEK, Sue, 1992 : *Genealogical Records on the Lac-Barrière, Grand-Lac-Victoria and Lac-Simon Populations and Their Ancestors to the Late 18th Century*. Canadian Museum of Civilization, Library, Ethnology document III-L-67M.

SPECK, Frank G., 1915 : *Family Hunting Territories and Social Life of Various Algonkian Bands of the Ottawa Valley*. Ottawa, Department of Mines, Geological Survey Memoir 70, Anthropological Series No. 8.

– , 1923 : "Algonkian Influence upon Iroquois Social Organization". *American Anthropologist* 25 (2) : 219-227.

– , 1929 : "Boundaries and Hunting Groups of the River Desert Algonquin". *Indian Notes* VI (2) : 97-120.

RELIGION

POLSON, Gordon, and Roger SPIELMANN, 1990 : "'Once There Were Two Brothers...' : Religious Tension in One Algonquin Community", in W. Cowan (ed.), *Papers of the Twenty-First Algonquian Conference*. Ottawa, Carleton University, pp. 303-312.

SPECK, Frank G., 1928 : "Divination by Scapulimancy among the Algonquin of River Desert, Québec". *Indian Notes* V : 167-173.

– , 1939 : "More Algonkian Scapulimancy From the North, and the Hunting Territory Question". *Ethnos* 4 (1) : 21-28.

ORAL TRADITION

ASSINIWI, Bernard, 1972 : "Aji-ji-wa-t'chig Manito-Akki", in *Sagana. Contes fantastiques du pays algonkin*. Ottawa, Éditions Leméac inc., pp. 95-108.

AUBIN, George F., 1982 : "Ethnographic Notes from Golden Lake", in W. Cowan (ed.), *Papers of the Thirteenth Algonquian Conference*. Ottawa, Carleton University, pp. 47-52.

BEAUDET, Rose-Aline, 1984 : *Comment l'ours perdit sa queue*. Val-d'Or, Commission scolaire de Val-d'Or et Bureau de coordination en milieux amérindiens et inuit. Manuscript.

BECK, Horace P., 1947 : "Algonquin Folklore from Maniwaki". *Journal of American Folklore* 60 (237) : 259-264.

CRAWFORD, Venetia (ed.), 1984 : *The Moose That Walked on Stumps. Narrated and Illustrated by Joe Ko Ko Ko*. Shawville, Quebec, Pontiac Printshop Ltd.

DAVIDSON, D. S., 1928 : "Folk Tales from Grand Lake Victoria, Québec". *Journal of American Folk-Lore* 41 : 275-282.

GAULTIER, Juliette (de la Vérendrye), n.d. : *Miscellaneous material : legends, drawings, illustrations, miscellaneous press clippings, album of photographs and bitten bark patterns, negatives, prints, etc.* Canadian Museum of Civilization, Library, Ethnology document III-L-64M. Manuscript.

INDIAN TRUTHS, 1976 : *Our People Talk*. La Macaza, Quebec, Manitou College, Thunderbird Press. Manuscript.

LEROUX, Jacques, 1992 : "Le Tambour d'Edmond". *Recherches amérindiennes au Québec* XXII (2-3) : 30-43.

PROVOST, Michèle, 1984 : *La Graisse du Castor*. Val-d'Or, Commission scolaire de Val-d'Or et Bureau de coordination en milieux amérindiens et inuit. Manuscript.

RADIN, Paul, 1914 : "The Boy Who Was Abused by His Older Brother. The Boy with the Magic Ball", in *Some Myths and Tales of the Ojibwa of Southeastern Ontario*. Ottawa, Department of Mines, Geological Survey Memoir 48, Anthropological Series 2, pp. 47-51.

SMITH, Annette, (ed.), 1976 : *Tales from the River Desert*. Maniwaki, The River Desert Band Council. Manuscript.

SPECK, Frank G., 1915 : *Myths and Folk-Lore of the Timiskaming Algonquin and Timagami Ojibwa*. Ottawa, Department of Mines, Geological Survey Memoir 71, Anthropological Series 9.

ETHNOSCIENCE – ETHNOBOTANY

BLACK, Meredith Jean, 1980 : *Algonquin Ethnobotany : An Interpretation of Aboriginal Adaptation in Southwestern Quebec*. Ottawa, National Museums of Canada, National Museum of Man, Canadian Ethnology Service, Mercury Series, Paper No. 65.

RANKIN, Jane, and Jackie KISTABISH, 1982 : *Remèdes algonquins. Anicinabe Mackiki*. Val-d'Or Friendship Center. Manuscript.

INDIGENOUS RIGHTS

ANONYME, 1987 : *La Revendication de la nation algonquine*. Maniwaki, River Desert Band Council, Manuscript.

COUR SUPÉRIEURE, 1989 : "Peter Decontie et autres c. Sa Majesté La Reine, et l'Honorable Jules Barrière mis en cause". *Recueil de jurisprudence du Québec* : 1893-1913.

FRENETTE, Jacques, 1988 : *Le pays des ANICENABE. La revendication territoriale globale de la nation algonquine*. Énoncé de revendication documenté et rédigé par Jacques Frenette pour le Conseil de Bande, Réserve algonquine de Maniwaki. Manuscript.

HESSEL, Peter, 1991-92 : "Algonquin Park and the Algonkins". *Valley. The Magazine of Eastern Ontario* 1 (2) : 6-8.

KISTABISH, Richard, and Jean-René PROULX, 1983 : "Constitution et mandat d'arrêt : La Conférence constitutionnelle vue du Grand lac Victoria". *Recherches amérindiennes au Québec* XIII (3) : 229-230.

LAPLANTE, Robert, 1979 : "Kipawa. Chronique des commencements". *Recherches amérindiennes au Québec* IX (3) : 219-236.

MATCHEWAN, Jean Maurice, 1989 : "Mitchikanibikonginik Algonquins of Barriere Lake : Our Long Battle to Create a Sustainable Future", in Boyce Richardson (ed.), *Drumbeat. Anger and Renewal in Indian Country*. Toronto, Summerhill Press Ltd., pp. 139-166.

SARAZIN, Greg, 1989 : "220 Years of Broken Promises", in Boyce Richardson (ed.). *Drumbeat. Anger and Renewal in Indian Country*. Toronto, Summerhill Press Ltd., pp. 169-200.

PRESENT LIVING CONDITIONS

ANICHINAPEO, Lise, Mary-Jane BRAZEAU, and Kitcisakik-Grand-Lac-Victoria children, 1988 : *Wamadisin!* Grand-Lac-Victoria. Manuscript.

COLLOQUE SUR LA SANTÉ ALGONQUINE, 1988 : *Rapport du colloque sur la santé algonquine*. Val-d'Or, Algonquin Council of Western Quebec. Manuscript.

CÔTÉ, Rémi, 1967 : "Sommes-nous des imposteurs?" *Kerygma* I (2) : 69-71.

EJINAGOSI, 1988 : *AKI*. Algonquin Council of Western Quebec.

KING, Paul R., 1971 *: Algonquin Portrait : A Study of the Rapid Lake Seasonal Agricultural Worker*. Geneseo, N.Y., State University College, Geneseo Migrant Center. Manuscript.

KISTABISH, Richard, 1982 : "La santé chez les Algonquins". *Recherches amérindiennes au Québec* XII (1) : 29-32.

– , 1987 : *Santé algonquine. Document de réflexion*. Val-d'Or, Algonquin Council of Western Quebec. Manuscript.

LAPLANTE, Monique, 1991 : *Les autochtones de Val-d'Or. Étude sur les autochtones vivant en milieu urbain*. Val-d'Or, Centre d'amitié autochtone de Val-d'Or/Native Friendship Center. Manuscript.

LAROSE, François, 1984 *: Systèmes interactionnels, modes d'apprentissage et adaptation scolaire autochtone*. Master's thesis, Department of Education, University of Sherbrooke.

– , 1987 : *Éducation indienne au Québec et prise en charge scolaire : de l'assimilation à la souveraineté économique et culturelle*. PhD dissertation, Department of Psychology and Education Sciences, University of Geneva.

– , 1988 : "Le jeu traditionnel algonquin au sein du processus d'intégration socio-économique dans une société semi-nomade et son utilité pédagogique". *Enfance* 41 (3-4) : 25-43.

– , 1991 : "Learning Processes and Knowledge Transfer in a Native Bush-Oriented Society : Implications For Schooling". *Canadian Journal of Native Education* 18 (1) : 81-91.

McDONALD, Jeanne, 1982 : "Nous marchons dans les traces de nos ancêtres : et pourtant il y en a encore pour dire que nous ne sommes plus indiens". *Recherches amérindiennes au Québec* XII (2) : 111-114.

MERVEILLE, Jean, 1987 : *La perspective anthropologique de la santé : le cas des patients amérindiens de Lac-Rapide au Québec*. PhD dissertation, Department of Anthropology, Université Laval.

MONTPETIT, Christiane, 1989 : *Trajectoires de vie de migrants autochtones à Val-d'Or*. Master's thesis, Department of Anthropology, University of Montréal.

PERREAULT, Guy, 1976 : "Visages de l'Abitibi-Témiscamingue", *in Cahiers du Département d'histoire et de géographie* 3. Rouyn, Collège du Nord-Ouest, pp. 130-163.

RANKIN, Sandra, Hanson McKENZIE, and Gordon McDOUGALL, 1985 *: En images et en mots. In Images and Words*. Amos, Imprimerie Bigot inc.

AUDIO-VISUAL DOCUMENTS

BLOCKADE : ALGONQUINS DEFEND THE FOREST
National Film Board of Canada, 1991
Dir. Boyce Richardson
Video or film. 26 min. Color.
"Blockade follows a small group of [Barriere Lake Algonquins] as they take on the government and the logging industry in a struggle to save their lands and way of life."

BUILDING AN ALGONQUIN BIRCDHBARK CANOE

Trust for Native American Cultures and Crafts Video, 1984
Dir. Henri Vaillancourt
¾" vt, ½" vt. 57 min. Color.
"In 1980, at Maniwaki, Quebec, Jocko Carle and Basil Smith built birchbark canoes so the process could be videotaped. Archival photographs and film introduce the documentation of this method of canoe building [...]".

CHEENAMA, THE TRAILMAKER. AN INDIAN IDYLL OF OLD ONTARIO

Dir. Harlan I. Smith under the supervision of Diamond Jenness, 1935
Film 16 mm. 45 min. Black and white. Silent with subtitles.
Description of traditional activities of the Algonquin with Mathew Bernard's family from Golden Lake.

KICHESIPI, LA GRANDE RIVIÈRE

Radio-Québec/Outaouais, 1983
Dir. Raymond Charette
¾" vt. 29 min. Color.
Description of Native People's traditional way of life and explanation of socio-cultural changes after contact.

LES MÉTIS ET INDIENS SANS STATUT (1 and 2)

Radio-Québec/Outaouais, 1982
Dir. Roger Gauthier
2 ¾" vt. 29 min. and 29 min. Color.
Socio-economic portrait of Non-Status Indians and Métis from Fort-Coulonge. Hunting Territories.

LE "MÉTIS STOMP"

Radio-Québec, 1980
Dir. André Dudemaine and Jacques Marcotte
¾" vt. 28 min. Color.
Situation of Non-Status Indians of Quebec and the Laurentian Alliance of Métis and Non-Status Indians of Quebec. Filmed in Abitibi-Témiscamingue.

MIKE BERNARD, DAN SARAZIN

Ontario Education Communications Authority (O.E.C.A.), n.d.
¾" vt, ½" vt. 19 min. Color.
"The Algonquins were the flower children of the forest long before hippies were heard of. Two Golden Lake chiefs try to define the fragile psyche of their band and their hopes for the future."

MOOWIS, WHERE ARE YOU MOOWIS?

Via le Monde, 1981-1983
Dir. Daniel Bertolino
Film 16mm. ¾" vt, ½" vt. 26 min. Color.
"Two young people lose each other through their stubborn pride and jealousy. (Algonquin)"
From the series *Legends of the Indian*.